W0006475

0571115373

LOUIS MACNEICE in the BBC

LOUIS MACNEICE

in the BBC

Barbara Coulton

FABER AND FABER
London   Boston

First published in 1980
by Faber and Faber Limited
3 Queen Square London WC1N 3AU
Printed in Great Britain by
Latimer Trend & Company Ltd Plymouth
All rights reserved

British Library Cataloguing in Publication Data

Coulton, Barbara
    Louis MacNeice in the BBC.
    1. MacNeice, Louis – Biography
    2. Authors, Irish – 20th century – Biography
    I. Title
    821'.9'12   PR6025.A316Z/

ISBN 0–571–11537–3

To Julia, Rachel and Helen

Contents

Illustrations

Acknowledgements

A great many people have helped in the compilation of the material for this book, and the formula 'without whom it would not have been possible' is in this case no empty courtesy. Friends and colleagues of MacNeice were generous of their time and memories, and BBC staff always helpful and co-operative. The kindness and interest shown by so many people has made the work a great pleasure.

First, I would like to acknowledge the help given by the poet's family: his sister Elizabeth, Lady Nicholson, his widow Mrs Hedli MacNeice, and his daughter, Corinna. Not everyone else can be mentioned here—some specific cases of help are acknowledged in the notes following the text—but gratitude is due to everyone who contributed, however small the contribution may have seemed: a great many pieces were needed to fill in as much of the picture as possible.

Others who have helped are listed in alphabetical order:

Dr and Mrs Gerald Abraham, Mr and Mrs Walter Allen, William Alwyn, Kevin Andrews, Professor Sir A. J. Ayer, Dorothy Baker, Sam Hanna Bell, Paul Bloomfield, Dallas Bower, John Boyd, Mr and Mrs D. G. Bridson, Cécile Chevreau, Mr and Mrs Douglas Cleverdon, Eileen Cullen, Mrs Joan Davies (Joan Coates), Mr and Mrs Dan Davin, Patric Dickinson, Mr and Mrs Francis Dillon, the late Professor E. R. Dodds, Sir William Empson, Elwyn Evans, Eric Ewens, Liam Gaffney, Val Gielgud, Frank Gillard, Robert Gittings, Margaret Gordon, Sean Graham, Harman Grisewood, Desmond Hawkins, Denys Hawthorne, Malcolm Hayes, John Hilton, Christopher Holme, Antony Hopkins, Richard Imison, Francis King, Laurie Lee, John Lehmann, H. A. Lidderdale, Sir Bernard Lovell, Elisabeth Lutyens, W. McAlpine, Mrs Mercy MacCann, Allan McClelland, Martha McCulloch, John Midgley, Stephen Murray, Howard Newby, Nesta Pain, Richard Pasco,

Robert Pocock, Mr and Mrs J. B. Priestley, Sir Victor Pritchett, Kathleen Raine, Goronwy Rees, John Sharp, R. D. Smith, Mrs Nancy Spender, Professor and Mrs Ernest Stahl, Leslie Stokes, David Thomson, Anthony Thwaite, Terence Tiller, Robin Whitworth, Angus Wilson, Ruth Winaver and the Revd Mr Wright of Carrickfergus.

Mrs Jacqueline Kavanagh and the staff at the BBC Written Archives Centre at Caversham went to a great deal of trouble to make available material in the files, and made the work very pleasurable, as did the staff in the Photograph Library, the Play Library, Sound Archives, the Script Libraries, the Drama staff at Bush House (where Dickon Reid kindly allowed the author to see a production of his), the staff at BBC Belfast, and the library staff at India House and Senate House. To these, and any others who helped, the author wishes to express gratitude.

Mrs Hedli MacNeice kindly lent personal papers from MacNeice's later years with the BBC. The author is very grateful to Mrs Valerie Eliot for allowing the use of unpublished letters from Eliot to MacNeice.

The author is grateful to the literary executors of the Louis MacNeice estate (Professor E. R. Dodds and subsequently Mr Dan Davin), and to the estate, for permission to quote from MacNeice's poems. These quotations are taken from the *Collected Poems* (Faber and Faber, 1979 edition).

Finally, the author would like to thank Michael Longley and the Arts Council of Northern Ireland, for a grant of £200 to help with the cost of research.

Chapter One

The Early Years: 1907–1940

Loves of the morning
'June Thunder'

In the BBC Archives there is a memorandum dated 9.1.1941: 'Louis MacNeice, a poet recently back from the United States of America, wrote to D.G. and said that he was anxious to do some propaganda to America. He came in to see me this afternoon and Harding talked to him.' It was signed by R. A. Rendall. As a result of this MacNeice joined the staff of the BBC and worked as a writer-producer in what was to become the Features Department. For some twenty years this was his full-time job, apart from a year and a half in Greece with the British Council, about halfway through his time with the BBC. In 1961 he went on a part-time contract, spending half the year in radio; when he died in September 1963 his last play had just been broadcast. His BBC career was a major part of his life and is worth examining in some detail.

Frederick Louis MacNeice was born on 12 September 1907, in Belfast; he was the youngest of the three children of John Frederick MacNeice, Rector of Holy Trinity Church, and his wife Elizabeth Margaret. The eldest child, Elizabeth, was four, and the elder son, William, two. In 1909 the family moved to Carrickfergus in County Antrim, at first to a house overlooking the harbour—the present main road had not then been built, and only a narrow quiet road divided the street of houses from the sea. In a poem, 'Carrickfergus', the poet recalls his childhood home:

> The little boats beneath the Norman castle,
> The pier shining with lumps of crystal salt;
> The Scotch Quarter was a line of residential houses
> But the Irish Quarter was a slum for the blind and halt.

As the rector's son, 'born to the anglican order', he was cut off from a whole section of the Irish people, but he had a strong attachment to the west of Ireland, as had his father. Both MacNeice's parents came from Connemara, though they had not met until they were in Dublin.

When the Rectory in Carrickfergus became available, the family moved there. It is a little way up the hill from the town and the harbour, a large, comfortable-looking, red-brick house, in a pleasant and sizeable garden. Photographs show the well-planted herbaceous borders, a summer-house, and the tall hedge which divided the garden from the cemetery, one of whose granite obelisks is just visible. The old gardener, Archie White, stands smiling with his spade—he was remembered with great affection by MacNeice. Unable to read or write, taking pride and pleasure in his work, white-haired and blue-eyed:

> He would talk to amuse the children,
> He would talk to himself or the cat
> Or the robin waiting for worms. . . .
>   'Novelettes', III, 'The Gardener'

Although the family had a sociable life, MacNeice himself was rather isolated in childhood. His brother was a mongol and retarded, and though he shared games and fantasies with his sister, she was four years older. His father seemed rather aloof to him, and he was closest to his mother. Other people in the household became important figures in his childhood lore, like the cook from County Tyrone who brought the world of fairy and folklore into the kitchen.

In *Autumn Sequel* MacNeice remembers Hallowe'en, when apples were dropped into a tub in the kitchen—'the black domain of the Will o' the Wisp' was conjured up, the dark with its ghosts and goblins:

> An ancient Celtic world had filled the air,
> The cropped black sow was waiting at the gate
> To seize the hindmost, and the empty chair

That creaked was creaking from the unseen weight
Of some dead man who thought this New Year's Eve,
The Celtic world having known a different date.

When the children went back to their small cold beds, the wind
rattling the window, Louis would think of an adult saying: 'you
never know where you will be when you wake up.' Miss
MacCready, the 'mother's help', would take the children up to
a top window where, as a treat, they could have a distant view
of a funeral, and hear the clods of earth thudding dully on to
the coffin. He remembered many sounds from these years: fog-
horns (the sirens of the poems) were menacing, as was the
curfew bell, rung twice daily by the sexton; but the trains which
passed not far from the house were comforting. Other images
from childhood are the Jack-in-the-box, 'Rock-a-bye-baby', the
sea, the hawthorn hedge, and—a sight which made an unforgettable impact—the apple trees in blossom in the Rectory
garden.

The church, of course, was prominent: he would sit in the
family pew, just a few feet in front of the pulpit, and see the
medieval nave, narrowed because the side aisles had been
removed. To his left would be the north transept with its marble
memorial to the Chichester family on the far wall. Sir Arthur
Chichester, in Jacobean costume, kneels opposite his wife
Lettice; between them is a small shrouded figure in a cradle,
their only child, who died in infancy. MacNeice thought of one
coat of arms as an old man watching him. This frightened him,
as did an old lady who dressed in black and knelt farther up the
church. For some reason of childish logic he assumed that she
was blind—he had a 'sort of savage, primitive fear of blindness'.

MacNeice's formative years were these spent in Carrick;
many of his images and myths go back to this time and place.
The most traumatic event was one which cast a dark backward
shadow over much of his childhood. His mother became ill in
about 1910, suffering uterine haemorrhages sporadically for
some three years, until a successful hysterectomy was performed.
But the knowledge that she must have this operation had
triggered a severe melancholic depression, which never really
lifted. She went into a nursing home and Louis, who was six,

never saw her again: she died in December 1914, from TB. The loss was a dreadful one to the child, and his last memories of her were sad ones: 'walking up and down the bottom path under the hedge that was always in shadow, talking to my sister and weeping', and then being driven away down the road from the Rectory as the children stood at the gate. Other memories were darkened by this. Even happy times at the seaside with his parents were clouded in retrospect by the thought of the dead gulls in the fishermen's nets. 'There was always a sense of loss because things could never be replaced.'

Another such memory was of some nestlings, in the same hedge by the bottom walk, which he inadvertently disturbed. 'I cannot remember seeing the nestlings fall out, but when I came past there again, there were hanging in the hedge little naked corpses, terrible, silent. I did not let on for years but I avoided that bottom walk.' This memory may be fused with the nursery rhyme in the 'Rock-a-bye-baby' references throughout his work. Shadows frightened him, and all his life he suffered from dreams. In the poem 'Autobiography', written in 1940, in his birth month, September, he indicates this childhood source of melancholy:

> My mother wore a yellow dress;
> Gently, gently, gentleness.
>
> Come back early or never come.
>
> When I was five the black dreams came;
> Nothing after was quite the same. . . .

Writing became an outlet from about the same time—diaries, poems, 'newspapers'. There was an ode to a parrot and one to a stuffed monkey. His father remarried, having engaged governesses for the children before this. When he was ten MacNeice went away to school in England.

His letters home from Sherborne are full of lively details, often illustrated with little sketches (he was very precise), of the gym, or the 'dormotories'. The number of slices of bread allowed at tea, poems he had been learning, rugby matches, the other boys—all are described in an intelligent and enthusiastic way.

He seems to have found great pleasure in the Dorset country-side, collecting fossils or playing games. For the first time he had plenty of companions of his own age. Photographs of him at home at this period show him smiling cheerfully, spade in hand, or with kittens climbing over him. He was known as Freddie during his childhood—the moody and aesthetic Louis did not emerge until he was about seventeen. At school he discovered the world of Malory and Arthur, of quests and grails; as late as 1961 he was wanting to do a radio programme on 'The Remorse of Sir Gawayne', but the suggestion was not accepted.

A dream that he recalled much later followed a holiday visit to a salt mine which was like a subterranean cathedral, the men 'like gnomes in the clerestories'. In the dream he was imprisoned by the gnomes, and could escape only by finding a certain jewel. He also recalled a holiday when his brother William was home too, from the institution in Scotland where he was at that time. He felt relief, and so guilt, when Willie went back there. A shadow had again fallen. 'And the bloom, I felt, had gone off the Dorset hills. And the boys at Sherborne seemed suddenly terribly young; I had learned their language but they could not learn mine, could never breathe my darkness.'

From Sherborne he went to Marlborough, to where he had won a scholarship. He enjoyed the chalk country, the Downs and the antiquities. His first close friendship was with Graham Shepard (the son of E. H. Shepard), whom he described as 'a surprising blend of precocious worldly-wiseness and faunal innocence'. A happy bicycle ride together, when 'the hedges were still fresh and lathered with mays, the laburnums were tumbling gold and the sun raking the downland', was remembered over twenty years later, in the poem 'The cyclist':

> In the heat of the handlebars he grasps the summer
> Being a boy and to-day a parenthesis
> Between the horizon's brackets; the main sentence
> Waits to be picked up later but these five minutes
> Are all to-day and summer.

This was written after Shepard was dead.

The Michaelmas term of 1924 saw a marked change in him. The ensuing year was, he said, the year of his most rapid intellectual development, when both he and Graham were 'itching to write'. The highbrow tradition at Marlborough encouraged a 'triumphant misfit' like John Betjeman, or an intellectual aesthete like Anthony Blunt. In Blunt, MacNeice found a sympathetic spirit: he became impatient with the apparent philistinism of his home town, and with Blunt he would wander around, posturing before imagined Baroque details of buildings, *pour épater le bourgeois*. Shepard was not influenced in the same way. 'He did not prefer Things to People and thought that Pure Form was nonsense. He was becoming more and more interested in the spectacle of contemporary English society, was trying his hand at writing social satire. He and I also collaborated in verbal fantasy.' These elements occur in MacNeice's writing for radio, including the play which he wrote after Shepard's death, 'He Had a Date'. During his last term at Marlborough, Shepard went to France and the three remaining close friends, MacNeice, Blunt and John Hilton, enjoyed 'an idyll'. It was a prelude to the Oxford days shared with Hilton and Shepard, while Anthony Blunt went to Cambridge.

When, in December 1925, MacNeice had gone to take his scholarship examination for Oxford, he had stayed at Merton; in walking from there to Christ Church Hall he had seen 'much decay and felicity'. He had thought to himself: 'I should really rather like to come up here.' John Hilton has written a memoir of the Oxford years. They were both surprised to find Oxford 'not only uninterested in the arts but violent in defence of superficial conventions'. So the small Marlborough group kept together. Hilton describes MacNeice in those days: 'his dark hair parted in the middle and curling back on to his forehead over each temple, large dark eyes flashing and crackling with raging rhetoric, opening to enormous size in mimed astonishment at some banality or narrowing to slits to put him at an infinite distance of sardonic scrutiny'. It was with Hilton that MacNeice made his first trip abroad, to Paris, at the end of the first summer term.

Oxford in the 1920s was a privileged and rather insulated world, but MacNeice found 'none of the geniuses around that there ought to be', and so felt let-down. The dons were not to be admired or emulated: 'becoming a don meant ossification'. Politics and social issues were not real to him; later he looked back on himself as something of a snob. Writing was the serious activity, with Auden as the doyen among undergraduate poets. MacNeice did not get to know Auden until later, in Birmingham, and Auden had only a vague recollection of 'a tall dark languid undergraduate from Merton, rather foppishly dressed'. Stephen Spender was there: 'his great beaming messianic face was an antidote to our conventional Oxford nonchalance', MacNeice recalled. Among the more frivolous pursuits were pubs, river-side picnics, canoeing.

When he was twenty, MacNeice made his first visit to the west of Ireland, with his father, now an archdeacon. In his myth-making way, MacNeice liked to think of this as his father's first visit there too, a shared homecoming, but the Arch-deacon had had a lifelong passion for his birthplace, the west, and a special love for Achill Island since 1911 when he had gone there alone. MacNeice's reaction was a romantic one: 'It was a country I had always known, mournful and gay with mournful and gay inhabitants, moonstone air and bloody with fuchsias. The mountains had never woken up and the sea had never gone to sleep and the people had never got civilised.' He retained this emotional attachment to the west; the remote, beautiful and timeless world became a country of the mind, an Arcadia. But he was aware of the ambivalences, as the poem 'Turf-stacks' shows:

> Among these turf-stacks graze no iron horses
> Such as stalk, such as champ in towns and the soul of crowds,
> Here is no mass-production of neat thoughts
> No canvas shrouds for the mind nor any black hearses:
> The peasant shambles on his boots like hooves
> Without thinking at all or wanting to run in grooves.

He cherished the inheritance of the irrational, the earthy, the romantic. With the self-conscious wit of the intellectual, he wrote, in 'Landscape of Childhood and Youth', that if he 'had one foot poised over the untrodden asphodel, the other was still clamped to the ankle in the bog'.

He got a first in Honours Moderations in Classics, in 1928,
and in the summer term began to read philosophy, for the
second part of his degree. He also met, for a second time, the
wife and step-daughter of Professor Beazley, a classical archaeologist who was a specialist in Athenian Black and Red Figure
Ware. (Mrs Beazley's first marriage had been to David Ezra,
who had been killed in the First World War.) There is a revealing comment in a later book, *I Crossed the Minch*: 'I have a
hatred of Greek vases, (a) because they are ugly in shape and
colour, (b) because they are viciously used to adorn school texts
of the classics, (c) because the house where I have most often
been embarrassed and disparaged was full of them, whole or in
fragments.' Mrs Beazley and her daughter were both named
Mary; they were attractive and exotic, with a Middle European
Jewish cosmopolitanism. Meeting them was a heady experience
for the young Louis MacNeice. He fell under the spell, and the
younger Mary fell in love with him. He describes her in phrases
that show the subjectivity of his response: 'bijou unreality',
'fragile as porcelain, dressed in the primary colours . . . always
scented with chypre'. She proved to have a passion for nature
and an unexpected sensitivity, but she could be melancholy and
temperamental, and her company could be exhausting.

The families were doubtful about the relationship, but the
idyll continued. Louis and Mary wrote to each other every day
during the Easter vacation of 1929, and the summer term was
one of picnics and boating on the river, Mary Ezra dressed like
'a nursery rhyme shepherdess'. In August Louis took Mary to
visit his family on Achill; in September they visited an uncle of
hers at St Tropez. A decade later, he wrote:

> They had nothing to ask
> Except that it should go on. Watching the vintage—
> A file of bullock carts and the muzzle of each
> Animal munching purple—he suddenly said
> 'We must get married soon.'
>
> 'Novelettes', V, 'Provence'

So, by his final year, they were engaged. Despite the distraction
he got his first in 'Greats'. A. J. Ayer remembers hearing
MacNeice during that final year, at a meeting of the Poetry

Club, 'deliver a metaphysical address which I found very impressive, though much of it passed my comprehension. It was a salutary shock for me to find someone who was so much more learned than myself and displaying a brilliance which I was sure that I could never match.' This is indeed a glowing testimony to the quality of MacNeice's mind.

On the last day of his last term MacNeice married Mary Ezra. Later he remarked with hindsight that, but for opposition, they might well not have married. So the Oxford days, and the decade, drew to a close. Quoting from Ezra Pound's 'Cathay', MacNeice wrote: 'But all this comes to an end. And is not again to be met with.' He added: 'All this did. And it was high time.' 'Much self-deception lay ahead', but in 1930 it seemed that real life had begun. He was married and he had a job: he had been appointed assistant lecturer in Classics at Birmingham University. E. R. Dodds, in his autobiography *Missing Persons*, recalled the Merton undergraduate, and his college's assessment of him as 'unquestionably gifted but unfortunately rather a difficult character and not always a steady worker—he spent too much time writing poetry.' This description attracted Professor Dodds, and MacNeice was appointed. In Professor and Mrs Dodds MacNeice found sympathetic friends who saw in him someone special, as did many other people. E. R. Dodds and he were fellow-Ulstermen with an affection for southern Ireland and a shared love of literature. But MacNeice was not really drawn to scholarly work—he wanted to write. His feelings about a provincial university were mixed: he endorsed the resentment felt by Professor Dodds at the superior attitude of Oxford and Cambridge, yet, faced with students who could not understand how the Greek philosophers could have sat together talking and drinking, he thought: '*Qu'allais-je faire dans cette galère?*' (This line he later gave to a character in a light-hearted radio play.) Perhaps the worst thing at this time was his inability to write. 'The trouble is that you cannot write in a hothouse,' he commented, in *The Strings are False*.

In marrying, MacNeice had come to 'recognise the existence of other people in their own right', but it was still an enclosed

world that he was living in. Professor Dodds describes the
marriage as an 'Enchanted Island', Louis and Mary like a pair
of 'grown-up children'. But there were new friends—the gardener Robinson, George, a young electrician, their maid Janet
and her family, and, in addition, Birmingham and businessmen
students. When Mary had a baby, in 1934, she became even
more immured, absorbed in child care, but MacNeice felt
happier and freer. This feeling was especially strong when he
went with Dodds to Ireland, where they met Yeats. It was at
this time that MacNeice and Auden became better acquainted,
meeting often at the Dodds' home. Another friend was Ernest
Stahl, a lecturer in German. With Ernest and his sister, and
Professor Dodds, MacNeice went to see Ireland play England
at Twickenham. 'What a lot of amusing things one might have
been doing before,' he thought—he was not, in future, to neglect the pleasures of rugby. He also became friendly with John
Waterhouse, a lecturer in English; they used to take MacNeice's
dog Betsy for walks.

During the early 1930s MacNeice's poems reflect a mood of
self-regarding sterility:

> Narcissus' error
> Enfolds and kills us—
> Dazed with gazing on that unfertile beauty
> Which is our own heart's thought.

In the same poem, 'Circe', there is an image which is to recur
in other poems and in plays: the 'parrot-ridden forest'. In
'Nature morte' he senses 'the appalling unrest of the soul', even
in a still-life painting. 'Sunday morning' has church bells to
sound a dead note, and weekly routine, without music or movement. Time and the fear of 'becoming stone' haunt the poems:
'The glacier', 'Perseus', 'Morning sun'; while in 'August' the
posed figures in a photograph epitomise life:

> Garlands at a set angle that do not slip,
> Theatrically (and as if for ever) grace
> You and me and the stone god in the garden
> And Time who is also shown with a stone face.

He wrote later: 'Sometimes in the night I woke and wondered
where we were going, but most of the time I was doped and

happy, most of the time except when I thought about time that most of the time is waste but whose is not?' After the birth of his son, Dan, he wrote an Ode in which he expresses greater contentment, a determination not to be haunted by Time, to take delight in the trees flowering in May—azaleas, syringa, laburnum, 'niched with the song of birds'. He prays for his son not to be caught between the 'jagged edges' of the world, and not to falsify it by 'taking it to pieces'. He feels that he has come home.

But, late in 1935, his wife left him, and their son, to join an American graduate student with whom they had become friendly. In *Autumn Sequel* Mary Ezra is remembered as

> Esther who stuck her black hair full of red
> Roses and ran away.

This was another loss that was difficult to forget—its traces are to be found throughout his writing. In 'Eclogue between the motherless' we have one key to the return to the past which was to recur again and again in poems and plays. Two voices talk of marriage: one is hoping to marry, but someone who is at present far away and who has only a year to live; the other has been married.

> A I thought 'Can I find a love beyond the family
>   And feed her to the bed my mother died in
>   Between the tallboys and the vase of honesty
>   On which I was born and groped my way from the cave
>   With a half-eaten fruit in my hand, a passport meaning
>   Enforced return for periods to that country?
>   Or will one's wife also belong to that country
>   And can one never find the perfect stranger?
> B My complaint was that she stayed a stranger.
>   I remember her mostly in the car, stopping by the white
>   Moons of the petrol pumps, in a camelhair rug
>   Comfortable, scented and alien.

These are wonderfully evocative phrases and images: the teasing play on words of 'the perfect stranger', the idea of Persephone, and the modern but exotic description of the car by the petrol pumps—the emotional quality of 'moons', and the suggestion of flight, journeying.

Company was more necessary than ever, as 'Homage to Clichés' suggests; this was written in December 1935. That Christmas was spent with his friends Graham and Anna Shepard, at a country inn near Tewkesbury. After this he returned to Birmingham, and saw more of those people whose company he appreciated: the Dodds, Walter Allen, Ernest Stahl, the sculptor Gordon Herrickx and Reggie Smith, whose vitality he admired. There was something more down-to-earth about Birmingham, with its admixture of working-class students—MacNeice always mistrusted what he called the 'Prolet-Cult' of Oxford and Cambridge. But he was ready to leave. First he completed, with Professor Dodds's help, his fine translation of Aeschylus' *Agamemnon*; then he obtained a lectureship in Greek at Bedford College, London. In many ways 1936 marked a new beginning, and before moving to London he made two trips abroad.

Easter was spent in Spain, with Anthony Blunt, 'while it was still peace there'; he enjoyed the paintings of El Greco, Goya and Zurbaran. In August he joined Auden in Iceland. With a group from Bryanston School they had a rough ten days trekking and camping in a barren part of the country, circling one of the icefields. Louis was totally lacking in both expertise and proper equipment: he shared Auden's tent, which collapsed slowly and soakingly on top of them, while MacNeice hid deeper in his sleeping bag. One of the group, Michael Yates, wrote an account of the trip—he recalls that 'Louis's endless dreams defeated Wystan's Freudian theories'—and there are photographs of a wild-Irish-looking MacNeice in oilskins and cap, with a growth of beard. There were rigours, with rain, and winds roaring down the icefield, but there were breathtaking views. After most of the party had left, the trip was less spartan, with warm hospitality at farms. Both Auden and MacNeice remembered the time as a happy one, despite the discomforts. Auden found MacNeice an 'ideal travelling companion, funny, observant, tolerant and good-tempered. I have very rarely in my life enjoyed myself so much as I did during those weeks when we were constantly together.' MacNeice never forgot Iceland, and he was to draw on this experience when he came

to adapt some of the sagas for radio, over ten years later.
Letters from Iceland was written soon after the trip—'a hodge-
podge thrown together in gaiety'. This is how the book reads:
lively, refreshing, humorous. The 'land of rocks and sagas'
provided a contrast to 'civilised' life, although it could offer
only a temporary escape; one could 'practise forgetfulness' for a
time. The comic side can be seen too: 'this cissy onslaught on
the open spaces'; and the 'Hetty to Nancy' section is very funny
indeed, with Auden transformed into the forceful Maisie, and
the Bryanston party into Miss Greenhalge and her girls. This
comic epistle, and Auden's 'Letter to William Coldstream, Esq.',
give us an amusing and vivid picture of the two poets, and the
London circle of writers and artists. There are details of the
Iceland trip, including Auden's glimpse of Louis, standing 'on
the quay muttering Greek in his beard Like a character out of
the Cantos'. Then there is MacNeice's 'Eclogue from Iceland',
where Ryan and Craven (himself and Auden) discuss the
materialism and violence of their world, a Waste Land of
'cosmic purposelessness', where Time sharpens his blade, 'among
the high rocks alone'. Grettir tells them of his struggles and
exile, and says that their only chance is to return where they
belong, to make an 'assertion of human values, which is now
your only hope'. In the background the jazzy voice of Europe is
heard, uncaring of what is happening. While Auden and
MacNeice were in Iceland war broke out in Spain.

When MacNeice came back it was to London. He took a flat
in Keats Grove, Hampstead, for himself, his son, a Scottish
nurse, and the dog Betsy. In November his divorce became
final. He had wanted to be in London to be at the centre of
things, and to meet writers. These appeared to be in two sets:
the 'old gang' who behaved as though everything were static,
and the 'new gang' who were involved with committees and
commitment. MacNeice was never very political, mistrusting
fashions and creeds. He observed the anomaly of Spender living
in a chic apartment and joining the Communist Party, and of
his friend from Oxford days, Goronwy Rees, 'a Fellow of All
Souls, a novelist, an editor of the *Spectator*, a playboy', thun-
dering on behalf of the proletariat and then going off to eat

oysters in an expensive restaurant. (Goronwy Rees has recently commented, 'We were an absurd lot.') The paradox of the intelligentsia seeking an escape from materialism in Marxism was noted by MacNeice. He met one inspiring Communist, John Cornford, giving him a lift back from Birmingham where they had both been visiting friends. Cornford was one of the first volunteers in Spain, fighting in the defence of Madrid, and dying at the end of December 1936 during the action at Lopera.

Soon after coming to London MacNeice became involved with the experimental Group Theatre. The commercial theatre offered Priestley, Bridie, Emlyn Williams and Noel Coward, and Drury Lane flourished with Novello musicals; while the smaller places like the Mercury at Notting Hill presented work by Eliot, Auden, Isherwood and Spender. The Group Theatre was formed by Rupert Doone and Robert Medley, producer and designer. Medley had been at Gresham's School with Auden; Britten had been there slightly later—he too joined in the work of the new group. Soon after his return from Germany, Auden, then at Helensburgh, was invited to London by Medley and Doone to discuss plans: at their Fitzroy Street flat Auden suggested writing *The Dance of Death* for them—it was performed late in February 1934, at the Westminster Theatre. In 1936 Auden collaborated with Isherwood on *The Dog Beneath the Skin* for the Group, and the following year they wrote *The Ascent of F6*. Spender contributed *Trial of a Judge*. In November 1936 the Group produced MacNeice's translation of the *Agamemnon*—an eccentric production with masks and dinner suits. Yeats came with Professor Dodds, and was moved to remark, of the production not the translation, 'We are assisting, my dear Dodds, at the death of tragedy.' The next year MacNeice wrote *Out of the Picture*, for which Britten composed music.

The Group Theatre was a short-lived but interesting 1930s phenomenon (it lapsed during the war, was revived briefly, but did not survive). Following Continental models, and drawing on dance and mime, it offered something original, if quirky, in London. MacNeice's interest in it shows his modernity, and his willingness to develop other forms than poetry. *Out of the*

Picture mixes comedy and satire with choric passages of verse, and a kind of revue double-act between a Listener-In and a Radio-Announcer. There is a mixture of earnestness and flippancy in the attack on the contemporary world. As a play it has its shortcomings, being rather too mannered. This and other productions were condemned by one reviewer as 'art-and-class snobbery'; this was in *New Verse*, but there were kinder notices in the same magazine from Kenneth Allott, and in the *London Mercury* from Dilys Powell. MacNeice agreed (in reply to the first reviewer) that his was hardly a good play, but he defended the production for giving the play a 'unity and drive on the stage which it lacked on paper'.

1937 was 'a year of wild sensation' for MacNeice: one passing affair ended in hurled teacups and laughter; a more important relationship was to change after a while into a lasting friendship. There was some journalism, and the commissioning of two prose books 'for which I had no vocation but which, I thought to myself, I could do as well as the next man'. These were *Zoo* and *I Crossed the Minch*, both with illustrations by Nancy Sharp. They are interesting books, easy in style, with excellent description, and a conversational tone that takes the reader into the author's confidence. In both he is the outsider, the layman, giving us his impressions and his thoughts. In fact, although he was presumably unaware of this, the books are not unlike the best kind of features being done, or which were to be done in the future, for radio. They prepare us for the ease with which he seems to have adapted to radio journalism. 'The crowd go to the zoo in much the same spirit as they go to Hampstead Heath or to the Wembley Stadium. Here I am at one with the crowd. . . .' We can easily imagine the introduction of sounds at this point. He digresses, reminisces, makes trips to various zoos—Clifton, Vincennes (at Bank Holiday with Ernest Stahl), Whipsnade, Regent's Park (where he went behind the scenes with James Fisher, then assistant curator). The personal response is found too in the book on the Hebrides—'a tripper's book written by someone who was disappointed and tantalised by the islands and seduced by them only to be reminded that on that soil he will always be an outsider'.

Twice during 1937 he went to the Hebrides, in April and July. He had had a 'sentimental and futile hope' that the Celt in him would be drawn out by the islands, but when there he realised that his affinity was after all with the London set of writers and artists. *I Crossed the Minch* is most enjoyable. There is humour, for instance the imaginary travelling companions, Crowder and Perceval, who make disparaging remarks about MacNeice. (Later, some of the radio features were to have 'Voices'.) There are humorous poems too: the well-known 'Bagpipe music' and the comic ballad about Lord Leverhulme's commercial exploits on the islands, all foiled by the native indolence:

> All that remained of Lever's plans
> Were some half-built piers and some empty cans,
> And the islanders with no regrets
> Treated each other to cigarettes.

At Heaven's gate, St Peter commiserates with Lever about the Celts:

> They've no team spirit, they won't take part
> In our study circles and community art
> And at garden parties they won't concur
> In speaking English—which is *de rigueur*.

So the Hebrides are left to the waves which creep over the lonely beaches.

There is pleasure in unexpected walks, often long and wet, as one on Lewis: 'The rain was now very heavy and every time I reached the top of a hill and the full force of it hit me, I would stand on a rock and enjoy it as if I was bathing. The desolate voices of the sheep, scattered grey among the stones, I found exhilarating also.' He liked the foam and the wind, the life and the barrenness, the melancholy attraction of a certain kind of loneliness. He shares his dreams, one of being a seal, his memories, the thought that he will be thirty in September. At times the cadences and alliteration of Anglo-Saxon verse ring through the narrative. There is a tersely effective account of the wreck of the Admiralty boat, *Iolaire*, bringing home men who survived the First War: 'The sea was dead calm for the crossing. In sight of Stornoway harbour the captain altered his course, took a steep angle to the right. The three hundred Lewismen knew the place like their hands, saw themselves go to their doom.' He took his farewell of the Hebrides with a certain regret, standing on deck at three in the morning. 'The moon had an aura like a peacock's eye, Venus lay on the low bank of cloud over Scotland, blue Vega was high over Skye.' He wrote the poem 'On Those Islands', about the peace there, but not for him, and not perhaps for long; and there is a beautiful love poem, 'Leaving Barra'.

More lasting than his fleeting acquaintance with the Hebrides was his affection for Ireland. His father was now Bishop of Down, Connor and Dromore, and the family home was in Belfast. On a visit there in 1938 MacNeice made a new friend in George MacCann, introduced to him in a bookshop by the poet Maurice Craig. MacNeice loved to visit MacCann and his wife Mercy at their cottage at Vinecash, in Armagh, where the water had to be drawn from the well. These friends were both artists, and also great hosts; MacNeice admired George for his humour and his vitality—he is the Maguire of *Autumn Sequel*:

> Whose Irish stories matched his Irish thirst . . .
> Who makes Belfast in all its grime seem gay.

The next year he met John Midgley, who has described the first meeting 'in the low-ceilinged bog-oak-furnished kitchen of a 200-year-old Armagh cottage . . . W. R. Rodgers and James Boyce were of the company.' Always, after this, MacNeice would love to go to Ireland and meet such friends.

In London, MacNeice was part of the literary scene. There were several magazines founded to provide an outlet for young writers: John Lehmann's *New Writing*, Geoffrey Grigson's *New Verse* and the Communist *Left Review*. A good deal of poetry was published in the *Listener*. The Left Book Club was founded by Victor Gollancz for propaganda writing. Not everyone believed, as Orwell did, that literature *was* propaganda. MacNeice did not. In 'A Statement', which he was asked to contribute to *New Verse* in summer 1938, he said that the poet should be both critic and entertainer—he is not some special breed, 'only the extension of the common man'. MacNeice was anxious to de-mystify literary production; he found literary critics too literary, he had written a year or so earlier; their method of looking at influences was 'over-rated and over-exploited; poetry is a natural and universal activity which we all practise from our earliest years.' He saw Auden and his 'group' as the contemporary poets of most significance, deriving partly from Owen, with elements of Lenin and Lawrence. Yeats, after his early escapism, had had a salutary influence. MacNeice mistrusted both propaganda and surrealism: 'bill-plastering on the one hand or visceral parrot-talk on the other'. The poet should write about his own society.

He himself was highly regarded as a poet. Grigson praised him for not having 'gone over to the Sitwells, the dons, to Bloomsbury', and for the 'certainty and peculiarity and delicacy of his rhythms'. He compared him to Horace, 'exiled in the wrong age', and Horace was indeed a favourite poet of MacNeice. In 1938 the volume *The Earth Compels*, dedicated to Nancy, was published. It contains some of his finest love poems, commemorating the intense love affair of 1937 and 1938, and the exciting, positive, sometimes trying, but always illuminating character of the woman he loved. 'June thunder' evokes some of the quality of this love, and of the early summer:

> as more appropriate
> To the maturer and impending thunder
> With an indigo sky and the garden hushed except for
> The treetops moving.

The storm blows the curtains, rustles the shrubbery, beats the flowers, but acts as a catharsis, a 'cleansing downpour':

> Breaking the blossoms of our overdated fancies
> Our old sentimentality and whimsicality
> Loves of the morning.

'Leaving Barra' compares her to the 'dazzle on the sea', to a fugue—alive and moving—'alive beyond question'. The vitality and tantalising excitement of the affair are caught in other short poems, like 'Trilogy for X', dated summer 1938, where her radiance invests everyday things with gaiety, and also in the long poem of 1938, *Autumn Journal*, in images of scent, dancing shadows, waterfalls, wind on wheat, music, movement and pattern. London is 'littered with remembered kisses'. The elegant and sophisticated love affair changed to friendship, as *Autumn Journal* records, though he sometimes thinks longingly of her as a companion, as when he is in Paris (they had a splendid supper together before he went).

Walter Allen has written of *Autumn Journal*: 'If anyone wants to know what it was like to be a young, very intelligent, sensitive man in the autumn of 1938, this is the book to read. It is a unique document.' It remains one of the finest poems of the decade. MacNeice described it as 'something halfway between the lyric and the didactic poem'. The personal story is set against the background of history, as war threatened Europe. Well-observed, sharp detail sets the scene of comfortable, complacent, middle-class England: 'summer is ending in Hampshire', where the neat lawns and clipped hedges protect the retired generals and admirals, 'And the spinster sitting in a deck-chair picking up stitches Not raising her eyes to the noise of the 'planes that pass'. The social system is unfair, the culture élitist; he is aware of his own 'cushy job', but sceptical about his classical education—dead languages and metaphysics. In protest at the conformity, 'The Fool among the Yes-men' may 'prick their pseudo-reason with his rhymes And drop his grain of salt on court behaviour.' When he came to write for radio, he availed himself of the tradition of light-hearted features to do the same himself.

The poem records his reaction to public events: the ranting of Hitler; Munich and the defeat of the Czechs; the civil war in Spain—he visited Spain at the end of the year. He also remembers his life in Birmingham, and his marriage, and reflects on his Irish heritage. He wants to be more outgoing, to have a share 'In a civilised, articulate and well-adjusted Community', where mind and body get their due. The past must sleep, the future wake; it is neither Styx nor Lethe which is before him, but Rubicon. Looking forward, he planned to try teaching in America, going at Easter to Cornell. Over there he met his former wife and her husband; they now ran a chicken farm and did not often come to New York. He fell in love again,

B

with an American writer, 'a woman who was not a destroyer. Something inside me changed gear, began to run easily in top.' Thinking that he had found the answer to his search, he felt nostalgic when he came back to England that summer.

He spent time with Walter Allen, Reggie Smith and Ernest Stahl—they were all doing research (MacNeice was writing his book on Yeats) and met in the Reading Room of the British Museum, adjourning promptly for a drink or a smoke. Then he and Ernest went to Ireland, Louis wanting to see the west in case it should be for the last time. They were in Galway when the war started, and returned to Dublin by way of Clonmacnoise, the thousand-year-old monastic settlement by the Shannon. MacNeice stayed in Ireland, dividing his time between Dublin and Belfast, until the New Year, when he went, as planned, to America. He wrote from Ithaca to George and Mercy MacCann: 'I have been having a lovely time though too much of it taken up with shouting about poetry from platforms. . . . my ladylove met me at the boat which was unexpected, so we went off and had duckling cooked with black cherries and oranges.' He had thoughts of staying in the States. Auden was in Brooklyn and thinking of becoming naturalised, but MacNeice writes that he does not think he would do that himself. He did ask his family to try to get his son Dan over to America, and his sister and father did what they could, although it did not seem a good idea—Dan seemed happily settled in Ireland with cousins. Then MacNeice wrote to say that he had changed his plans: he did not want Dan to be sent over, he was coming back to England. He intended to do this in the summer, but he was dangerously ill with peritonitis and had to remain until December.

1940 was a year of reassessment for MacNeice. There was the decision about America, while the war in Europe reached a critical stage, and the Blitz began on London. Among the poems that he wrote in the autumn of that year was 'Autobiography', in which he considers his early life. The poems written from 1925 to 1940 were collected for publication, and appeared in 1941 as *Plant and Phantom*. In his introduction to the volume, MacNeice wrote: 'When a man collects his poems, people think he is dead. I am collecting mine not because I am dead, but because my past life is. Like most other people in the British Isles I have little idea of what will happen next. I shall go on writing, but my writing will presumably be different.' At the end of 1940 he was also at work on a prose autobiography, not published until after his death, *The Strings are False*. In the November he visited Auden in Brooklyn, spending Thanksgiving Day with him, Britten and Peter Pears, Carson McCullers and Gypsy Rose Lee. Then in December he sailed for England, 'to a past which is not there . . . returning somewhere I belong but have not as it is now, been. . . . Yet I am not so gloomy as I might be.' On board the *Samaria* he worked at some of the prose drafts, trying to sum up his life: 'I am 33 years old and what can I have been doing that I still am in a muddle?' Within weeks of his landing, he was contacting the BBC (Ogilvie, according to the memorandum of Rendall's) and on 9 January 'Harding talked to him.' His new career was soon to begin.

Chapter Two

The BBC: the Growth of Drama and Features to 1940

From that silence
Are borrowed ear and voice and from that darkness
We borrow vision. . . .

'The Stygian Banks'

The institution that Louis MacNeice was to join in 1941 had been in existence for less than twenty years. In October 1922 a consortium of leading wireless manufacturers, the British Broadcasting Company, advertised for a General Manager. The choice made for this appointment was decisive in establishing the course and character of what was to become the BBC. John Reith saw his new post as not just a job but a mission. He had his responsibility to the trade, but he saw too 'something of the inestimable benefit which courageous and broad-visioned development of this new medium would yield'. He had only a small team to work with, and large vested interests to withstand, but he was determined to avoid the dominance of political influence and commercial power. Nor was he content that radio should be used merely for entertainment, 'in the narrow sense'. Its informative and educational potential should be recognised, and the cultural pursuits hitherto enjoyed mainly by those with leisure and money were to be made available to everybody.

Reith had had to make his way largely by his own efforts, so he was not biased in favour of the privileged classes, and his Scottish Calvinist upbringing can be discerned in the stern and uncompromising way in which he pursued his aims. Certain of his own beliefs put their stamp on broadcasting; those

concerning religion and the monarchy, for instance. This, doubtless, was acceptable to the majority. One thing which may, as
Reith claimed, have been in advance of its time was the social
concern: 'The Savoy Hill conception of the part that broadcasting could play in national and international affairs was
ahead of public opinion.' Apart from a very brief initial period
in Kingsway, Savoy Hill was the home of the BBC for nearly a
decade. The small staff were enthusiastic: using the nautical
imagery which seems to attach itself to the BBC, Reith wrote of
the new craft which a 'devoted, adventurous crew launched
into uncharted and treacherous seas, where never sail was
carried before'. *Radio Times* made its appearance in September
1923—the 'Bradshaw of Broadcasting' it called itself, changing
the metaphor. New possibilities, in technique and output, were
explored by the broadcasters, while at a higher level the future
of the Company was being considered. The Crawford Committee, reporting in May 1926, favoured a public service
monopoly to replace the Company at the end of the year. So the
British Broadcasting Corporation began life on 1 January 1927,
with Sir John Reith as its first Director General.

The Productions Director, R. E. Jeffrey, shared with Cecil
Lewis, his Assistant, a belief in the possibilities of radio drama;
both wrote articles for *Radio Times*. There was a huge potential
audience (by the end of 1926 over two million licences had been
issued, an almost fourfold increase in three years). A great deal
of the output was music, and talks were another staple. Outside
broadcasts increased, covering more and more sporting events
and 'special occasions'. Sometimes a miscellany of verse and
music would occupy an hour or two of the evening. A great
attraction for the family audience was the radio play, usually an
adaptation of a stage play or a novel; plays specially written
for radio were rarer. R. E. Jeffrey, in an article headed 'Seeing
with the Mind's Eye', wrote of the power of the imagination to
create a great range of scenes. Cecil Lewis, writing of his own
production of Conrad's *Lord Jim*, pointed out that the key to
radio drama was simplicity—audiences must not be confused
by the action. More imaginative programmes were possible
after the inauguration of the Daventry 'experimental station'

in the late summer of 1927: there was a version of Goethe's *Faust* (anticipating MacNeice's version by twenty years), Synge's *Riders to the Sea* and Karel Căpek's *R.U.R.*

Technical developments included the use of multiple studios, all controlled by the producer who could fade them in and out from his 'dramatic control panel'. Different acoustics could thus be used, and effects separated from musicians and actors; great skill and accurate timing were needed. One play broadcast in April 1928 used five studios: this—'definitely a radio play'—was 'Speed', by a pseudonymous 'Charles Croker'. It was 'a satire on the efforts of man to conquer the universe . . . a tragi-comic fantasy', alternating its setting between the modern world and Olympus: 'the gods speak in blank verse, the mortals in colloquial prose. Need I say more?' There was difficulty in getting playwrights for radio: competition from films; a kind of censorship that was felt to operate in the BBC, turning a blind eye to some of the realities of life; and perhaps a kind of snobbishness on the part of some writers—all hindered development.

Writing in September 1928, in *Radio Times*, Jeffrey confessed that he did not yet know what was to be 'the ultimate technique of radio drama'. It would need time, of course, but also 'a single-minded artistic genius who will envisage its tremendous potentialities and devote himself to moulding them to his own use'. Good writing, finesse, taste—these would be essential. So far, there had been nothing 'worthy of superlative praise'. He felt that Strindberg's thirty-year-old work *The Dream Play*, virtually impossible on stage, would prove an almost perfect 'wireless play'. Such a work, 'overflowing the limitations of the theatre and the crudity of stage appurtenances, uses the wide plains of human fantasy . . . and materialises subconscious thought for its characters'. Our immediate reply might be that stage limitations did not deter the great Elizabethans, but the points about fantasy and the subconscious drama are pertinent: much of MacNeice's work for radio was to be in those very fields. An audience would need to be appreciative of such drama, and Jeffrey concludes, in rather a condescending tone, that 'so long as the multitude thinks superficially, we must in part offer superficial drama, that is, the drama of infidelity, of fear, of unhappiness, of love that embraces death; it would neither be effective nor fair to accept financial tribute from the many, and feed only the few.'

In 1929, Jeffrey was succeeded by Val Gielgud, who was ready to encourage creative radio, although principally interested in the stage. One of the most enthusiastic experimenters was a friend of Gielgud's, Lance Sieveking. Another important figure was Tyrone Guthrie. Val Gielgud has paid tribute to these writer-producers: 'It was due mainly to Lance Sieveking and Tyrone Guthrie that it was learned that plays could be written which owed nothing in their writing or construction to conventional stage models.' In October 1928 Sieveking devised and produced his first 'Kaleidoscope': 'A Rhythm Representing the Life of a Man from Cradle to Grave'. This was a dramatic compilation of prose, verse, dialogue and music, showing conflicting influences on the man, and certain turning points in his life. The following May a companion piece on the life of a woman was broadcast. The same month, Guthrie's 'Squirrel's Cage' told of the frustrations of city life for a young man. Lasting an hour, it was constructed in a novel way, with six scenes and five interludes, without breaks, and without narration. His later play, 'The Flowers Are Not For You To Pick', broadcast in 1930, used the device of a drowning man's recall of his past life, the voices from his past alternating with the sound of the waves. Guthrie's note on the play comments that 'the many short scenes rise out of and sink into the rhythmic sound of splashing, moving seas. . . . it may be possible to suggest not merely the water in which Edward is engulfed, but the beating of a heart, the tumult of fear. . . .' Another of his radio plays, 'Matrimonial News', relied on internal monologue, the thoughts of a woman sitting alone in a Strand restaurant. It was Guthrie who made the comment that the imaginative listener 'will create illusions infinitely more romantic than the tawdry grottoes of the stage'. Richard Hughes's play 'Danger', about three people trapped in a mine, is another example of outstanding radio drama. Thus the tradition was being established which Louis MacNeice was to inherit.

The 'Harding' who spoke to MacNeice when he called at the BBC in January 1941 was E. A. Harding, another pioneer of radio. Originally an announcer at Savoy Hill—an Oxford man with a beautifully modulated voice and a rather mannered syntax—he became interested in producing and in experimenting. He wrote a play on the legend of Roland, setting the speeches of his four characters against a background line of music. It was produced by Peter Creswell in November 1929. Two years later, Harding himself produced 'an interesting experiment in the kind of impressionism that is only possible over the microphone, or, perhaps, in a sound film'. This was Ezra Pound's 'Villon': the original poetry was combined with Pound's own 'hobo' dialogue, and with his music. Less recherché pieces also showed imaginative use of radio: E. J. King-Bull's dramatic sequence, 'Yes and Back Again', based on Walter de la Mare's anthology *Come Hither* (with the author's blessing), was broadcast in September 1930 and revived twice the following year—a programme note draws attention to its pervading 'other-worldly atmosphere', ideal for radio.

Fantasy was one thing, but radio could also deal with actuality. 'He Went to China' was of this kind, produced in June 1930 by Lance Sieveking and Victor Purcell. Historical subjects and topics of regional interest lent themselves particularly to this kind of 'feature' programme. This term had been in use from early on, as early as 1924, although the programmes referred to were usually only miscellanies. Cardiff Director, Mr Corbett-Smith, is hailed as 'father of the feature programme' in an undated article in the BBC Archives. There came to be great variety in the application of the technique of features, but in the main they were documentary, non-drama, although using dramatic techniques to deal with one of any number of subjects—the originality of feature writers was astonishing. Ultimately, Features became a separate department, after the section had attained great importance and prestige during the war. Another early feature, anticipating some of the war-time pieces, was 'Crisis in Spain', broadcast in June 1931: it told the story of the Spanish Revolution, through words and music; no comment was added to the actual speeches of the protagonists and the news bulletins. The same technique was used for 'Waterloo', and for a programme showing the events leading to the First World War. Peter Creswell's feature on the trial of Charles I initiated a whole series of famous trials. By 1935, it seemed that the future of radio drama might lie with the feature rather than with the play.

By the 1930s, nine out of ten homes in Britain had a wireless set, and the popularity of this family entertainment affected (in A. J. P. Taylor's words) attendance at 'churches, chapels, clubs and literary societies. . . . The Englishman still belonged to a community, though shut up in a box listening to a tinier box.' As the BBC grew there was greater specialisation and organisation. The 'slap-happy' days were over by the time of the move, in 1932, from Savoy Hill to Portland Place, from sail to battleship. The former Productions Department had already been divided into three: Revue under John Watt, Variety under Eric Maschwitz, and Drama and Features under Val Gielgud. A new Empire short-wave transmitter was operating from Daventry in 1932, so that it was felt that the new Broadcasting House would be the radio headquarters of the Empire. Now it was possible to produce the round-the-world link-up programmes which were to be famous, on Christmas Day and Empire Day (24 May). Harding organised these during 1932 and 1933, until he went to Manchester as Head of Programmes in the North Region.

Although it could not have been foreseen at the time, the move of Harding to Manchester was to have important consequences. On the one hand, he made a decisive impact on broadcasting in the north, which was to have widespread effects later; on the other hand, his place in London was taken by a producer who had formerly worked on *Radio Times*— Laurence Gilliam, who organised future round-the-world feature programmes, and to whom Gielgud was happy to delegate the documentary side of the department's work. In Manchester, new and creative talent was brought into broadcasting by Harding: D. G. Bridson and Francis Dillon came into the BBC in this way, and were to be among the leading members of the future Features Department (the department to which Louis MacNeice belonged). Geoffrey Bridson's account of his own career in radio, *Prospero and Ariel*, includes a portrait of Archie Harding. The Oxford intellectual, with strongly Left sympathies, was a 'true exotic' in Manchester; he had a passionate interest and belief in radio: 'his whole attitude to the medium was stimulating and somehow exciting.' His ideas about the use of radio were also original: 'In Harding's view *all* people should be encouraged to air their views, not merely their professional spokesmen. . . . The air at least should be open to all, as the Press quite obviously was not.'

So it was that a very lively development of actuality broadcasting took place in Manchester. One of Bridson's features, on May Day, was praised in a letter to *Radio Times* by one 'George Potter'—a disguise for Laurence Gilliam. There was the series of 'Harry Hopeful's Northern Tours', in which local people were given their chance to speak their minds or display their humour. These seem to have been less appreciated in the more sophisticated south, since they are described in a *BBC Year Book* as interviews with 'peasants from remote northern districts'—a reminder of regional and class differences so pronounced in the 1930s. As examples of the work that was being done, we may instance, from 1935, Bridson's documentary reconstructions 'William Cobbett' and 'The Death of Bede', and Francis Dillon's adaptations of Andersen's 'The Nightingale' and 'The Snow Queen'. Another acclaimed feature was Bridson's 'March of the '45', which told its story in narrative verse with a strong beat and movement. It was frequently used by Harding when he became Chief Instructor, in 1936, at the newly instituted Staff Training School. Francis Dillon was one of the first to 'graduate', along with Guy Burgess, later to find fame in other fields. After this, Dillon went to the West Region; among his recruits was Douglas Cleverdon, one of the most distinguished of BBC producers.

Throughout 1938 the question of feature programmes was taken up with particular insistence by the drama critic of the *Listener*, Grace Wyndham Goldie. They could, she maintained, be the strength of the BBC's Drama Department. Among the year's productions she praised Bridson's 'Coronation Scot' (produced in collaboration with Scottish Region) and his dramatisation of *The Waste Land*; Stephen Potter's historical documentary on the Armada, 'The Last Crusade'; Olive Shapley's sympathetic feature on 'Homeless People'; and Laurence Gilliam's 'Job To Be Done', which dealt in a very moving way with American unemployment. All these made very effective radio programmes. The local importance of some of this work came home to Mrs Goldie when she visited the small mining town of Willington, in County Durham, to see a feature being made by Geoffrey Bridson and Joan Littlewood. The chance to speak for themselves and to take part in a radio programme meant a great deal to the people of the town.

The new Head of Programmes in the North Region was a very able man, John Salt. He proposed that programmes 'of greatest national value' should be selected from the quarterly output of the regions, and of London, without preference being given automatically to the capital. He also advocated the gradual building-up of a school of writers with experience of actuality work, and the freedom to tackle wider subjects for which they might be fitted. Producers need not, he argued, be confined to one particular region, and outside writers could be called in. 'I believe that this kind of approach, by applying a sociological sense to the whole field, would direct creative ability to the right quarters and give feature programmes a new lease of life.' J. H. Dunkerley, of the Midland Region, also held features to be important. He felt that the high quality which such work should aim at was not always being reached; a more generous allowance of time, and a team of good writers in the Features Department, would be necessary. Regional producers should meet each other and the London producers in order to keep up with developments and exchange ideas. He acknowledged the help that Gilliam had given to his regional producers on a recent programme.

In the autumn of 1938, and the spring of 1939, Gilliam was urging regional directors to take news items, social problems and 'personality' stories and treat them more fully and in perspective. There were difficulties: the regions had small staffs; there was the problem of editorial opinion, and of maintaining responsible impartiality; but at such a time listeners should be informed and made to think, not just entertained.

> To-day was a beautiful day, the sky was a brilliant
>   Blue for the first time for weeks and weeks
> But posters flapping on the railings tell the fluttered
>   World that Hitler speaks, that Hitler speaks
> And we cannot take it in and we go to our daily
>   Jobs to the dull refrain of the caption 'War'. . . .

MacNeice captures the atmosphere of suspense and fear in September 1938 in *Autumn Journal*. He was returning to his lecturing job in London; 'But work is alien' and metaphysics seemed irrelevant, as 'conferences, adjournments, ultimatums' followed one another.

> And the individual, powerless, has to exert the
>   Powers of will and choice
> And choose between enormous evils, either
>   Of which depends on somebody else's voice.

MacNeice was not at that time aware of the potential part that broadcasting could play, but he shared with many educated middle-class liberals the belief in some kind of socialism, and the disillusionment with the ineffectiveness of government; he was not committed to actual political involvement. As for the BBC, it was for him an occasional outlet for some of his poems, and the source of a little extra money. A relation of his former wife was a producer and MacNeice persuaded him to let him broadcast a short talk, 'In Defence of Vulgarity', in December 1937. He wrote later that he did listen in to radio, but 'I then thought it a degrading medium, both vulgar and bureaucratic and not even financially rewarding. I may have been a snob at the time. . . .'

He cannot have been too snobbish, however, for in December 1938 he was writing a letter to the *Listener* to the effect that entertainment value should be put before highbrow attitudes in compiling programmes of poetry. He added: 'Poets should certainly write plays, and probably certain other forms of verse, expressly for broadcasting purposes.' Mrs Goldie took him up on this, asking why poets were not writing for radio, when

Auden, Day Lewis, Spender, and MacNeice himself, were writing the sort of verse that radio could use, and the plays put on at the Group Theatre had the right vitality and freshness of approach. 'Why, then, don't poets write for radio? Have they overlooked this market, these possibilities? Or do they refuse to tackle the problems of the medium? Or have they found it impossible to get help about these problems from the B.B.C.? ... Or doesn't it offer them enough money? What *is* the difficulty? Will Mr MacNeice tell us?' It is interesting that this most perceptive and influential critic and later exponent of broadcasting should have made her comments on both features and poets.

Although music and light entertainment were using radio, the literary establishment was still wary. John Pudney received some 'cautious advice' from T. S. Eliot: 'some young fellows in the B.B.C. are interested in what they call radio drama. . . . they have got hold of poets and teach them what they need to know about the technique.' Eliot had met Gilliam, whose ideas are possibly reflected in this remark, and he thought it might be useful for Pudney to contact him, although 'the B.B.C. usually gets shifted about before anybody has time to do anything.' This suggests a strangely vagrant circus, luring poets to teach them new tricks. Pudney did join for a while. 'I listened to some good angel whispering to me that five years in the B.B.C.—no more, no less—was just the right stay.'

The rather cloistered and gentlemanly attitude of some of those at Broadcasting House could not be maintained: it had become clear that broadcasting could play an important part in national and international affairs. But there was opposition from official circles. Reith had wanted foreign language broadcasting to be considered. 'I had tried periodically and urgently for three years to have this matter taken seriously. Almost every month brought news of extensions of activity in totalitarian lands.' In the summer of 1937 the subject was at last put on the Cabinet agenda, although it was October before the BBC was invited to send representatives to the Cabinet committee. There was the threat of direct governmental control to be resisted; the BBC must continue to be 'independent', its news service based on telling the truth. At this time Reith was feeling increasing dissatisfaction with his job—having greater and more political ambitions—and increasingly isolated in the institution that he had created. Committees and controllers put a restraint on individuality and vitality; there was frustration at some of the administrative controls; it was not a happy time.

1938 saw Reith's departure from the BBC. He was succeeded as Director General by F. W. Ogilvie, Fellow of Trinity College, Oxford, formerly Professor of Political Economy at Edinburgh, and President and Vice-Chancellor of Queen's University, Belfast. This was at a time when Louis MacNeice's father was Bishop, so the two families had met; his sister recalls taking Louis to a party given by the Ogilvies in London. (Ogilvie was the 'D.G.' to whom MacNeice wrote at the end of 1940, or early in 1941.) Harman Grisewood has described this period at the BBC as a 'weak interregnum'. The BBC's indecisiveness and lack of constructive action aroused criticism. Reith, briefly Minister of Information (until his old adversary Churchill came to power) had to see the Director General in April 1940 to tell him that the BBC 'should be doing much more on the home front'. There was not as yet much general approval of the war, and radio could help in informing, exhorting, entertaining and countering enemy propaganda. The BBC was aware of its responsibilities, but official statements seemed remote: the *Hand Book* for 1940 spoke of 'the information and encouragement of a people whose temper and manner of living could not fail to be changed by the coming of war'.

Outside the BBC there was also a distance between classes, and regions. There was a notorious early poster exhorting the populace: YOUR COURAGE YOUR CHEERFULNESS YOUR RESOLUTION WILL BRING US VICTORY. 'You' and 'us' is revealing; the work of Mass Observation was needed to bring about a more realistic campaign. In George Orwell's *War-Time Diary* the entry for 3 June 1940 quotes a letter to the *Daily Telegraph* from Lady Oxford, Margot Asquith, on the subject of war economies. 'Since most London houses are deserted there is little entertaining. . . . in any case, most people have to part with their cooks and live in hotels.' As Orwell comments:

'Apparently nothing will ever teach these people that the other 99% of the population exists.' His entry for 3 July 1940 reveals the mood 'of something near despair among thinking people because of the failure of the Government to act and the continuance of dead minds and pro-Fascists in positions of command'.

There were some features being produced to inform and unite people: 'Shadow of the Swastika', 'The Land We Defend', 'Go To It'; but the Drama and Features Department had been evacuated from London at the outbreak of war. They went first to Evesham, bringing an exotic flourish to the quiet countryside, but gloom set in at the inactivity and the restrictions. Rustication ended after two months, when they moved to Manchester. This brought northern and southern features producers together, the nucleus of the section which Laurence Gilliam was anxious to have working nearer the centre, especially when the Blitz began. Through 1940, however, he had to chafe at the delay, and try to work from separate 'centres'. We get a glimpse of London in September 1940, again from Orwell's *Diary*: 'Can't write much of the inanities of the last few days. It is not so much that the bombing is worrying in itself as that the disorganisation of traffic, frequent difficulty of telephoning, shutting of shops . . . wear one out and turn life into a constant scramble to catch up lost time.' Orwell had misgivings about joining the BBC (he was in the Indian Service) but he reasoned that it was better to work inside such an institution, and perhaps improve it, than to remain ineffectively outside, to do 'the dirty work because it's needed'.

MacNeice had been wondering what attitude he should take to the war. In November 1939 he wrote to Professor Dodds that 'in this case it seems quite feasible to be agin the Govt. and still support the war.' In August 1940, he wrote again to Dodds, from America: 'By this stage I am on for doing anything— cleaning sewers or feeding machine guns, but preferably something not too intelligent.' His return was delayed, as we have seen, by a serious illness, until December. He wrote about his feelings in articles for *Horizon* and *Penguin New Writing*:

'Traveller's Return', 'Touching America', 'They Way We Live Now'. He was glad to be back, and responded to the spirit of Londoners, the feeling of being besieged and making a stand for freedom. The liveliest impression is found in an article he wrote for *Picture Post*, describing the morning after a severe raid on 16 April. Amid the excitement and violence, the 'drunken flamboyance' of the fire, the chaos of shattered glass, burning buildings and wrecked shops, he was 'half appalled and half enlivened by this fantasy of destruction'. He was stirred by the people's ability to cope. 'That London can take it may no longer be news, but it remains—and will remain—a national asset. Thursday, April 17, 1941, was a day with a very strange feeling in the air—partly hysterical, partly fatalistic, but partly —I should like to say—epic.'

MacNeice had approached the BBC almost as soon as he was back; his friends the Stahls remember him commandeering the dining-room in their Oriel Square flat in Oxford, while he wrote what must have been his first script, later broadcast. 'The March of the 10,000', about Xenophon, was produced in March. Before that he compiled a programme of poems and songs from America, and wrote 'A Cook's Tour of the London Subways'. He went home to Belfast for a fortnight, but once back in London he continued his free-lance work. This included reviewing films for the *Spectator*, between January and April 1941. Most of the films were just 'entertainment for a drab afternoon', but two were more serious: Anthony Asquith's *Freedom Radio* and Humphrey Jennings's *This is England* with a commentary by Ed Murrow. MacNeice found the latter 'a moving and vivid picture of England, particularly industrial England, at war'. It was a parallel to the work of Features section, in which MacNeice now became more involved.

The first series that he worked on was one aimed at America; he had made his interest in such propaganda clear in his original application to the BBC. The series was 'The Stones Cry Out', taking as its subject the buildings which represented traditional values and which were being bombed. Moves were made to get him on to the staff of Features, which was being increased to meet the needs of war-time broadcasting. Gilliam at last won his argument and he and his team returned to London in May 1941, with quarters at Bedford College where MacNeice had worked before the war. He was appointed on 26 May, for a trial period of three months, and then confirmed in his post. So his new career began, with his new colleagues: Harding, Gilliam, Bridson, Dillon and the others whose work earned Features such high esteem during and after the war.

Chapter Three

Features in War-time: 1941—1945

This new crusade
Autumn Sequel, Canto IV

MacNeice commemorated an early meeting with his new colleagues in *Autumn Sequel*: Harrap is Harding, Herriot is Gilliam and Devlin, Jack Dillon.

> As Harrap said
> Suggesting I might make an air-borne bard
>
> (Who spoke in parentheses and now is dead),
> 'On the one hand—as a matter of fact I should
> Say on the first hand—there is daily bread,
>
> At least I assume there is, to be made good
> If good is the right expression; on the other
> Or one of the other hands there is much dead wood
>
> On the air in a manner of speaking which tends to smother
> What spark you start with; nevertheless although
> Frustration is endemic (take my brother,
>
> He simply thinks me mad to bother so
> With people by the million) nevertheless
> Our work is aimed at one at a time, you know,
>
> And by and large and at an approximate guess
> If poets must live (perhaps I am wrong to think
> They must but if they must) they might find this mess
>
> No more a mess than wasting wits and ink
> On scratching each other's backs or possibly eyes
> Out or half out (no wonder they take to drink;

We might have one by the way) but it could arise
They found it in fact less messy; after all
Homer liked words aloud.' Harrap's blue eyes

Twinkled between the brackets. . . .

The studied Oxford nonchalance, assumed by both men, would
have been understood by both; beneath lay a genuine desire to
do something useful, and to communicate. So MacNeice agreed
to 'join this new crusade', to undertake the purely ephemeral
work of war-time, persuading neutral nations and reassuring
their own 'blacked-out compatriots' that values still mattered.
Meanwhile,

Herriot filled his pipe
(Who was going to be my boss) and Devlin, who
Was going to be my colleague, took his swipe

At both their dignities. . . .

For MacNeice, Features was a new world. He had been
dissatisfied with academic life, rejecting both common-room
and campus. War had interrupted everyone's lives, setting
people unsuspectingly on new courses, if they survived. Before
the war, in *Autumn Journal*, MacNeice had written of his hope
of finding a community where 'the individual . . . works with
the rest . . . where the people are more than a crowd'. No longer
squandering oneself in 'self-assertion', working skilfully and
with expertise, mind valued but body not neglected—he might
have been setting out some of the qualities he was to find in
Features. It may have been a necessary but it was a none the less
congenial niche. Francis Dillon, who knew him well, says that
Louis was an introvert trying to grow an extravert skin; the
department was a suitable place for such an attempt, especially
as convivial habits eased the way. In Laurence Gilliam he was
to find a friend and a superior whom he could respect. Among
those who worked with Gilliam was Douglas Cleverdon, whose
description we may quote. 'Gilliam himself was experienced in
journalism, and had a particular enthusiasm for radio documentaries; he was also a man of wide-ranging interests and of
inspiring integrity; he was compassionate and courageous, and

would always back a project that had a chance of success rather than reject it because it might fail. He was also a *bon viveur*, unpunctual, extremely good company, and a tower of strength to his subordinates. To him mainly was due the development of BBC features as a radio form.'

Francis Dillon was MacNeice's mentor and friend, an old hand from whom Louis was good at picking up hints, and an irrepressible 'Lord of Misrule', to use Gilliam's nickname for his Features staff. His humour, folk-singing and love of schnapps are used to characterise him in *Autumn Sequel*. Dillon and MacNeice often went through war-time London to get material for their features: 'Devlin and I fished in this troubled air.' Once they went to St Paul's, to help as well as observe, when it was ablaze after being bombed. (Jack insisted that Louis was after a state burial.) On another occasion they went to the bombed Museum of the Royal College of Surgeons, and found bizarre specimens afloat—a panda skin and a foetus 'like a small soapstone Buddha'. Jack recalls that Louis was shaken by some of the sights; in MacNeice's words, in *Autumn Sequel*, they were 'humbled and exalted day by day'. He went further afield with Dillon, going halfway across the Atlantic on an American destroyer to get material about convoy ships for a radio series, 'Freedom's Ferry'. After the war they were to go together to India for four months.

Much of the wandering through London, punctuated by welcome stops for drinks, was for the scripts that Louis MacNeice was writing for the series aimed at America, 'The Stones Cry Out'. The message continued: 'but the people stand firm'. His first contribution was on Dr Johnson's House in Gough Square, broadcast on 5 May, when he was still an 'outside' writer. Evocative street names are listed, and the alphabet forms a motif: 'A is for art, A is for arson, B is for bookcase, B is for bomb. . . .' Harpsichord music suggests the period, while an indomitable old lady represents war-time Londoners. His next script, for 27 May, was on Westminster Abbey. An account of the raid on 10 May is interwoven with historical references and themes from the Bible. At first his scripts were produced by Harding or Gilliam, but by September he started to produce some of his own work. He acquired the skills readily and became one of the best producers in the BBC. Radio and he seemed perfectly suited to one another. Other buildings in that first series were Madame Tussaud's, the House of Commons, the Temple, the Plymouth Barbican, St Paul's and the Royal College of Surgeons; he also did one feature on Belfast.

Louis MacNeice was still an important member of literary London, which though reduced in numbers was brought more closely together by the war. There was Cyril Connolly and *Horizon*, making a stand for aesthetic values (but he did publish Goronwy Rees's 'Letter from a Soldier'); John Lehmann and *New Writing* with more emphasis on the social role of the writer; and the editor of *Poetry London*, Meary Tambimuttu, who was generous in his assistance of poets, whether established or unknown. Social occasions brought these 1930s survivors together: parties at Elizabeth Bowen's Regent's Park house, or John Lehmann's flat, or special events like the wedding of Stephen Spender to Natasha Litvin, in April 1941. John Lehmann records this, in his autobiography: the occasion 'in reuniting our literary world, painfully marked the absence of Christopher and Wystan. William Plomer and Joe Ackerley were there, acting once more the satiric chorus in undertones which grew disturbingly merrier as the alcohol began to work, Cecil Day Lewis and Louis MacNeice, Julian and Juliette Huxley . . . Rose Macaulay, Stephen's fellow-editors on *Horizon* Cyril Connolly and Peter Watson, and Tambimuttu. . . .'

Some of the younger authors served in the war; others experienced the Blitz. Even to soldiers on leave London seemed an exciting place. The mood is reflected in the work of Elizabeth Bowen, Henry Green, Graham Greene, Anthony Powell, William Sansom. Some of these acted as wardens, fire-watchers, or members of the fire service. Spender remembers the sense of being on 'a little island of civilization surrounded by burning churches—that was how the arts seemed in England during the war.' John Lehmann recalls: 'We were united in a this-has-got-to-be-seen-through attitude towards the war which was taken for granted, and also in a determination to guard the free world of ideas from any misguided military encroachment. We *needed*

one another, and for purposes larger than our own security or
ambitions. This sense of cohesion was extraordinarily stimulating.' Not only writing, but theatre, music and painting were
valued more intensely; war artists were commissioned, and plays
and concerts flourished amidst the danger. Musicians and
actors served in the forces, but were often given leave to perform
in a civilian capacity.

Much of the writing, acting and musical talent was afforded
an outlet by the BBC, and the Drama and Features Department
made a notable contribution. New writers and producers were
taken on—including MacNeice—during 1941 and 1942. Among
them were Robert Barr, Leonard Cottrell, Patric Dickinson,
Robert Gittings, Robert Speaight, Igor Vinogradoff. One of the
music assistants was Edward Sackville-West; and the pre-war
television producer, Dallas Bower, joined for a time before
returning to film-making. Bower was to be instrumental in
giving MacNeice his first major radio assignments. In 1942
Features moved from Bedford College to Rothwell, near
Broadcasting House, and the neighbouring pubs, the Stag and
the George, became havens for artists of all kinds: at any one
time there might be a gathering of leading poets and composers—MacNeice, Dylan Thomas, William Alwyn, Elisabeth
Lutyens, Humphrey Searle, William Walton. Benjamin Britten
returned from America during 1942. In the pubs, company
could be enjoyed, ideas exchanged, contacts made with
Features producers, and outside writers who came to Broadcasting House could meet fellow-artists. It was an exciting time.
Gilliam in particular should be credited with encouraging so
much talent.

We have occasional glimpses of MacNeice in the memoirs of
other writers. Kathleen Raine gives a poet's view of him—one
of the faces that emerge for her from 'the shadows of war-time
London'. 'Louis MacNeice I did not know very well . . . but he
occasionally took me out to dinner, and gave me odds and ends
of writing to do for the BBC. . . . Louis was most kind to my
struggling and largely worthless efforts. I remember sitting in
his company one evening, in the Café Royal probably, and his
making up a half serious fantasy, about people who either had,

or did not have, "a little candle" alight in them. He himself still shone, in those days, with a poet's soft interior light which one might imagine coming from the rath of the *Sidhe*.' In different mood, Victor Pritchett recalls, from his war-time diary: 'Sometimes one was excited, sometimes careless in these raids. Sometimes angry and scornful. Once Louis MacNeice and I wandered down the streets in St John's Wood and tried, unsuccessfully, to carry away a stone lion from the garden of a destroyed house. The thing was too heavy.' (And they, presumably, not best fitted for such exploits after a convivial evening.) V. S. Pritchett also recollects how he occasionally stayed with MacNeice (who lived then in Wellington Road, St John's Wood), and was persuaded by his host to crawl into a shelter with the family and the dog, during the raids, despite his reluctance—polite insistence always won the day.

The sense of cohesion described by John Lehmann was to be found in Features too. War lent an immediacy and shared purpose—the job was worth doing, the enemy clearly evil. So it was in special circumstances that MacNeice began his BBC career. The work that Gilliam, Bridson, Cleverdon, Dillon, Cecil McGivern and Stephen Potter had been doing before the war was now more urgent, and really came into its own. Apart from the enlightening and informative features, Val Gielgud wanted entertainment to be provided, so the fund of creative talent had varied outlets. (The famous 'ITMA' and 'Brains Trust' were provided by other departments.) Outside the studios also, Features and other BBC colleagues met and were a social group. As for the 'offices' in Rothwell, they were distinctive: really a series of flats, 'front doors' were propped open, and there were bathrooms and kitchens attached. These were not supposed to be in use, but Jack Dillon could twist the charladies round his little finger—they even cleaned the bath for him—so the office provided a convenient pied à terre for very late nights in town.

This is the setting for MacNeice's work. He later wrote about the group experience of Features: 'In this age of irreconcilable idioms I have often heard writers hankering for some sort of group life. . . . we cannot but envy playwrights, actors or

musical executants. And here again I for one have found this
missing group experience, in a valid form, in radio. Radio
writers and producers *can* talk shop together because their shop
is not, as with poets, a complex of spiritual intimacies but a
matter of craftsmanship. . . . we are fully entitled to discuss
whether dialogue rings true, whether the dramatic climax is
dramatic, how well the whole thing works. This is refreshing
for a writer.' MacNeice's enjoyment of radio work is clear here:
he enjoyed working with actors, musicians and engineers; he
liked the valid nature of the co-operation—it was not a self-
indulgent coterie, but a purposeful team. As for the intellectual
stimulation: he held that his colleagues would compare very
well 'with almost any contemporary salon of literati'; they
were, on the whole, 'quicker-witted, more versatile, less ego-
centric, less conventional, more humane'. (We may remember,
too, that during the war one of MacNeice's BBC colleagues and
friends, although not in Features, was William Empson.)

While MacNeice was halfway across the Atlantic with Francis
Dillon in June 1941, the captain of the ship picked up on his
radio the news that Russia had been invaded and was now an
ally. After their return home, MacNeice was asked to write a
feature on Chekhov—the BBC might be unwilling to play the
'Internationale', but there was no objection to celebrating
Russian culture. Stephen Potter produced the script, and when
MacNeice revised the piece in 1944 he paid tribute to Potter for
tackling the original version, 'almost unproduceable in places',
written when he 'had not envisaged the studio set-up'. In
October 1941, Gilliam produced another feature written by
MacNeice. 'The Glory that is Greece', to commemorate the
first anniversary of Greece's entry into the war; he juxtaposes
the soldiers of 1941 with those of Thermopylae holding out
against the Persians. The suggestion came from the Foreign
Office that a large-scale feature might be appropriate to
celebrate the heroism of Russia. The producer was to be Dallas
Bower; he chose MacNeice to write the script.

The subject, also selected by Bower, was the story of Alexander
Nevsky's defiance of the Teutonic invaders, as told by Eisenstein
in his film. Bower, before the war, had used a copy of the film

to illustrate the art of camera to trainees in television. So he, MacNeice and Dillon saw the film, with its stunning visual effects—these would have to be rendered in words and sound. Prokofiev's score was used, and MacNeice wrote some splendid descriptive passages, as well as maintaining the sense of drama. The terrifying black helms of the Knights and the battle on the frozen lake are described by two onlookers (this device he used again, in 1959, in his play about the battle of Clontarf). The production, done 'live', with cast and orchestra, was from Bedford Corn Exchange, where the Music Division was based during the war. The cast was headed by Robert Donat. As the large 'open' studio broadcast was about to begin, in December 1941, an indefinite delay was ordered: when the awaited bulletin came, it was to report the attack on Pearl Harbor, thus adding to the drama of the occasion.

America was at last in the war. Another major BBC feature was required. Again Bower was asked to produce it; again he chose MacNeice to write the script, and suggested the subject to him—a play based upon Samuel Eliot Morison's *Admiral of the Ocean Sea*. This is the story of Columbus, and 1942 would be the 450th anniversary of the 'discovery' of the New World. It was certainly an epic theme, one which might catch the stayed with MacNeice (who lived then in Wellington Road, St imagination of a poet. It was in this way that 'Christopher Columbus' came to be written, one of the most important radio scripts up until then, and one of MacNeice's major radio plays. Dallas Bower has commented: 'MacNeice's task in breaking down Morison's vast narrative into a manageable dramatic whole was formidable and in general I think he succeeded admirably. I was determined that the musical counterpart to MacNeice's text should match the latter in quality.' In January 1942, he contacted William Walton, with whom he had worked before; Walton said that he would like to write the score, but other commitments would mean a delay. Dallas Bower preferred to wait until Walton could do the work, rather than ask another composer, so arrangements went forward. On one occasion Bower asked Walton to meet him and MacNeice for dinner at the Etoile in Charlotte Street, more of a literary haunt then than now. Originally planned for March, the radio play was finally placed on 12 October—the actual anniversary of the arrival of Columbus and his ships in America.

MacNeice continued his activities outside the BBC: he gave lectures and poetry readings, to the Poetry Society and to students; wrote articles; worked on film scripts for the Ministry of Information; produced a pamphlet on the American army. At the BBC he was busy with routine features as well as the 'Columbus' script. One feature was on Vienna, the 'city which never dies', for the fourth anniversary of its occupation by Hitler; another was on Greece, for Greek Independence Day: these were broadcast in March. In April there was a light-hearted piece: 'Calling All Fools'. April Fool programmes were a BBC tradition, which MacNeice came to enjoy. 'Salute to the USSR' continued the work of tributes to the Allies (after the war he would write a 'Salute to All Fools'); 'The Debate Continues', in May, showed that the long history of free debate in this country had not been stopped by the bombing of the House of Commons the year before. He contributed features on Hitler and Goebbels to the 'Black Gallery' series. An hour-long feature on Yugoslavia, 'The Undefeated', went out in June. No wonder, then, that a note in *Radio Times*, in May 1942, called MacNeice 'a man who seems capable of turning out the most stately contributions to broadcasting with a scarcely credible facility'. That year, too, he might have been called up, but it was decided that he was doing more valuable work in radio. Naturally most of the output was propaganda, as was essential in the early years of the war. But the play on Columbus was offering him more scope. The routine features continued with 'Britain to America' in July, and 'Salute to the Army' in September.

During 1942 two important events occurred in MacNeice's personal life. In April his father died; he held him in great respect and remembered him with affection, as poems like 'The Strand' and 'Woods' reveal, or the passage in 'The Kingdom':

> dead in daffodil time
> Before it had come to Easter. All is well with
> One who believed and practised and whose life
> Presumed the Resurrection. What that means

He may have felt he knew; this much is certain—
The meaning filled his actions, made him courteous
And lyrical and strong and kind and truthful,
A generous puritan.

The influence of his father was not overt, but it was real. The poem 'The Strand' describes him affectionately, paddling in the sea; there is a photograph of the Bishop, trousers rolled up, hand in hand with his grandson, Dan, walking by the sea, in just the way the poem describes. Later poems reveal MacNeice's admiration of his father, and the ways in which he carried out his pastoral duties and withstood prejudice. Then in July he wrote to Mercy MacCann, from a flat in Maiden Lane, next to Covent Garden: 'I got married this Wednesday to someone you will like very much. Her name is Hedli. . . . We both hope to come over to Ireland about July 20th for at least a fortnight.' They stayed with Mercy at Vinecash, and had a very happy time. Hedli Anderson was a singer who had known Auden and Isherwood before the war, and had worked with the Group Theatre. During 1942 she won praise for her interpretation of *Pierrot Lunaire*, and she was to take part in several of her husband's radio plays and give recitals from time to time, often coupled with poetry readings by Louis. Louis's son had been living with relatives in Ireland; he could now rejoin his father. A year later, Louis and Hedli had a daughter, Corinna, so the family was complete. In January 1943 they had moved from Hedli's Maiden Lane flat to St John's Wood.

MacNeice continued to write poems, although there can have been little time for this. Following *Plant and Phantom* in 1941, the war poems included some vignettes: 'Bottleneck', 'The conscript', 'The mixer', 'The libertine', 'The satirist', as well as the better-known poems about the Blitz. An effective poem is 'Alcohol' (it was published in *Horizon* in January 1943): quoting Bacchylides, the poet writes of 'golden seas of drink', which make everyone equal.

Looking around in war
We watch the many who have returned to the dead
Ordering time-and-again the same-as-before:
. . . . Bacchylides was right
And self-deception golden. . . .

In September of 1942 MacNeice was thirty-five, and
'Prayer in mid-passage' surely refers to this; he often wrote
birthday poems. The poem echoes the hymns of his childhood,
and has a valedictory quality:

> O Thou my monster, Thou my guide,
> Be with me where the bluffs divide
> Nor let me contemplate return
> To where my backward chattels burn
> In haunts of friendship and untruth—
> The Cities of the Plain of Youth.

Some poems still express yearning 'for the hollow Heart of the
Milky Way', a longing 'for what was never home', but others,
like 'Prospect', express hope for the future:

> Though Nature's laws exploit
> And defeat anarchic men,
> Though every sandcastle concept
> Being *ad hoc* must crumble again,
>
> And though to-day is arid,
> We know—and knowing bless—
> That rooted in futurity
> There is a plant of tenderness.

The longer poems of the 1940s have a meditative strain—this
would seem to have been a time of personal fulfilment.

In October 1942 'Christopher Columbus' was broadcast.
Notes and comments in the BBC Archives show that he conceived it as 'essentially a one man, one idea programme'.
Columbus would be shown as 'permanently motivated by a
mystical *idée fixe*', and as 'an egoist, uncompromising and
difficult in his dealings with other people'. The main emphasis
of the programme was to be on 'the excitement of achieving the
impossible'. So this is an epic tale, a tale of quest, with a
romantic yet ruthless hero. The inhuman dedication is shown
in the episodes involving Beatriz, who loves Columbus; there is
also a touch of lyricism and melancholy:

> Though he is my love
> He is not for me;
> What he loves is over

Loveless miles of sea
Haunted by the West. . . .

His obsession drives him on despite failure and the opposition
of the official commission; eventually, after the defeat of the
Moors, Queen Isabella does help him. The second part of the
play shows the quest beyond the sea, and the triumphant
return, when Columbus tells them all: 'I have brought you a
new world.'

MacNeice realised the potential of his medium, and the part
that music could play. He sent an outline to Walton, so that the
music could 'illuminate the dominant themes'; it would also
suggest transitions, from a quayside tavern, with its guitar
music, to the ship, with sea shanties, or to the chant of the monks
at the monastery of La Rabida. The 'Te Deum' is sung
when Columbus reaches his goal, contrasting with more exotic
music that suggests a native atmosphere. Processional music
marks the progress through Spain after the return. As well as
the music there is the evocative use of words: names and
description allow the mind to create the scene. Seville, the
Sierras, Cordoba, Alicante, Valencia, Tarragona—

With its dark cobbled alleys clambering up the hill
And the smell of fish and wine
And the broken Roman arches that betoken
So much glory of the past . . .

The grandiloquence of the court scenes and official proclamations is in contrast to the poetry of inner soliloquy—perfect for
radio. Columbus, alone at night on deck, hears voices of faith
and doubt: choruses are effectively used here. The text was
later published, with an introduction by MacNeice which
makes an interesting essay on radio drama. He stresses the need
for clear and economical construction, the freedom from the
constraints of time and place, the appeal to the imagination.
Further, 'you can, with less fuss and more credibility than on
the stage (and perhaps than on the screen) introduce—if you
want to—Allegorical speakers or choruses.'

The BBC Symphony Orchestra and Chorus were conducted
by Sir Adrian Boult. The cast was a fine one, to match the

quality of words and music. Laurence Olivier played Columbus (Vivien Leigh, who Drama Bookings Department thought would not be free, sat with the producer through the performance), Marius Goring and Robert Speaight read the Choruses of Faith and Doubt, Gladys Young was Queen Isabella, Margaret Rawlings Beatriz, and Hedli Anderson played a waiting-woman. Among others in the large cast were actors who often took part in works by MacNeice—radio actors like Laidman Browne, Mark Dignam, Stephen Murray and Alan Wheatley. These early 'live' productions had all the excitement and tension of a theatre performance, a team effort involving producer, actors, musicians, technicians. Fortunately, a recording was made, although this was before the days of tape, so the performance survives. Not only was it 'a major creation for radio', in the words of Douglas Cleverdon, but a valuable precedent for many of MacNeice's subsequent plays in the saga or quest tradition.

The next series of features was wider in range than those done previously. For 'The Four Freedoms' MacNeice was encouraged to present his own ideas. These he outlined in notes and a memo to Gilliam, dated 28 December 1942. 'Start with a big bang with the French Revolution as fountain head of so many of our modern conceptions and as also linking up with the struggle for revival and/or survival of the French People today.' To follow this, he proposed a switch to Early Christians, and then Pericles. He also suggested the Renaissance, Milton, Lenin, and a final programme 'to summarise these various contributions to human liberty and to balance the pros and cons'. These ideas are amplified in two and a half pages of typescript, handwritten marginalia stressing certain points. The tone shows enthusiasm: he wanted to avoid 'whitewashing', and to deal as fairly as possible with the examples chosen. He wrote features on all but one of the suggestions, Lenin, and produced all except 'The Renaissance'. Benjamin Britten wrote the music for 'Pericles'— MacNeice had asked him for music 'of a rather special nature, being an impression of early Greek music'; it would require 'skilful rendering'. The series was broadcast during February and March 1943.

The radio work was an outlet for many ideas and skills, while the poetry was a more private exercise. At the same time that MacNeice was busy with the early stage of his career, Eliot was also trying to combine private poetry and public war effort—of a more exhausting and less rewarding nature (many talks and travels were undertaken). In a letter to E. Martin Browne, dated 20 October 1942, Eliot commented: 'It is one thing to see what was best worth one's while doing, in a distant retrospect, but in the midst of what is going on now, it is hard, when you sit down at a desk, to feel confident that morning after morning spent fiddling with words and rhythms is a justified activity. . . . And, on the other hand, external or public activity is more of a drug than is this solitary toil which often seems so pointless.' Much of the BBC work was a chore, but generally it was enjoyable and had a sense of purpose; and there was the companionship of the group experience. During the summer of 1943 there were two literary features: 'The Death of Byron' in May, and 'The Death of Marlowe' in June. Those more concerned with the war were 'Sicily and Freedom' in June, and 'Independence Day' (produced by Gilliam) in July. 'Four Years at War' was broadcast in September. But one feature that autumn was suggested by MacNeice himself: the true story of a young Italian poet, Lauro de Bosis, who, in 1931, had sacrificed his life in a gesture against Fascism.

'The Story of My Death', as MacNeice called this short play, was to reveal techniques which would influence later plays. It was a contrast to the grandeur of 'Columbus', and brought in colloquial conversation and modern argument (when de Bosis visits America and talks to students). The mainstream of the play, however, is poetic: the poetry of Shelley, beloved of de Bosis's father, forms one thread; de Bosis's own poetry another. Shut in his tower in Ancona, he had written a verse play, *Icaro*, which provides an apt metaphor: de Bosis emerges from his artistic isolation and flies over Rome scattering leaflets against Mussolini. On one flight his plane disappears: the radio form allows for a last soliloquy on this flight. In a programme note for a later rebroadcast, MacNeice made the comment: 'I have always thought of it as *technically* one of my more interesting

programmes.' (First broadcast on 8 October 1943, it was
revived in 1952.)

That same autumn MacNeice received news of a death that
affected him deeply—that of his friend Graham Shepard who
had been serving with the Atlantic convoys. Ernest Stahl, a
friend of both men, recalls that Louis was shattered by the
news. The memory was still keen ten years later, when Mac-
Neice was writing *Autumn Sequel*:

> But Gavin's cradle sank and the dark defiled
> Atlantic scrawled its flourish of cold foam
> Above him, while on shore we drank our mild
>
> And bitter, wondering when he would come home.
> Until one day (I was living in St John's Wood
> In one small cell of London's half empty comb)
>
> His sister called and came upstairs and stood
> Quietly and said quietly, 'We have lost
> Gavin'; a cobra spread an enormous hood
>
> Over the window and a sudden frost
> Froze all the honey left in the looted hive. . . .

At the time, in 1943, MacNeice wrote 'The casualty', in
memory of his most 'accordant friend' with whom he could no
longer share an 'articulate silence'. The next year he wrote to
Gilliam about a script in preparation, then called 'Portrait of a
Contemporary'. It was to be a biography of 'a serious-minded
young man (born 1905–10 and died in action at sea some time
in the war)'. This was to be a commemoration of his friend in a
very moving play, called eventually 'He Had a Date'.

Outlining the play, MacNeice pointed out that despite the
middle-class, public school, Oxbridge background, the young
man 'avoided being moulded and so can serve as a symbol of
the various discontents of this country between the two wars'.
Throughout a series of unsatisfactory jobs and relationships,
including marriage, the character was 'gradually clarifying his
outlook', eventually having a closer understanding of the working class, experiencing the Blitz, then joining the Navy: 'and
there for the first time be really happy through experiencing

that peculiar and revitalising community of feeling which is said to characterise a "good ship". . . .' Two things may be said at this point: the correspondence is not necessarily a close one in detail between the character, Tom Varney, and Shepard himself; and some of the experiences are close to MacNeice's own. It was meant to be representative, not entirely personal. It is the first of MacNeice's radio plays which is a 'biography' of a modern type—he tried several variations on the theme, with mixed success. This play remains a very effective one, both from the point of view of feeling and technically. It marks an important development in MacNeice's work for radio, and stands in the line begun by Sieveking and Guthrie.

The biography takes the form of a flashback of his life as the character drowns: the play opens with him on watch aboard ship—he sights something approaching and is asked for the bearing. 'What bearing?' is then applied to his own life. Motifs are used like poetic images; some indeed were to be used in poems. At six months old Tom's mind is likened to a Japanese paper flower, which will unfold only in water; there is the Jack-in-the-box, a frightening symbol; 'Rock-a-bye-baby'; a rock on the seashore; the sea itself. Another device which MacNeice first used in this play is the suggestion of period and mood through snatches of popular tunes—he wrote to his friend John Waterhouse, at Birmingham University, to ask for a list of suitable songs. Tom's childhood, schooldays and Oxford period are traced; then he learns some truths about class during the General Strike. After this he abandons 'Greats', disillusioned by university life. He works for a time on a provincial newspaper, and marries a Scots girl, Mary; the marriage does not work. The key points after this are Spain, Munich and the war. One hopeful interlude is set at Lords, when Tom meets Jane, whom he knew at Oxford. She still loves him and they indulge in brief nostalgia and hope:

> I dreamed I walked still to and fro
> And from her company I did not go
> But when I waked it was not so. . . .

C

He joins the Navy, arranges to meet Mary again, but is recalled to his ship.

'Effects' are always an important, and intriguing, part of radio production: here they are used sparingly and with good results. There is the telegram boy's knock on the door, the bat hitting the ball at Lords, the bleak wind as the captain announces the disbanding of the International Brigades in Spain. As in *Autumn Journal*, we have a personal life set against a background of public events. MacNeice's poems read well, and his longer ones use easy conversational tones and more lyrical moments; the extension of these uses of language into radio work, where effects and music could be added to the range of possibilities, is understandable. In this play the challenging role is that of Tom Varney, whose inner meditation holds the whole piece together; interspersed are the sections of narrative-through-dialogue. Variation comes with different voices—some regional accents are used, like that of the Scottish sailor who sings a ballad about a dead man. It was chance that the play about de Bosis preceded this one, but some of the techniques had been tried there. The patterning is very satisfying, and the overall structure controlled. The discipline of the work of art is given force by the depth of feeling animating the play.

Something of this feeling may be found in the poem, 'The casualty':

> Yes, all you gave were inklings; even so
> Invaluable—such as I remember
> Out of your mouth or only in your eyes
> On walks in blowsy August, Brueghel-like December,
> Or when the gas was hissing and a glow
> Of copper jugs gave back your lyrical surprise.
>   ... O did you
> Make one last integration, find a Form
> Grow out of formlessness when the Atlantic hid you?

The 'inklings', promise unfulfilled, echo Tom's regrets at the end of the play: 'Believe it or not, I did have ideals of a sort. But I could not quite get my bearing.' The play struck a chord in some of the listeners—in those who (according to the report of the Listeners' Panel) found it 'heartbreakingly true' as a picture of a representative of their generation, a frustrated idealist. Others, however, found it 'unworthy'; a few, especially women, refused to believe that anyone could be such a 'selfish brute'. One personal letter of appreciation, written to MacNeice himself, was from Gilbert Harding. 'The people who listened with me found it most moving—for want of a better word and we are grateful to you.' The original broadcast was on 28 June 1944; there was a revised production for the Third Programme in 1949, and there have been more recent productions. Douglas Cleverdon describes it as 'a brilliant example of sceneless composition', but MacNeice himself seemed to under-rate his play.

The war had now moved into its last phase—features were less propaganda than reporting of the progressive victories after D-Day, when the famous 'War Report' series began, broadcast after the nine o'clock news each evening and continuing until the end of the war. MacNeice had more freedom, although he was still assigned some features. As preparations for the Second Front opening were being made, Gilliam planned programmes 'to catch and repeat the greatest moment of tension of our time almost as it was being lived'. He wanted MacNeice to write a feature for D-Day. Val Gielgud was not enthusiastic, but would not stand in the way if the proposal 'struck a really creative note' in the poet. MacNeice pointed out, in a note accompanying a draft of the script, that he wanted to avoid grandiose phrases. (Gilliam's style often tended to be rhetorical.) MacNeice explained: 'I have used the narrator as a bridge between the inarticulate fighting man and the listener who wants to hear expressed those things which the fighting man *acts on* but does not normally express to anyone.'

He had already begun to widen the range of his own writing for radio. In March 1944 there was the first of his plays based on a folk or fairy tale. 'The Nosebag' is 'a direct and very simple dramatisation of a Russian folk story'. The published text was to be dedicated to Francis Dillon, but this play is not in Dillon's vein of topical satire (though other plays by MacNeice are of this kind). The story of Death and the Soldier is told in a more straightforward, but jaunty, manner, reminiscent of Stravinsky's

'Soldier's Tale'. The Soldier acquires a magic pack of cards and a nosebag that will always provide food. In one village he hears of a haunted palace, and offers to help the Tsar (played by Peter Ustinov). The midnight haunting provided a marvellous opportunity for sound effects: howling wind, jabbering and screeching of devils, the clock striking midnight. A note to the play lets us into some of the secrets: 'the bestial noises of the devils were achieved by a mixture of discs on the turn-tables and voices in the studio; my key disc was a recording of jabbering apes.' Later, for the clanging in the smithies of hell, MacNeice had to decide between 'spot effects' in the studio or a gramophone record. ('Spot effects' involved anything which ingenuity could contrive to get the correct sound.) 'In the end I disregarded realism and plumped for a ringing noise. The records of real smithies being too unpoetic, I used a recorded bell-bird.' MacNeice enjoyed working out his effects meticulously.

Death had to be represented in the play: when the Soldier tries to help the Tsar he finds Death standing at the bed's head, and bargains with her. MacNeice commented: 'The voice of Death would be out of most actresses' compass. Miss Gladys Young attained it. While this programme was meant to be fun, I had no intention that "Death" should be merely funny. She had to be frightening—and, in a way, pathetic.' This play gave MacNeice the freedom to employ fantasy and humour—two qualities which became characteristic of some of his radio work, extending the range that he had already encompassed in 'Christopher Columbus' and 'He Had a Date'. The Soldier tricks Death, but is finally repaid by her, and condemned to eternal life. He takes part in battles throughout history, until the present: 'I added this piece of homage to the moujik because of what was happening as I wrote—at the beginning of 1944. . . . I greatly admired and admire the courage of the Russian soldier; this story after all was about the same type of man and it was the same type of man who made this story.'

In July came the anniversary of Chekhov's death, when MacNeice revised an earlier feature, this time producing it himself. Such a piece, a literary biography, was expected to give accurate information, but there could be interpretation. MacNeice's own intention was 'to correct the popular fallacy which uses the word Tchehov as a synonym for melancholia and which, incidentally, vitiates so many English productions of his plays'. The action takes place on the day of Chekhov's death, earlier phases of the story being told through the memories of the writer and his wife. MacNeice was aware of the possibility of such a device sounding contrived, but he preferred it 'to the cold-fish voice of the Narrator'. Another device, used at the end of the play, was the dream, deriving from an actual dream recorded by Chekhov. This gave a more poetic turn to the end of the play, a sense of foreboding and the echoing of voices heard before (the last of MacNeice's radio plays was to have the same kind of ending). The dream also made 'a better prelude to the death itself than could have been contrived through any further dialogue'. So 'Sunbeams in his Hat' ends with Chekhov's voice, 'speaking slowly in a great space', asking where he can book a passage to Odessa.

An outstanding aspect of MacNeice's work for radio was the conjunction of words and music. The Walton score was the first major example, and MacNeice's friend Britten had written music for the short feature on Pericles. For 'The Nosebag' he used excerpts from Russian composers. His friend, Gerald Abraham, the music historian, and at that time Director of the Gramophone Department, had advised on the music for 'Salute to the USSR', and did the same for 'The Nosebag'. MacNeice's next plays were to be adaptations of Apuleius: 'The Golden Ass' and 'Cupid and Psyche'—these would offer an opportunity to commission special music. One member of the Features section who was also a musician was Eddie Sackville-West; in November 1944, with less than two weeks before the productions, MacNeice asked him if he could recommend someone. Sackville-West suggested a young man fresh from college, with only one score to his credit. This was Antony Hopkins. In fact, back in 1941, he had acted as rehearsal pianist for Walter Goehr (whom he knew from Morley College) at a BBC rehearsal of 'Alexander Nevsky'. He did not meet MacNeice then, and had no idea that it would be through this poet—only a name to him—that his own career in broadcasting would come about. The first time he heard his music played by a full orchestra was for MacNeice's plays. It was a good partnership, although MacNeice was rather 'a dark horse', withdrawn and laconic. Hopkins added enthusiasm and inventiveness, and they shared a sense of humour—there was always something of the schoolboy in MacNeice, Hopkins recalls.

In a programme note in *Radio Times*, MacNeice warned that some listeners might be shocked at the picaresque story of 'The Golden Ass', but it should please those who like surprise, strangeness and laughter. 'Cupid and Psyche' provides a contrast, with its lyricism and gentler humour. Music gives the atmosphere and effects, and really is, as MacNeice hoped, integral to the play. It makes delightful listening. 'Oracular music' signifies the visit to Miletus, while funeral music accompanies the sad procession of Psyche and her family to the mountain top, where they presume she will die. Instead, 'zephyr music' wafts her to a 'deep and flowery valley', and an enchanted palace. The magic is suggested by the music, and a musical motif signals Cupid's nightly visits. When Venus decides to destroy the beautiful mortal, she sets her seemingly impossible tasks. Animal helpers, represented by music, are ants, giant sheep and an eagle. The climbing of the mountain to the black cascade which is the source of the Styx, and the descent to Hell, to Proserpina, are also rendered musically; as are the weaving women and the ascent from the Underworld. Among the jokes is the overblown fanfare which annoys Jupiter: 'This prelude is not really necessary *every* time I have visitors.'

By the end of 1944 MacNeice and Hopkins were at work on 'A Roman Holiday', in which the tradition of Saturnalia is used to comment on the state of society. This came from a sudden idea of MacNeice's, to use a group of Roman types at a banquet. It could not be placed during Saturnalia, from 17 to 25 December, but on 10 January, another programme being postponed to make way for it; this was Gilliam's doing, so that MacNeice's feature should not be lost. (MacNeice rarely had a programme suggestion turned down—his superiors valued his work and were anxious to encourage him.) In this short play (it lasts half an hour) an old aristocrat regrets the passing of the Republic; Calvus, a rich profiteer, is the host; a *nouveau riche* freedman and various idle and hedonistic young men are among the guests. Some of the music, MacNeice wrote to Hopkins, should suggest 'banal sensuality'—there is something spiritual missing from Augustus' ordered society; but the slave-girl, Philinna, was to be characterised by a pastoral and plaintive flute solo. She uses the licence of Saturnalia to tell the others that they are not really happy—they are 'lonely in this world'. The future holds little hope for her and her kind. Then, suddenly, she has an intuition that somewhere, at that time, something might be happening to bring hope. The possible Christian solution is suggested by Palestrina's 'Hodie Christus Natus Est'. (MacNeice had asked Antony Hopkins to choose some 'appropriately moving piece of Christian music'.)

After preaching national propaganda, earlier in the war, MacNeice was beginning to transmit his own message to his audience, in his own terms. We find similarities in the poems of the same period: looked at in this context, they yield a clearer meaning. 'Epitaph for liberal poets' expresses the fear that civilised ways of life are being destroyed, along with the freedom of individual thought. No longer paid to be themselves, the poets will be superseded by

> The tight-lipped technocratic Conquistadores ...

It has happened in the past:

> The Individual has died before; Catullus
> Went down young, gave place to those who were born old
> And more adaptable and were not even jealous
> Of his wild life and lyrics. Though our songs
> Were not so warm as his, our fate is no less cold.
>
> Such silence then before us, pinned against the wall,
> Why need we whine? There is no way out, the birds
> Will tell us nothing more; we shall vanish first,
> Yet leave behind us certain frozen words
> Which some day, though not certainly, may melt
> And, for a moment or two, accentuate a thirst.

When the obvious Fascist danger was in sight of being overcome, other dangers began to reveal themselves, and the mood of disillusionment set in early.

In 1944, for example, there were plans for after the war: the party political truce would be at an end; would a 'brave new world' be instituted? There were warnings of the power struggle ahead—as when Britain helped impose a reactionary government in Greece, not to appear to be countenancing Communism. The Big Powers of the Cold War were already asserting themselves. The duplicity of politics and international affairs could hardly be reassuring. Then, too, people were in danger of becoming cyphers in a bureaucratic code. Dating to 1944 is one of MacNeice's best-known poems, 'Prayer before birth':

> I am not yet born, console me.
> I fear that the human race may with tall walls wall me,
>   with strong drugs dope me, with wise lies lure me,
>   on black racks rack me, in blood-baths roll me.

The unborn child asks, in advance, for help in the roles he will have to play, when

> old men lecture me, bureaucrats hector me, mountains
>   frown at me, lovers laugh at me, the white
>   waves call me to folly and the desert calls
>   me to doom and the beggar refuses
>   my gift and my children curse me.

(This section contains some of the images to be used in 'The Dark Tower'.) The final cry is for

> ... strength against those who would freeze my
>   humanity, would dragoon me into a lethal automaton,
>   would make me a cog in a machine. ...

It is a prayer to resist being dehumanised, turned to stone, or having his 'entirety' dissipated and spilt.

Also dated to 1944, to June, is 'When we were children', which recaptures the freshness of early life, with images of light and blossom, the hawthorn and laburnum in the Rectory garden. After the hard work and stress of war-time it is not surprising that the poet harks back to days

Whose winds and sweets have now forsaken
　　Lungs that are black, tongues that are dry.

Now we are older and our talents
Accredited to time and meaning,
To handsel joy requires a new
　　Shuffle of cards behind the brain
Where meaning shall remarry colour
　　And flowers be timeless once again.

Meanwhile, he could tilt at the system in another way. A favourite figure with MacNeice was the Fool: there was 'The Fool among the yes-men' in *Autumn Journal*; later, he would combine fool and jongleur in 'The Stygian banks'; there were the playing-card fool and April Fool. In 1945 he wanted to do another 'half-hour programme of fun and games . . . a kind of satirical fantasy which will pan around a large number of topical subjects, and should make an agreeable catharsis for the large company of the browned off'. Val Gielgud approved the idea, but, because of the date of Easter, the feature had to be placed on 31 March. So MacNeice switched to the March Hare—another anarchic figure—who could embody 'poetic madness as contrasted with the prosaic madness' of everyone else. He would act as a variant of the Fool with his grains of salt.

In 'The March Hare Resigns', the Hare canvasses the country for support to get time stopped, so that he will not be ousted on 1 April. The tour visits Ministries and other bureaucratic institutions, an academic anxious to return to the gastronomic delights of All Fools College, idle workers and idle rich. Those about to plunge into the mediocrity of domestic life are warned: 'Goodbye to the neiges d'Antan, the perquisites of passion. And then middle age . . .' The Hare can convince nobody, and he gives up. The programme seems to have been great fun to do, with a splendid Hare in Esmé Percy. MacNeice could indulge his liking for puns and satire, the whole team enjoyed the work, and the conviviality—the tour of clubland, after the Hare's tour, as MacNeice put it. Antony Hopkins composed music, based on the theme of 'Over the hills and far away'. MacNeice wrote him a note the next day (this is perhaps characteristic, that he found it easier to do this than to speak to

Hopkins) : 'I feel it is time that I put on paper my appreciation of your Grade A plus work in all our joint programmes.'

By this time, MacNeice had worked for almost four years for the BBC, in a time- and energy-consuming job, in the stress of war-time. In the early months of 1945 he was also working on a film script. In August 1944 he had been invited by Two Cities Films (a subsidiary of the Rank organisation) to write the script; this was at the suggestion of Dallas Bower, whose idea, plot and setting provided the basis of 'Pax Futura'. It was written partly at Dallas Bower's flat in Tite Street (Whistler's old studio) and partly at Louis's St John's Wood home. The contract was signed in the Rising Sun pub in Tottenham Court Road, with Cecil Day Lewis as witness. But the film was never made—it would have been a very costly production, a pro-genitor of the *Star Wars* genre.

'Pax Futura' was to have been a 'film fantasy of the Future of Aviation', set in 1995; as well as being futuristic, it preaches a warning about power being perverted. The opening setting is the flight deck of a stately 'Cunarder' of the air, captained by a hero who has clearly suffered, but is withdrawn. His name is Flavius; other classical or semi-classical names are used: Xanthias is shifty and self-indulgent, the villain of the piece, whose Bible is Nietzsche; Galba is a scientific rationalist, with a mistress named Delia; Zoe, the actress, and Crito, are 'types' like some of the figures in his radio plays. Helen is an idealised woman—beautiful, intelligent, practical, but also tender and romantic. The battle for power was to be a theme of several of MacNeice's radio plays. There is something of a 'quest', too, in Flavius's work for universal peace, and in his fight against the totalitarian threat. Xanthias leads a secret group: he considers that people 'are like flies in the desert'. Flavius points out

> The mark of the beast, Helen, the evil eye,
> The spiteful finger of hate, the underground of greed,
> Blood-lust and lust for power—conspiracy
> Against the House that Jack built.

Simon, a cynic, says that 'the world has become a prison. Where everything runs to schedule.' As Flavius tells his passengers, the 'anti-men' are attacking.

Worked into the action aboard the airship are flashbacks to earlier years, in documentary film in Flavius's archives. In this way, the fifty years between the end of the war and the time of the film are covered. Shots of 1944 (bombs, D-Day, tube shelters) and reminiscences of older passengers recall Churchill's oratory during the war, and the sudden feeling of emptiness when it was all over. Conferences, international control—all attempts fail, until 1960. Then Flavius, as a young man, inspires those present at an international conference and indicts the selfish vested interests which prevent peace. In a new world, a Pax is achieved, at the cost of constant vigilance; until now, 1995, when danger is imminent. Some of the ideas are very striking, given that it was written in 1945. Much of what follows is exciting and inventive—perhaps a *Boy's Own*-ish sort of adventure (to use a phrase that MacNeice used of his own work some years later). The hero defeats the villain, and wins the ideal lady. There are also some very typical MacNeice touches in the more lyrical parts: the nostalgia for 'Corn in the wind and sweet peas in the sun', for the 'bonfire smells in autumn'; Flavius's search for 'something unknown. . . . Unknown and perhaps unattainable'. He had lost his mother when young, and remembered his father's example of an old-fashioned idea of service. The village where he takes Helen also recalls MacNeice's own past—the Downs: 'The earth is old and the air is clean.'

In April, MacNeice went to Ireland—a welcome respite from London after the four years he had worked there. He was collecting material for features and looking for new writers. He was there when the war ended (as he had been when it began) and he had to hurry back to London to produce an already planned 'London Victorious', the feature he had been assigned as part of the celebrations by Features section. He wanted no naturalistic 'news-reel', nor 'the kind of dramatised incident which we did so much on the air around about 1941'. The mood, it seems, was to be more subdued, serious but not grandiose. His choice of music is interesting: a solo instrument, 'played of course by someone who is both sensitive and expert', perhaps Dennis Brain on the horn. His friend William Alwyn

composed the music; Dennis Brain could not get leave from
the RAF band, so Norman del Mar deputised. There is a
similarity in mood, and in the music, to the feature 'A Roman
Holiday'. 'London Victorious' was broadcast on 18 May, soon
after the war in Europe ended.

So the war was over; 'Goodbye to London' written nearly
twenty years later sums up its effects and the aftermath:

> Then came the headshrinking war, the city
> Closed in too, the people were fewer
> But closer too, we were back in the womb. . . .
>
> From which reborn into anticlimax
> We endured much litter and apathy hoping
> The phoenix would rise. . . .
>
> And nobody rose, only some meaningless
> Buildings and the people once more were strangers
> At home with no one, sibling or friend.
> Which is why now the petals fall
> Fast from the flower of cities all.

Chapter Four

Early Post-war Developments: 1945–1947

I stayed. On my peacetime feet
Autumn Sequel, Canto IV

Weary with the war, and work, MacNeice enjoyed his stay in Ireland. He was there with his family in April 1945, Dan home from his boarding-school, Corinna full of boisterous energy. His wife, however, was ill and needed to rest, as he wrote back to Gilliam; it would be best to stay where they were, and he could go on with BBC work in Ireland. He also wanted to work on a new play: 'my old idea of a programme on "The Dark Tower" has suddenly blossomed out and I should like to get on with writing it within the next few weeks.' Gilliam backed him up, as he always did when he felt that his staff needed support. In an official memo he noted that MacNeice would be 'at the disposal of Northern Ireland Programme Director with a view to preparing Features programmes on Ulster subjects either by himself or writers that he can discover and encourage . . . Mr MacNeice will also be working on various agreed projects for the Home Service, including "The Dark Tower" and "The Careerist".'

During May and the early days of June, MacNeice worked on 'The Dark Tower', sending synopses and comments to Gilliam. The work was not easy. 'I am writing the Tower but it comes slowly—partly because virtue has gone out of me and partly because the subject is so austere that I can't do it in long sessions.' He was wondering, in fact, if it would be possible to have perhaps three months 'free from obligations to the

institution'. His stay was extended until 10 July, but Gilliam
was abroad so further possibilities could not be discussed. He
went to southern Ireland, partly to work, but his 'allergy to
England' was forcing him further west, to Achill Island, where
he and Hedli had taken a holiday home for a month. The need
to stay away was pressing. He offered to have a month's pay
docked: Laurence could tell 'them' that Louis was '(1) Irish—
and have not been in my own country for three years and not
for so long then—and (2) an (for lack of a better word) artist—
which means that I can do some hackwork all of the time, and
all hackwork some of the time but not all hackwork all of the
time.'

Although weary himself he was encouraging to his little
'flock' of new writers. One was the clergyman-poet from
Armagh, W. R. Rodgers. Gilliam had approved a programme
on Armagh, to be written by Rodgers, helped by MacNeice.
Rodgers had long been an admirer of his fellow-poet, and after
MacNeice's death he acknowledged his debt in a Belfast programme about him: 'He taught me how to write for radio at its
most formative and exciting period. I cannot be grateful enough
for the encouragement and affection he gave me over many
years.' Another writer who received help and kindness from
MacNeice was Sam Hanna Bell. Louis took the script of 'Ill
Fares the Land' away to Achill with him, returning it with
congratulations and meticulously detailed comments. 'Here
follow some page by page notes (disregard them if they irritate!)', he wrote. He made helpful suggestions about radio
technique. Sam Hanna Bell also remembers how reassuring
Louis was in the studio, calm even when things went wrong.
Outside the studio, in the Elbow Room (now deserted and
boarded up) or the Bodega, he could be good company. In
Belfast there was a more relaxed atmosphere than in the BBC
in London, as a producer who knew MacNeice from pre-war
days recalls: Ursula Eason was working in Belfast then and after
the war and she remembers the pleasant times spent with Louis,
in the studio, the pub, or at rugby matches. It was rather
difficult to start 'small talk' with him, but on rugby and broadcasting he was always willing to converse. Sam Hanna Bell was

to make his career in broadcasting in Northern Ireland;
Rodgers was persuaded to come to London later that year.
These two were with MacNeice, in the Bodega in Belfast, in
August 1945, when news came of the bombing of Hiroshima.
MacNeice's worst fears were perhaps surpassed; he was horrified.

He was back in London in September, preparing for his
production of 'The Dark Tower'; Britten was to write the
music. Features having become a separate department in July,
for this one programme MacNeice was attached to Drama. He
wrote to Britten that he liked the idea of using mainly strings.
Val Gielgud liked the script 'immensely' and offered to let
MacNeice produce it himself. It was scheduled for 21 January
1946. Before that there was a pleasant jaunt to Ireland, in
November, to produce the feature about Armagh by Rodgers,
'City Set on a Hill'. MacNeice's friend William Alwyn, who
composed the music, recalls the occasion. Most of the music was
pre-recorded in London, but additional music for flute was
performed at the live broadcast, with Alwyn as soloist. Afterwards, before their drive to Bertie Rodgers's home in Armagh,
they became 'convivial, to say the least'. Stopping on the way,
a sudden impulse persuaded them to dance

> a solemn jig at midnight
> in peaty darkness by an Irish bog
> to mournful pipings on my flute.

These pipings were improvised jigs and reels, played by Alwyn,
'to which Louis solemnly cavorted'. The conviviality continued
by candlelight in the country manse, but when they at last went
to bed Louis insisted that they should be called in time to catch
the train to Dublin next morning, for the rugby match—which
they all thoroughly enjoyed. (We must admire MacNeice's
dedication or ingenuity, in achieving a correspondence between
dates of programmes and of international matches.)

'The Dark Tower' is one of the most celebrated of all radio
plays. Having written the script, and entrusted the music to
Britten, MacNeice wrote to the cast, lightly but clearly indicat-
ing his concept of the characters. The subject was suggested by
Browning's poem 'Childe Roland to the Dark Tower came',

with its impressive nightmarish description of the waste land
through which the knight has to travel, until

> looking up, aware I somehow grew,
> 'Spite of the dusk, the plain had given place
> All round to mountains. . . .

> Burningly it came on me all at once,
> This was the place!

In the midst of the mountains lay the Tower itself, 'squat' and
'blind as the fool's heart'. This is the focal point from which
MacNeice develops his poetic parable. Roland is a quest-hero,
destined to fight some nameless evil; he is a representative of
the human race, the last son of a family which has sent all its
men to their death on the quest. It is the dominant mother who
spurs them on.

The brother before Roland is Gavin; when he has gone, the
Tutor takes over Roland's education. The young man is an
unlikely hero, lacking concentration, tending to be flippant and
sceptical—a modern man. (He is less like the forceful Columbus,
more like the young man of 'He Had a Date'.) He is susceptible
to the gentler influence of love, rather a romantic, as we learn
from the passages with Sylvie, the girl he loves. Images from
'The Dark Tower' are found also in the poems, and in later
plays, especially 'Nuts in May'.

> Today is a thing in itself—apart from the future.
> Whatever follows I will remember this tree
> With this dazzle of sun and shadow—and I will remember
> The mayflies jigging about us in the delight
> Of the dying instant—and I'll remember *you*
> With the bronze lights in your hair.

Sylvie tries to make him stay, to enjoy a 'sane and gentle life'.
The Tutor tells him that man lives on a sliding staircase, which
takes him downwards, but he must keep trying to ascend. The
Sergeant tells him how to sound the challenge on the trumpet:
'Hold that note at the end.' His mother gives him a ring with a
blood-red stone, representing her will; as long as that remains
firm, the stone's colour will hold.

One person whom Roland visits is Blind Peter: he lost his

sight and his belief fifty years before, when the Dragon got to
his part of the world, and 'everything went sour'. He became an
informer, sending men to their deaths, then having to watch his
own child die after her mother's suicide. This is described by
MacNeice, in his synopsis, as a 'parable of fascism'. Another
symbolic figure is the alcoholic whom Roland meets at the
port—'a sort of cartoon of the despairing intelligentsia'. The
whole scene is conjured up through music, and as the solipsistic
'soak' rambles on with his thoughts Roland wonders if his whole
quest is not a dream. But a stentorian voice is heard, ordering
everyone aboard:

> For the Dead End of the World and the Bourne of No Return.

On the ship there is a scheming steward, in league with the
seductive Neaera—a haunting violin is her motif. Roland is
nearly diverted from his mission, but sees Sylvie at the quayside
of the next port; she too tries to hold him back. He tells her of
his vision of the land:

> the deserted port,
> The ruined shacks, the slag-heaps covered with lichen
> And behind it all the frown and fear of the forest.
> This is the Dragon's demesne.

Giving in to her, Roland goes with Sylvie to a haunted chapel
(there are echoes of Malory here); in time, he hears the voices
of father, brother and those as yet unborn. Sylvie will return to
a house with an apple orchard (image of an Eden), while he
will go through the forest, with its 'gibbering guile', and the
desert of 'silent doubt'. Mocking him are the voices of a parrot
and a raven; a mechanical clock expresses the tedium of the
desert. These are counterparts of poetic images, and they are
very effective.

An unwilling hero, Roland is glad to find that his ring has lost
its colour—he is reprieved. At this point he considers the question of his own free will: he has decided to let chance govern his
movements, then refuses to be so guided. His humanity asserts
itself with the exercise of free will. Then the mountains appear,
as in Browning's poem, and the ghosts of those who have gone
before. Music creates the Tower itself, rising out of the ground

—a brilliant passage. There is also the crescendo of heartbeats, before the music stops suddenly. Then comes the challenge call on the trumpet—the play ends with this call 'enriched and endorsed by the orchestra'. MacNeice himself said that Britten's music added another dimension to the play. The verse, however, is the mainstay, approaching conversation, with evocative poetic imagery. The total appeal to the imagination is very powerful—all that the early advocates of radio could wish for. Motifs like the ruined port, the chapel, the desert, the Tower itself, are particularly suited to sound. It is a well-constructed play, and MacNeice derived satisfaction from the production. He praised, too, the sensitive acting of Cyril Cusack as Roland. 'The Dark Tower' has something serious to say, and this is underlined by the context of the war and the preoccupations of MacNeice's earlier scripts. Nor were the themes of evil and humanity exhausted: they would recur in later radio plays. 'I have my beliefs and they permeate *The Dark Tower*. But do not ask me what Ism it illustrates or what Solution it offers', he wrote in his introduction to the published text (dedicated to Britten).

In the same introduction, MacNeice places the play in the line 'of writings which include *Everyman*, *The Faerie Queene* and the *Pilgrim's Progress* . . . Man does after all live by symbols.' The same tradition of double-level writing was to be the subject of his last critical work, *Varieties of Parable*, given as the Clark Lectures at Cambridge in 1963. He was to write a series of 'parable plays' for radio, as well as other kinds, but at the end of the war he was not certain that he would stay in the BBC. The reaction against London and the work he had been doing in the war made him unwilling to commit himself during the stay in Ireland. The success of 'The Dark Tower' may have played a part in his continuing in radio. It won praise from many people, including C. Day Lewis ('magnificent') and W. R. Rodgers ('most memorable broadcast I have yet heard'). After a repeat broadcast in November, Henry Reed also wrote to MacNeice: this letter is doubly interesting, for Reed was to write several plays for radio during the next decade or so. 'Dear Louis, Forgive a fan-letter. . . . I found I was listening with an

intentness I had never before been forced to give to anything
except music on the wireless. . . . I am sure yours is the way
radio must go if it is to be worth listening to; I have always
thought your claims for its potentialities to be excessive; I now
begin, reluctantly, to think you may be right, and am very
glad.' In a postscript he added: 'it is difficult to rise and cheer
in a letter.' MacNeice thanked him for his 'flattering letter',
admitting it was his favourite programme. 'Of course I was
terribly lucky to get music from Benjamin Britten. . . . I thought
he did a superlative job on it.' Back in February he had said in
a letter to George MacCann that it was his 'favourite programme
to date. The public either loved it or loathed it (I have a heap
of letters—ecstatic or virulent).' In the same letter he writes of
an impending move to Essex (perhaps he was still 'allergic' to
London, if not to England). He was looking forward to 'going
all moujik', although Hedli had 'bouts of alarm and despon-
dency'. For a year or so the MacNeices lived at Tilty House,
near Dunmow, but then returned to London.

Among the changes in the BBC after the war was the separa-
tion of Features from Drama, as an independent department
under Gilliam, in July 1945. As there were still poets and playwrights in this section, 'Features' was not a very accurate name.
In 1946 the Third Programme was instituted, giving more scope
to creative writers. There was an infusion of new blood in
Features Department: Bertie Rodgers came over from Northern
Ireland, and shared an office with MacNeice. (They went over
together in September 1946 to produce a programme in Belfast
—'The Country Parson'—and returned with an illuminated
address from Rodgers's former parishioners—this they hung in
the office.) The poet and ex-academic Terence Tiller joined the
department on his return from Egypt; Louis's Birmingham
friend Reggie Smith did the same on his return from the Near
East. An ex-student of MacNeice, Dorothy Baker, joined a
little later on. Rayner Heppenstall, from the Army, and Alan
Burgess, from the RAF, increased the strength of Features.
This distinctive radio team, Gilliam's creation, was rather a
law unto itself, and unlikely to bow to bureaucrats. One
comment in a letter from MacNeice to George MacCann at

about this time suggests the spirit: writing of Francis Dillon he
says, 'working for Jack is great fun. . . . the main qualification
is getting on well with the fellows in the public bar.'

Such a group would offer an attractive haven from the drab
realities of post-war Britain. The mood is reflected in the
memoirs of certain writers. Patric Dickinson (who continued,
and continues, to do radio work after leaving Features, where
he was mainly concerned with poetry programmes) has remarked that 'England was becoming increasingly unpleasant
and materialistic'; that 'we were being occupied by the
Philistines.' Rupert Croft-Cooke (who also did work for radio,
including programmes with Jack Dillon) has described, in *The
Dogs of Peace*, 'those very strange years immediately after the
Second World War'. He remembers 1946 to 1950 as 'years in
which there was a faster and more futile rate of change than
perhaps ever before'. There was the sleaziness of post-war
London—not only did the servicemen return, but the 'spivs'
flourished. Officially, there was austerity and regimentation,
against which Croft-Cooke rebelled. He sums London up as 'a
shabby, disgruntled, impoverished society'. Neither was he in
tune with the Features style. The BBC atmosphere and the
nearby pubs, 'where the staff drank garrulously for long and
boring sessions eventually became tiresome and I was content to
read short stories of my own for Roy Campbell'. However,
Campbell was one of the set of writers to be found in the pubs,
but he was in Talks, not Features, Department.

Apart from the returning soldiery, and the people in broadcasting, there were literary people for MacNeice to meet. One
figure who occasionally held court was Edith Sitwell. John
Lehmann records that 'Edith's policy at these gatherings was to
mix old friends and almost total strangers. . . . Poets, from Tom
Eliot, Stephen Spender, Louis MacNeice and Dylan Thomas,
to some penniless unknown young man whose verses had caught
Edith's attention, were always to be found in abundance.'
MacNeice continued to write poetry during the late 1940s,
developing a longer, more meditative type of poem, like 'The
Stygian banks'; these are too discursive at times, but express his
personal philosophy and are an important phase in his output.

In his introduction to the published text of *The Dark Tower and Other Radio Scripts*, in 1947, MacNeice expresses gratitude to Laurence Gilliam for his willingness to accept spontaneous suggestions, and for his flexibility in allowing 'an elastic treatment of those other programmes which "have to be done".' One of the spontaneous suggestions was for a follow-up to the March Hare programme of 1945. MacNeice was fond of this creation, brought alive by Esmé Percy—something which only radio could do without distorting the intention of the writer. Esmé Percy played the part again in 1946, in 'Salute to All Fools', broadcast on 1 April. Once more Antony Hopkins wrote the music, this time taking as his theme tune 'Alleluia, I'm a Bum'. After the Hare, the next main character was an Agent, Nonesuch, played with a 'common' voice by one of MacNeice's favourite actors, Howard Marion-Crawford. The Agent deals in anything beginning with T: theatre, television, test-matches, trout-fishing, thaumaturgy. The Hare wants his help in finding a bride, Truth. This allows for some neat satire: on Fleet Street truth, Tory and Marxist truth, photographic truth, poetic truth ('of a foolish and tiresome kind of poet', as MacNeice comments in a note).

MacNeice's delight in parody and pun, akin to Hopkins's musical pastiche and variations on a theme, is clear from the writing. The poet, for instance: 'I beat in the void my ceaseless wings in vain. And only those can escort me who are also winged. Those who have inspiration.' The Hare claims to have inspiration, and is questioned by Poetic Truth: 'What is a poet?' 'A poet is the unacknowledged legislator of the world.' 'How does he legislate?' 'By sitting in a corner. And burning always with a hard gem-like flame.' (It is appropriate that the style of the catechism should be echoed.) Actors enjoyed MacNeice's scripts and his production, and there are jokes for them too, as in the 'ham' section when Tory Truth confronts Hodge: 'There will always be happy peasants like ... like ... Ahoy there, Hodge, come here! Now then, Hodge, show these people how happy you are.' Hodge, 'quavering with misery', replies: 'Oh, ma'am, it be bitter cold today.' 'He loves the cold, he loves it.' 'Ah—if I could only get a bellyful of bread—and excuse me,

Colonel, touching my forelock, sir, but if you could see your way to repair my roof—' There is an Analyst, who claims that Truth lies in the Unconscious; a Gael, who claims that Truth is Cathleen ni Houlihan, 'Takin' up her entrenched position over the graves of kings'; and a fake yogi. A programme note, in *Radio Times*, explained that 'the Neo-Yogi was inspired not by the East but by California. It was Laidman Browne (who played the part brilliantly) who had the idea of adding an extra facet by making the Yogi a cockney in disguise.' Finally, a Scientist splits the Hare in two—two sets of discs were dubbed together for the two hares quarrelling—but the character survives everything, bounding off, free and easy, proclaiming spring: 'The daffodils blow their trumpets, there is green fire in the hedge-rows, there is even a new note in the ring of the office telephone.' The play is fun to read, and must have been fun to take part in and to produce.

Both the March Hare programmes were published, and MacNeice wrote of them that 'the first object . . . was, I must admit, entertainment. I am fond of nonsense literature. But even Lewis Carroll, in passing, throws light on his own times, gives a "criticism of life". . . .' The basic theme of the earlier play was 'the clash between the poetical (and sympathetic) madness of the Hare and the pedestrian (and repellent) madness of everyone else'. The second play 'rubs in much more salt'— he considers that all dogmas and institutions need to be mocked, but he is not a cynic. At the end of the 1950s, he wrote a similar piece, taking the literary and academic world as his target. One of the strands of his radio work is this comic-satirical line. The next play in 1946 of this kind, 'Enemy of Cant' (not his own title), is based on the plays of Aristophanes, to whom MacNeice wanted to pay homage as 'an author of infinite fantasy, a lover of slapstick and beauty, a good hater and a hard hitter, a live man, an Enemy of Cant'.

The broadcast on 3 December was introduced with that comment about Aristophanes; what followed was a compilation and adaptation (with free translation by MacNeice) from the plays. The struggle between democratic Athens and totalitarian Sparta reflected recent history; the question is posed, 'What

good's this war done anyway?' Extracts from *The Clouds* are
used to attack certain ideas in education, and contemporary
sophistry: 'How sweet it is to belong to the avant-garde of
thought.' Aristophanes complains that Athens is a dead city:
'Why, even my plays can't be properly staged.' He also warns:
'The next few years are going to be pretty unpleasant. You mark
my words, there'll be witch-hunts and things like that. They've
got to take it out on someone.' How true that was to prove.
Once again, Antony Hopkins collaborated with MacNeice,
providing musical jokes—effects such as 'solemn chord, then
raspberry, on orchestra', or a 'short blasphemous fanfare'.

Another 'joker' was a poet admired much by MacNeice—
Dylan Thomas, who played the part of Aristophanes. He was
to take part in several of MacNeice's plays. These early post-
war years were the period when Thomas was living in Oxford-
shire, and frequently working for the BBC. (Officialdom did not
always approve: he was once listed in minutes as an actor to be
less frequently used; producers seem to have taken little notice.)
He took part in one 'Country Magazine' programme with Jack
Dillon, who had introduced Thomas and MacNeice early in the
war, taking Dylan to Louis's flat. Their host commented that
he had seen the other's latest book of poems, and thought some
of them good. Some? The praise was too faint for Dylan—'they
were all bloody good.' MacNeice came to admire Thomas
greatly as a poet; he also praised his acting for radio. In an
article for *Encounter*, soon after Thomas's death in 1953, he wrote
of his 'roaring sense of comedy', his 'natural sense of theatre'.
Subtle and versatile, he 'took production', capable of the
sonorous or the comic, 'such as the friendly Raven . . . in a
dramatised Norwegian folk-tale'. In *Autumn Sequel* that unique
voice is commemorated:

> A whole masque
> Of tones and cadences—the organ boom,
> The mimicry, then the chuckles; we could bask
>
> As though in a lush meadow in any room
> Where that voice started.

The Norwegian folk-tale was 'The Heartless Giant', a

delightful play, broadcast on 13 December 1946. The lines given to the Raven are a playful echo of some of Thomas's own Gothicism: 'I speak to you in extremis and de profundis'; he lives, he tells us, by 'churchyards. And ruined towers. And under gallows.' In October MacNeice had suggested this play for the Christmas season on the Home Service. Antony Hopkins worked with MacNeice for the last time on this play; it was a pity that the very fruitful partnership could not continue. In a way, MacNeice is gently satirising his own most famous radio play: like Roland, Boots has a quest, following his brothers who have been turned to stone by the Giant with no heart. Aided by a charming princess, with hair 'like a waterfall of sunshine', and all her wits about her, and by some amusing animal helpers, he finds the heart at the bottom of a well on an island in the middle of a lake, and destroys it. Cyril Cusack played Boots, as he had played Roland—so the cast were included in the fun. Peter Ustinov again had a regal role—the rather fussy and harassed king. Hedli MacNeice sang the words of the Picture Book, urging Boots on to the happy ending of the fairy tale.

The more serious side of MacNeice's radio writing is also represented by work during 1946. (Although, in *Autumn Sequel*, he records his staying on after the war without enthusiasm— 'So I stayed. On my peacetime feet. There was little alternative' —the next few years were very productive.) In September there was 'Enter Caesar', on the theme of power: Caesar is a ruthless opportunist and egoist. The programme note makes this plain: a warning against any 'gush about his idealism or even about far-sighted statesmanship (even if he did make the trains run on time)'. The Republic was ended by him, and Caesarism flourished. This is a dramatised feature rather than a play, and uses the device of the schoolmaster (this became a device overworked by MacNeice in the 'compulsory' pieces—perhaps the schoolmaster in him continued to survive). Elisabeth Lutyens wrote music for the feature, echoing military music of oppressive regimes.

Another serious play, an original one, was 'The Careerist' (first mentioned in the memorandum by Gilliam when MacNeice wanted to stay longer in Ireland). It is a variation

on the theme of power, a more personal one. MacNeice chose
to exclude the character of Caesar himself in the earlier play;
in 'The Careerist' he not only presents the protagonist (a publisher) but explores his inner thoughts. MacNeice called the
genre a 'psycho-morality', and the name Jim Human is indeed
a reminder of one of the medieval morality plays, *The Castle of
Perseverance*, which traces the life of 'Humanus Genus'. The
earlier hero begins in childish innocence, is led astray by
tempters and his bad angel, but is eventually saved. Jim goes
through a similar process, but ends by committing suicide.
There are echoes of Sieveking's 'Kaleidoscope' plays, tracing a
man's life from birth to death, each section heralded by a voice
crying the hour—'Past eleven o'clock on a dark manic morning'. Choruses of male and female voices are used, and there is
a flute solo—composed and played by William Alwyn. Alwyn
remembers the happy nature of all the work he did with Louis,
who trusted him 'as a fellow technician'.

An experimental aspect of the play was the personification of
the warring elements of the human personality. Margos
clamours for immediate satisfaction; Philia has a romantic
yearning for the unattainable (symbolised by a glittering witchball); Scolios is the sceptical intelligence; Eris the lust for
power, the mainspring of Jim Human, while Eusebes is his
conscience. The inner and outer worlds confront each other
when the boy goes to school: 'the multiple self faces the world of
others.' Oxford follows, then publishing; in the war he is a
crypto-Nazi. Finally he is unmasked. Eris becomes Satan: 'All
this power, I said, I will give thee', and leads him to a mountain. He has reached the top—but he commits suicide. Another
student at another Oxford tutorial considers the question of
evil. . . . After a pause there is a flute finale. There are certain
images which recur in poems: the fingers groping like sea
anemones in a pool, 'For what is never there'; the witchball is
like the 'hanging lamp' in the poem 'Hands and eyes'. Man's
life is an 'ocean liner packed with celebrities. . . . But she never
makes more than one voyage', like the *Titanic*, which MacNeice
had seen as a child, sailing from Belfast Lough. Later, MacNeice
was to produce a skit on this play, written by Laurence Kitchin.

'The Careerist' was the first play that MacNeice wrote for the Third Programme (there were repeats of 'The Dark Tower' and 'Enter Caesar' but they were written for the Home Service). The idea of an 'Arts' programme came about before Haley's time as Director General; Nicolls and others had discussed it early in the war. Haley furthered the idea, and 'Programme C' was planned. The feeling in some quarters was that a new 'civilising' element was needed, now that the war had revealed the public's desire for serious and intelligent entertainment. It was hoped that audiences would 'include the most intelligent, receptive people in all classes, persons who value artistic experience all the more because of the limited opportunities they have of enjoying it'. Nicolls had first advanced the argument that a third service should be free from the rigid time schedule of the Home; it could also have more freedom in choice of material. As soon as the war was over the Heads of the three programmes were announced: Lindsay Wellington was to be Head of the Home, Maurice Gorham of the Light (replacing the Forces Service—Gorham soon left for television and was succeeded by Norman Collins), and George Barnes of the Third. Barnes had persuaded Harman Grisewood (formerly in Talks, from which he had resigned) to return as his assistant, when he officially took up his post in July 1946. Talented planners like Etienne Amyot helped give shape to the new service, which began on 29 September 1946. Leslie Stokes, who had been a producer in Drama and Features Department from 1943, was in charge of publicity. The small staff thus combined experience of talks broadcasting, music and theatre. In 1948 Barnes became Director of the Spoken Word (titles were very grand then) and Grisewood became Controller of Third Programme. In the same year Christopher Holme, a contemporary of MacNeice at Oxford, joined as Chief Assistant.

While many felt that the new service would be a great cultural force, and while it stated its aim as attracting all listeners, who would select what they wished to hear, there were fears among some people—including Features producers— that the service would be divisive, that it would create an élitist audience, and that their own programmes would reach fewer listeners than they had done on the Home Service. But the Third did offer extended opportunities. Features Department took advantage of these: indeed, the very first programme put out on the Third was 'How to Listen', by Stephen Potter and Joyce Grenfell. The series of Chaucer's *Canterbury Tales*, translated by Nevill Coghill, was also produced by Potter, beginning in 1946. Among other early programmes were the serialisation of John Hersey's *Hiroshima*; 'Atomic Energy', by Nesta Pain; the first of the 'Imaginary Conversations' edited and produced by Rayner Heppenstall (various established writers contributed scripts); Laurie Lee's 'The Voyage of Magellan', also produced by Heppenstall; Douglas Cleverdon's feature about the poet Sir John Suckling; and MacNeice's 'Enemy of Cant'. (His translation of the *Agamemnon* was one of the earliest Drama offerings, but was not specially written for the Third, nor indeed for radio.) Henry Reed was one of the writers to make an art of radio writing: his adaptation of *Moby Dick*, with music by Antony Hopkins, was produced by Stephen Potter, and his 'huge and marvellous script' (in the words of the producer, Heppenstall) on Giacomo Leopardi gave the radio actor Carleton Hobbs one of his best parts. Francis Dillon wrote and produced a biographical feature on Hans Andersen; and MacNeice did a new production of 'Cupid and Psyche'.

The first meeting of Features to discuss specifically Third Programme plans had been held in January 1946. Among suggestions recorded in the minutes were those of MacNeice: 'satirical fantasy' and 'psycho-morality'. By the summer two plays had been commissioned from him by the Third, 'The Careerist' and the Aristophanes feature. He was concerned also with some of the poetry programmes put out during 1946. The possibilities of the new service next led him to suggest, in December 1946, that he should dramatise two Icelandic sagas. MacNeice's synopsis comments on the fierce individualism and the aristocratic pride of those small communities, who were trying to set up a democratic order, founded on law rather than on blood feuds.

Gilliam approved the idea and it was agreed that MacNeice should start with two programmes based on the Njal saga. At first each was to have been an hour long but at MacNeice's request they were extended to seventy-five minutes. They were scheduled for March 1947, and were to be broadcast on successive evenings. This is a perfect example of the new freedoms of the Third in practice. The music was conducted by another composer friend of MacNeice, Alan Rawsthorne, and composed by Arnold Cook.

Artistically the subject was a challenge: the strong drama would have to be brought out from the detail of the original (he used Dasent's translation); the dialogue needed to be pithy; and the characters had to be made alive. The choice of cast was very important: a 'Grade A actor' would be needed to play the brave but gentle Gunnar. Stephen Murray took the part—MacNeice had known him since the Birmingham days, when Murray was in rep there, and he admired his acting. The first programme tells of the death of Gunnar, after much feuding, and largely because of his vengeful wife, Halgertha, played by Sonia Dresdel. The second play is the story of Gunnar's friend Njal. Both plays are introduced by the Watcher (reminiscent of the *Agamemnon*). 'The Burning of Njal' begins with an eerie apparition of Gunnar in his cairn: '. . . the moon was shining. I saw him as clear as I see you now—there he sat with his hell shoes on and four lights shining around him and none of them threw a shadow.' Only radio could so appeal to the imagination. The halberd which Gunnar had won from Hallgrim sings when a man is about to die; it sings now, at the beginning of the feuding which ends with the burning of Njal and his family in their hall—a fate met with great dignity.

MacNeice suggested that recordings should be kept in the Archives (they were on disc in those days), as both programmes had been major undertakings. They had presented difficult technical problems, and the music had had to be so carefully adjusted to the rest of the play that it could not be pre-recorded. The challenge and the subject seem to have inspired him, because he was by this time working on the second saga that he had originally suggested, 'Grettir the Strong'; this was broadcast in July 1947. MacNeice had been fascinated by Iceland since his visit there with Auden in 1936. In *Letters from Iceland* he had imagined a meeting between himself and the saga hero:

Grettir: And you with your burglar's underlip,
In your land do things stand well?
. . .
Ryan: I come from an island, Ireland, a nation
Built upon violence and morose vendettas.
My diehard countrymen, like drayhorses,
Drag their ruin behind them.

'Ryan' says he is an exile; so too was Grettir—a 'doomed tough', a 'surly jack', 'joker and dressy', kept witty by disaster and preferring mundane pleasures to mysticism. There is a hint here of the personal sympathy that MacNeice felt for his hero.

The radio play starts by showing us Grettir as brawling and flippant, but as the story of his ill-luck progresses he gains our sympathy. Afraid ultimately to be alone, he is nevertheless brave. In his programme note for *Radio Times* MacNeice stresses the tragic irony, the blend of realism and epic grandeur, and the humanity of the saga heroes who, like their Greek counterparts, were 'railroaded to their doom', partly by errors of judgement, partly by flaws of character, partly by circumstances. The play is marvellously effective radio, swiftly moving and neatly constructed, poetry and music matched. The composer this time was Matyas Seiber: his score is wonderfully in keeping with the text, conveying sombreness and mystery, and replacing 'effects' for most of the play, for sea and storm, for instance. It is particularly good in the supernatural sequences: when Grettir fearlessly digs into Kar's burial mound on the headland to wrest the treasure from the dead warrior; or when he fights with the terrible spectre of Glam, whose eyes will haunt him for the rest of his life. Grettir has cleansed the valley, but from now on he 'will be a hunted man—and a man alone'.

Although the story covers several years, it is easy to follow: punctuated by brief fanfares and proclamations of the yearly Assembly, the play exploits the freedom of radio. The characters are clearly presented: the sympathetic King Olaf, the affectionate younger brother Illugi, who stays with Grettir at the end; the sorrowful mother who knows how her sons will die.

Radio is also the perfect medium for the sequences where Grettir assumes disguises. (Howard Marion-Crawford played Grettir.) There are also the 'Saga Voices', adding the choric comments which MacNeice found suitable in 'Christopher Columbus'.

> The years, Grettir, the years,
> and every year made up of haunted nights.
> So you think one is company. Do you? Do you?
> Your hands may pull in nets—but what goes on in your head?

Poetry of the strongly rhythmical kind, with lyrical undertones, comes over well, as in the description of the hidden, glacier-encircled glade, or the island of Drangey:

> A prison of your own choice with the cold waves all round you . . .
> A hundred fathoms high and the black cliffs alive with puffins . . .

Enchantment, magic—good or evil—can be conveyed well on radio, words and music weaving their spell. This is another element of the Grettir play: his downfall and death are brought about by witchcraft; the storm is raised and a curse put upon the hero. After his death, the story continues briefly: his half-brother Thorsteinn follows the killer to Constantinople to join the Emperor's guard (a short passage of martial and eastern-sounding music suffices for the transition) and avenge Grettir's death. The ending is compelling, a strong vibrant 'folk' voice singing of the 'cold lands of ice and wind' where 'Man is not just nor nature kind', while a plaintive note is sounded by the violin which plays between verses; at the end the orchestra joins the solo instrument to make a moving close. The play still rates as a major achievement, although not so well known as 'The Dark Tower'.

It is pleasing that the credits include 'technical direction' by Bea Samuels, a programme engineer who worked closely with MacNeice; they used also to bet on rugby matches, especially when Scotland played Ireland. A junior programme engineer who started working with MacNeice at about this time was Joan Coates. She was a teenager, straight from school, and very awed at the thought of working with a famous poet. She expected him to be remote, 'quite unable to communicate with simple mortals like me'. Her first meeting with him was at a script conference; he was extremely kind, gentle, and very clear about the effects he required of her. She was always impressed by his firm grasp of the technicalities of radio production, and the complete confidence that he had in his team. He used effects sparingly, often dispensing with conventional fade out– fade in from scene to scene, cutting to a completely different acoustic and trusting the listeners to follow what was happening. Joan Coates's memories of Louis MacNeice's productions are of 'calm happy days with lots of laughs and no temperaments. . . . He was always grateful for a job well done and generous in his praise.'

The BBC wanted new writers, especially with the Third Programme in operation; the *Year Book* for 1947 had an article by MacNeice asking for contributors. He mentioned some of the prejudices against radio, and various false assumptions, such as thinking that the BBC was a government department and its staff, civil servants. He explained what happened to a script from an outside writer: 'Once the theme of the script has been approved (and that not so much on moral grounds as on entertainment grounds), the script will probably be read by one man only—either the Director of Drama or the Director of Features—and handed straight over to the producer. The producer will welcome the author's co-operation till the moment of transmission. The author therefore has far more to say about the performance of his piece than in any other medium which involves teamwork.' He mentioned his own scripts—fairy stories, morality plays, satires, a translation of Aristophanes and dramatisation of Apuleius. He ended with a practical inducement: 'Were I not on the staff of the BBC, a single recent programme of mine would have brought me— from three guaranteed performances—rather more money than I once used to earn as a University lecturer. So aren't you lucky to be "outside writers"?'

Some outside writers do not seem to have taken radio very seriously, however. At about the time that MacNeice was writing that article, Cyril Connolly was publishing the result of a questionnaire about the need for writers to earn a living. The problem of supporting themselves by a 'secondary occupation' was one of the issues. We may sympathise with John Betjeman's dream of being a station-master on a small, country, one-way branch-line, or admire Robert Graves's vow of poetic independence, but for most people it was a problem to be faced more realistically. C. Day Lewis felt that literary hackwork could have some relation to a writer's serious work—'serious writing, in one sense, is any writing you take seriously'— although he thought that a routine job that brought him into contact with other people, but left him enough time to spare, would be best. George Orwell thought that the secondary job should be something non-literary. Stephen Spender stressed the things to avoid: lowering one's writing standards, exhausting oneself, becoming too absorbed in the other task, or taking on a self-important role which would 'usurp one's creative personality'.

For some writers, any job in an institution was anathema— and MacNeice himself was no lover of institutions. J. Maclaren-Ross complained that occupations like the BBC left one without time or energy 'when the day's dull work is done'—it is not clear how much experience he had had of this. Dylan Thomas conceded that 'shadily living by one's literary wits' is as good a way as any of making too little money, 'so long as, all the time you are writing BBC and film scripts, reviews, etc., you aren't thinking, sincerely, that this work is depriving the world of a great poem or a great story.' These two writers were partly maintaining their own images; it would also be necessary to consider how much time could be wasted in other ways. Edward Sackville-West gave a more balanced reply: 'any employment that continues to absorb most of the would-be writer's energy can hardly fail to sap his creative vitality and will quite soon destroy it altogether. On the other hand, there are, of course, all kinds of daily chores and interests which, far from diverting a writer's energy, nourish and promote it.'

MacNeice had not contributed to this debate, but at about the same time he was writing of the group experience he had found in Features. (The introduction to the radio scripts published in 1947 contains these comments.) He also considered the

1. Louis MacNeice: BBC script-writer and producer; 1.4.1942. He had been nearly a year with the BBC at this time.
(*BBC copyright photograph*)

2. 'Britain to America'—a series of programmes telling the United States about events in war-time Britain.

(*a*) A run-through of the script. With the producer, Laurence Gilliam, and the writer, Louis MacNeice, are programme engineers Harry Baine and Charles Ladbrook, secretary Thelma Kelley and the narrator, actor Leslie Howard; 11.10.1942.

(*b*) In the dramatic control room, during a broadcast.
(*BBC copyright photographs*)

3. Rehearsals of 'Christopher Columbus'; 12.10.1942.

(a) The producer Dallas Bower, with MacNeice beside him, takes some of the large cast through the script.

(b) MacNeice, his wife Hedli, and the actor Robert Speaight.
(*BBC copyright photographs*)

4. Mahabalipuram.
(*Archaeological Survey of India, Southern Circle, Madras*)

5. (a) MacNeice with William Empson. MacNeice was the producer of a
programme of Empson's poems, read by the author; 1952.
(b) A scientific collaboration: for the Christmas Day round-the-world
broadcast 1955, recordings of stars and moon signals were made at Jodrell
Bank. Professor Bernard Lovell is shown sitting with MacNeice; standing
are the co-producers Laurence Gilliam and John Bridges.
(*BBC copyright photographs*)

6. Four of the actors who took part in many of MacNeice's plays, and were friends of the poet.

(*a*) *above, left*, Howard Marion-Crawford; (*b*) *above, right*, Stephen Murray; (*c*) *below, left*, Allan McClelland; (*d*) *below, right*, Denys Hawthorne. (*a and b BBC copyright photographs; c photograph by Edward Hutton*)

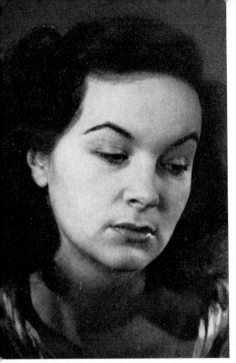

7. (a) *above, left*, Cécile Chevreau and, (b) *above, right*, Mary Wimbush, were two of the actresses who acted in MacNeice's plays.

(c) *below*, A scene from MacNeice's television play 'Another Part of the Sea'; 6.9.1960. *l.* to *r.*: Liam Gaffney as Con Ryan, Margaret Gordon as Portia, Russell Napier as Tom Carstairs and Sheila Brennan as Bridie.

(*a Sacha-Masour; b and c BBC copyright photographs*)

8. Louis MacNeice: poet, writer and producer; 17.11.1955.
(*BBC copyright photograph*)

various media of communication. He hoped that television would not supersede sound broadcasting. 'As with many other media its narrow limits are also its virtues, while within those limits it can give us something unobtainable from print (though print of course will always retain its proper autonomy). When I first heard a piece, which I had written for broadcasting, broadcast, I was irritated by details of presentation but excited and delighted by the total effect (there was more to my script, I felt, than I myself had realised).' There is satisfaction to be gained from hearing one's words spoken by actors—the writer does not normally see his books being read. As a producer, he had control over the presentation, and there was pleasure and excitement in a shared experience. 'This pleasure in a thing-being-performed-and-shared, while obtainable in all sports and some of the arts, is sadly lacking in the world of literature today.' Of course, some broadcasting would be hackwork, but not all of it. As for the question of being in an institution: 'with ingenuity and a little luck a creative person can persuade (or fool) at least some of the administrators some of the time.' We should recall, though, that he was in Gilliam's department, and Gilliam shielded his creative writers as much as he could, giving them a great deal of freedom.

There were other advantages, including travel abroad, for some of the Features producers. Always wanting to be on the spot to record history, or to have his producers there, Gilliam encouraged not only the journalists on his staff, but his poets too, to write documentary features. In April, MacNeice had visited Rome as part of the preparation for an hour-long feature on the city. He devised a 'mosaic' of Roman history, juxtaposed with contemporary post-war Rome, with all its problems. It was the kind of feature that was to be largely superseded when tape-recording became widely used in the 1950s. One of the most important events of British history in 1947 was to take MacNeice further afield, to record his impressions of India.

Chapter Five

From India to 'Faust':
1947–1950

Not strange for all their ingrown iconography, not so strange as
our own dreams
Because better ordered, these are the dreams we have needed
Since we forgot how to dance.

'Mahabalipuram'

'India is the most *foreign* country I have ever visited. If we use
the word "foreign" for Italy or Iceland, we should really find
some other word for India.' This most foreign country made a
deep and lasting impression on MacNeice. He first went there
with Francis Dillon in 1947, on behalf of Features Department,
meeting up with Wynford Vaughan Thomas. The occasion was
the independence and partition of India that summer. The
BBC had great prestige, so they were met with a special
welcome, although MacNeice describes their arrival at Karachi
airport, on 8 August, in lighter vein: 'the Customs man looked
at our papers and said, "Lots of funny people we get these days".'

The difficult and disputed decision about how and when to
hand over power to an independent India and a newly created
Pakistan was eventually made hurriedly. The task of presiding
over the last rites was given to Lord Mountbatten, as Viceroy:
the date was to be 14–15 August, at midnight. The news came
as a shock to some of those concerned with winding up the work
of administration. Sir William Tennant was acting as Auditor-
General in Simla; in his unpublished memoir he tells of
'distressing reports of the plunder and murder of travellers of all
communities across the new frontiers'—this had been happening

since March. He was sad to see the hitherto loyal and trouble-free department becoming 'disturbed and unhappy'. 'Our final glimpse at Delhi station was of a refugee train crammed with unfortunate souls fleeing from the wrath to come.'

The newspapers told the story: 'unprecedented scenes of enthusiasm' greeted the August ceremonies, but there were the horrors of massacre and flight, columns of refugees stretching for up to sixty miles, making for the border in the Punjab. Trains crossing the border arrived crammed with slaughtered bodies and running with blood. MacNeice saw some of all this. 'I arrived in a town called Sheikhupura the morning after a communal massacre. The survivors of the minority community were cramped into a schoolhouse and overflowed into the street; flies swarmed on the stumps of their arms and legs, and their eyes were haunted or, what was worse, quite blank. Never again shall I believe those romanticists who maintain that war was clean when people used swords and spears.' In *Autumn Sequel* he described another occasion, when he and Wynford— 'Evans'—found the refugees too terrified to get into the lorries, and the British and Indian soldiers

> tired and nervous under an angry sky
> With a stench of death from those already dead
> And a stench of fear from those about to die. . . .

'Remembering half that scene I remember enough.' In the main radio feature that he wrote on India, MacNeice includes the refugee camps, the cholera, the dead bodies, a woman looking for her son, whom she will never find. But these do not predominate, and he stresses that murder, rape and atrocities occur not only in India; political capital should not be made out of people's miseries. He was anxious to show India in perspective, and to inform listeners of her long history.

The visit was unforgettable for more reasons than the horror: there was the splendour, the hospitality and the friendliness, and the antiquities. In Delhi they were guests at Viceroy's House, and entertained to lavish feasts, invited to all the parties, and given places in the Council Hall on the night of Independence. It was a last great durbar, with all the pomp and

panoply, maharajahs and ranees resplendent in robes and
jewels. MacNeice's fame as a poet brought an invitation to
speak to students. Some young men came hoping to meet
another poet too, Dylan Thomas; they were puzzled to meet
Dillon and Thomas (was the bard two men?). Wynford
Vaughan Thomas has written of how 'Louis, that lone walker
with the probing mind, brought the classicist's detachment to
the warm chaos of India and Pakistan. His long, highly intelligent face gave him the right appearance of indrawn
meditation. He was a yogi whose sacred books were Greek.'

Going north from Lahore they followed the age-old road into
Kashmir, through Peshawar, past Taxila where the armies of
Alexander had stopped, past all the frontier forts, to the Khyber
Pass. MacNeice remembered the halt at the frontier to get
petrol, and how they looked for the District Commissioner. 'We
found a very handsome, very courteous, very busy young man
scoring out things with a blue pencil. "Excuse me, gentlemen,"
he said, "I shall be at your service in a moment, but just at the
present I am composing . . . a curfew." ' Jack Dillon recalls how
Louis enjoyed that. In Kashmir they met some 'Homeric
characters', chiefs and tribesmen, and also saw the legendary
beauty of the valley, rich with flowers, and the majesty of the
mountains. They rode along some of the ridges, and one night
Wynford woke the other two to see Nanga Parbat, far away
across the ranges, like a tiny lion with snow on its mane,
floating in space as the day dawned. Jack stayed on in Kashmir
for a while after his companions had left, trusting to his luck to
get out. He got a lift with a pilot and joined up with the others
in Delhi.

Meanwhile, MacNeice visited Calcutta and Benares. In
Calcutta, 'that hideous city', he met a Bengali poet who took
him on a picnic ('a lot of wet food in paper bags from a Chinese
restaurant') when it poured with rain, and they laughed a lot.
In Benares he stayed in an eighteenth-century palace by the
Ganges, entertained by two Hindu-ised Frenchmen. After the
official part of their tour they had several weeks in which to see
southern India, although Wynford Vaughan Thomas was called
back to London to rehearse for the commentary on the Royal

wedding in November. He had set his heart on seeing some of the famous caves, so Jack sent a telegram to the BBC to say that Thomas must stay for some recordings or they would have to make do with 'Dillon's voice'. When those who knew him explained to the administrators that Jack had a uniquely rasping voice, a legacy from First War gassing, they gave in. Mortimer Wheeler gave them introductions to leading archaeologists in south India, and they were state guests in Hyderabad and Madras. Wynford could not accompany them on the whole tour, but they first visited the famous painted and sculptured caves at Ajanta, cut into a curved gorge above the river, and almost deserted. The preaching halls and monastic dwellings of Buddhists of centuries ago were calm and impressive. At Ellora they visited the elaborate rock-cut temples, Buddhist and Hindu.

Further on, they went to once-rich Golconda, its ruby mines and houses now abandoned. At Madras they enjoyed what MacNeice described as 'two of the best but most dissimilar meals of our lives'. One was with a Shell-Mex official who, uncertain of the near future, opened the century-old Madeira for them. The other was with a Brahmin archaeologist, their guide in the area, at a vegetarian restaurant. 'Here we ate off banana leaves—chutney at the left top corner, turmeric at the right top corner, rice in the centre, etc., etc., and, of course, chappatis to eat with. At the end of it Dillon and I were garlanded with wet pink roses.' They went to the abandoned site at Mahabalipuram, a former royal capital, on the Tamil coast. A granite outcrop is shaped into a huge temple, beside an immense rock face carved with reliefs of Hindu gods. In his poem 'Mahabalipuram', MacNeice captures the desolation, and the awesomeness of the site, facing the empty sea:

> All alone from his dark sanctum the lingam fronts,
> affronts the sea,
> The world's dead weight of breakers against sapling, bull and
> candle
> Where worship comes no more,
> Yet how should these cowherds and gods continue to dance
> in the rock
> All the long night along ocean in this lost border between

>   That thronging gonging mirage of paddy and toddy and dung
>   And this uninhabited shore?

As he imagines the feelings of the artist, thirteen hundred years before, he finds the vision less strange:

>   But the visitor must move on and the waves assault
>   the temple. . . .
>   Still from to-day we know what an avatar is, we have seen
>   God take shape and dwell among shapes, we have felt
>   Our ageing limbs respond to those ageless limbs in the rock
>   Reliefs. Relief is the word.

'Ageing' is an exaggeration; during the months in India he had his fortieth birthday.

After the enormous empty palaces of Tanjore, and the temple of Trinchinopoli, they reached the tip of India at Cape Cormorin, where they bathed and were served with a lavish picnic. They began their journey home in November. One stop on the return was at Cairo; the cholera epidemic kept most people away so they had the Pyramids to themselves. Louis gazed at the Sphinx for a long time, Jack recalls. Told of this later, Francis Worsley commented that 'she' probably couldn't make head nor tail of him. Back in London they began their programmes. They had done their homework before going, and collected a wealth of impressions while away. The months there made a great impact on MacNeice, and he tried to suggest the richness and complexity in the script for 'India at First Sight'—an avowedly personal portrait of the country. It breathes with the life of first-hand experience and response, and is a sympathetic attempt to understand and present the subject. It is seen, of course, through western eyes, and the visitor 'is attended by the western familiars of the mind'.

Gilliam held that a good feature gained artistry and shape from the mind of the writer-producer, and MacNeice's documentaries have his personal stamp. This tends to reduce objectivity, and occasionally to introduce a note of sentimentality, as in the use of the figures of the Nanny and the young Edward. But it also has MacNeice's honesty and imaginative power. Edward feels that he ought to visit India just because he does not want to go there—he is suspicious of 'all this yogi-cum-swami stuff'. His knowledge is slight: 'a spot of Kipling and a spot of Tagore'. The shock of his encounter with India is recorded, and the aspects of the country are represented by voices; there is also the Still Voice, the inner voice of the poet. The history of India is traced through its more striking episodes. The emphasis is not the usual one: not the victories of Alexander and Asoka, but the message that grandiose ambition is futile— the lesson that Asoka himself had had inscribed on a rock. The Raj is represented by 'bewigged, madeira-drinking nabobs', by the missionary whose gravestone reads, 'Destined to labour in a peculiar vineyard', and by Kipling's 'deserted cantonments'.

Understanding and tolerance is the theme—even Nanny and Uncle Howard become more tolerant, at least at a subconscious level. There are also vivid descriptive passages: the 'efflorescence of grace-notes' of the sculpture, India's 'mosques and temples and sacred trees, her stupas and chaityas and towers of silence', the 'gods that dance in the rock'. The programme ends with evening scenes: the domes of the mosques turn lavender, the granite boulders purple, while 'the tarnished mirrors of the paddy-fields are stained red and soon, very soon, it will be dark—the quick curtain of the tropics.' India goes on with the flow of the Ganges, and morning may bring new vision. The piece still makes interesting listening and is a useful example of the kind of documentary work that came from Features, although each producer created his individual pieces. As far as MacNeice's career is concerned, this sort of work is not unlike his early journalism—*I Crossed the Minch*, for instance. Later, he thought of drawing on some of the scripts of documentaries about places he had visited to incorporate into a book.

The first feature went out on 13 March 1948; two further programmes were broadcast in May—'Portrait of Delhi' and 'The Road to Independence'. Both were contributions to series, and they lack the inspiration of the first programme. They are more like hackwork, with rather tired devices: 'stooges' of history, geography and literature, visitors with a guide, a school-master instructing a class. It was not that MacNeice had exhausted his interest in India; he put forward suggestions of his own for programmes on the Mogul Empire and Hindu

culture, and these doubtless would have been more interesting.
A year after the visit to India, MacNeice surprised Maurice
Collis, at the Sligo funeral of Yeats, by his conversation on
'Indian sculpture, a subject alien to the occasion'. And while in
Greece, in 1950, he wrote a poem, 'Didymus', about that
apostle's mission to India.

Feeling perhaps that it was time for something lighthearted,
as a change from routine, MacNeice suggested a fairy story.
This was accepted in May, and 'Two Wicked Sisters' was
written, in a Dillonesque manner, as topical satire. It is more a
counterpart of the April Fooleries than of the other fairy tales
that MacNeice dramatised. This variation on the Cinderella
story has a king and his factotum who have to deal with reports
and white papers, Ugly Sisters who are in advertising, and
astrologers who complain that psychology has reduced the art
of prediction to absurdity. One prince is a slick smooth-talking
American looking for a princess with perfect measurements,
another wants to marry so that he can claim tax allowance for
a queen. Prince Paragon is superior, and literary: '*Qu'allais
je faire dans cette galère?*' he asks wearily. (MacNeice himself asked
this question, of his Birmingham job, and in *I Crossed the Minch*—
is there an element of self-parody?) Paragon and Elise lead off
the Danse Existentialiste. There are the MacNeice puns:
'Tomorrow the sun will be in conjunction with Oedipus—a
complex of the first magnitude'; 'a twelve years' course of
psycho-paralysis'; 'he studies the Cominform'. Paragon's gift
for predicting winners deserts him, and he seeks refuge in NW11,
where he becomes a free-lance journalist. Elise becomes his
secretary, and Paragon decides to write something original—
the story of three sisters. . . .

This facetious protest has an interesting correspondence with
a longer poem written at about the same time, 'The Stygian
banks', where the poet expresses his everyday philosophy of
renewal and life, in blossom and Spring.

> Yes, let the teacher of ethics
> Reduce all acts to selfishness, let the economist
> Confuse conditions and causes and the psychologist
> Prove and disprove the rose from manure and the scientist

Explain all value away by material fact—
What do I care? It is Spring and it always will be
However the blossoms fall; and however impure
Our human motives. . . .

Before MacNeice went on leave that August, Gilliam wrote
to remind him to submit his autumn schedule. He was working
on one feature for the opening of the UN Assembly in Paris that
September ('No Other Road') but other work had to be decided
on. Back in March 1947, MacNeice had put forward some ideas
for a Features meeting (which he could not attend); Gilliam
asked whether he was still interested in any of these. 'I take it
the "Return Journey to Cork" is a certainty'—this was the
production of a script by Sean O'Faolain which involved a visit
to the city to make some recordings, an opportunity not to be
missed. It was broadcast in November. 'You also said you
would like to do an adaptation of Petronius' *Satyricon*. How
about "The Queen of Air and Darkness"? Let me know if you
want special working facilities for this, and if so how long.' Two
plays, following these ideas of MacNeice, made up most of his
work during the next six months, before he had leave to work
on a collaboration with Ernest Stahl, to translate *Faust* for
the Third Programme's Goethe bi-centenary celebrations in
1949. That same list of programme suggestions included a play
on the battle of Clontarf—not written until 1959—and a long-
term project which he never got round to: 'I still hope in the
latter end to get down to my panorama of slavery through
world history but as you will realise one has to feel very fit even
to start research on this.'

By this time, in 1948, after seven years in the BBC, MacNeice
was one of its most distinguished writer-producers. From the
start, Archie Harding and Laurence Gilliam felt that they had
a great 'catch', and by 1948 the official *Year Book* accorded him
a 'Profile'. 'At the coming of peace he . . . continued to explore
broadcasting as a medium of publication without ceasing to
write and publish poetry and criticism. It was an important
decision, and on its results depend to a large extent the direction
and quality of original imaginative writing for radio in this
country.' There are some personal touches too: 'one who walks

by himself . . . his stillness, as he watches and listens at Lord's or
Twickenham, in a Delhi bazaar or a Dublin pub . . . some are
perturbed by his presence, call him aloof. Actors love the sinewy
quality of his writing for speech, the sharp contemporary tang
of his scholar-poet's idiom.' The picture is supplemented by
other people's memories.

Auden made an acute comment, after MacNeice's death:
'On anybody who did not know him well and had never
witnessed his powers of concentration and the rapidity of his
mind, the first impression must have been of a lazy over-
gregarious man who spent more time than he should pub-
crawling.' He did enjoy the pubs, but he would peer carefully
around the door of the Stag or the George before entering, so
that he would not be saddled with the company of some bore.
He might stay silent for hours, but his presence added something positive to the company. Another Features producer was
Michael Barsley who wrote *Those Vintage Years of Radio*, in
collaboration with John Snagge. 'Louis was one of the quietest
and best-mannered of a rowdy bunch of writers and producers,
and since he was Irish this seemed a remarkable thing. He
would as soon have beer as wine or spirits, and was often to be
found at lunch-time in "The George". . . . His voice was slow
and rather nasal, and he had a way of curling his lip in argument as if slightly contemptuous, which was quite unlike him,
unless the contempt was deserved. His passionate hobby was, of
all things, following and watching Rugby football.' MacNeice
looked distinguished, usually elegant in tweeds; his sense of
humour was real, though often slow to reveal itself, and it could
be laconic and caustic. Some people thought him shy, some
aloof; neither adjective is quite accurate.

Despite appearances, he was able to work hard and meticulously, and he could work anywhere, cutting himself off from
surrounding noise and distraction. He enjoyed the company of
all kinds of people, if they were not boring or pretentious. He
kept his poetry private, but he was always observing. He could
communicate a warmth, but he could take a long time to get to
know someone. The writer Dan Davin first met MacNeice late
in 1948, introduced to him by Jack Dillon; he recalls this in

Closing Times. 'There was no instant exchange of liking, no immediate synapsis. He was wary of new men. . . . When he talked it was, as it were, through interpreters, distanced by formal courtesy and protocol.' Even after a night of drinking in company with Bertie Rodgers and Dylan Thomas, in Oxford in 1949, the distance persisted. 'They were all three very tight. . . . Dylan boisterous, Bertie portentously grave, and Louis' normal vigilant taciturnity betrayed by the fixture of his smile.' It was Louis who realised that Dan Davin was uneasy, probably because he was sober, and who tried to redress the imbalance by getting him a quick succession of drinks.

In September 1948 MacNeice went to Ireland for the re-burial of Yeats in Sligo, in Drumcliffe churchyard. Maurice Collis's lively account of this tells how his brother gave MacNeice a lift in his car. 'MacNeice had many friends in Dublin and was lavishly entertained by them on the evening of the 16th.' So he turned up an hour late in FitzWilliam Square, his eyes not quite open. He sat in the back of the car with Maurice Craig: 'for all the poets of Ireland, great and small, were setting out for Yeats's funeral that day.' After lunch in Sligo the cortège started for Drumcliffe, in pouring rain; a clouded Ben Bulben provided a backcloth for a desolate scene. The occasion was not as solemn, Collis says, as Yeats would have liked, what with the rain, and the umbrellas and a slight difficulty in lowering the coffin into the grave. MacNeice added a bizarre touch by insisting that it was the wrong body—a Frenchman with a club foot, he maintained, had been dug up by mistake. 'Can't do anything now, he said. Everyone then went back to the hotel for tea.'

That same month MacNeice produced an additional pro-gramme, a short play satirising his own 'Careerist'. Laurence Kitchin, an outside writer, had submitted this in 1947, while MacNeice was in India. Dorothy Baker read the script and found it 'very amusing . . . really a very good take-off of some of Louis' tricks of style and it might be very nice if he himself could be persuaded to produce it. . . .' When he returned MacNeice invited Laurence Kitchin to call at the BBC—he was surprised that Kitchin could remember 'The Careerist' well

enough to parody it as he did in 'The Life of Sub-human'. He
was prepared to produce it himself and sent a memo to Gilliam:
'I have just seen Mr Kitchin, who seems highly intelligent. We
both agree that the skit on "The Careerist" is essentially Third
Programme stuff, so I hope it can be accommodated there.' It
was; and a repeat of MacNeice's own play was put on two days
before so that the parody would gain point. Unfortunately,
MacNeice's awkwardness with strangers spoilt any potential
collaboration with Laurence Kitchin, for whom it amounted to
two hours in the Stag, standing at the bar and talking about
rugby, and a rather uneasy transmission. Laurence Kitchin did
not like to proffer suggestions, although MacNeice might have
welcomed them had the two men known each other better.

By November, MacNeice was working on 'Trimalchio's
Feast'. Gilliam assured him that he was not to regard it as
a task; he could drop it if it did not look promising. But it was
promising. Alan Rawsthorne was commissioned to write music
for it; Trimalchio was to be played by Wilfred Pickles; and the
sycophantic professor, Agamemnon, by Dylan Thomas. Although intended for the Third Programme, there was some
concern at the indecency of the subject. The Controller wrote
to Gilliam: 'there are certain well-established British sus-
ceptibilities to bear in mind.' MacNeice wrote an explanatory
note for *Radio Times*, but his references to homosexuality and
the 'workings of the bowels' were deleted—not from the play
however. The work became more than a satire, having a strong
sense of character, especially in Trimalchio, played with splendid ease and warmth by Pickles. Perhaps the character becomes
too sympathetic, but the play is very enjoyable listening.

In adapting the material for radio, MacNeice had to break
up long monologues, and invent dialogue. He used regional
accents, to convey the variety of the geographical backgrounds
of the freedmen and the *nouveaux riches*, and also to suggest
character. The Irishman is a good storyteller, the Welshman
severe in his censure of decadent pupils, the Cockney husband
and his French wife suitably sly and smooth-talking, the Soho-
mafioso Italian devious. Above all, the Yorkshire accents of the
host work well: 'ye've had nowt yet', 'when I were a lad I used

to read that in 'omer.' In sharp contrast are the superior tones
of the Professor, a flattering parasite. The music adds its effects:
brash and blaring, but buoyant, to start with; fanfares and
tongue-in-cheek chanting from the slaves; solemn for the mock
funeral. There is also a 'spiritual', 'A slave is a man', sung by
Inia Te Wiata. After reminders that no one is immortal, the
play ends on a muted note. It was broadcast on 17 December,
and repeated on the 25th—the beginning and end of Saturnalia.

Early in 1949 MacNeice was working on his new play, 'The
Queen of Air and Darkness'. Once again the theme is misguided power, idealism perverted to evil. The starting point
was a poem which greatly intrigued MacNeice; it was by
Housman, a favourite poet of his:

> Her strong enchantments failing,
>   Her towers of fear in wreck,
> Her limbecks dried of poisons
>   And the knife at her neck,
>
> The Queen of Air and Darkness
>   Begins to shrill and cry,
> 'O young man, O my slayer,
>   Tomorrow you shall die.'
>
> 'O Queen of Air and Darkness,
>   I think 'tis true you say,
> And I shall die tomorrow;
>   But you will die today.'

Writing to MacNeice in April 1952, after reading the play,
Eliot commented: 'I am most interested ... that you should
have made this development of Housman's theme, because this
has always seemed to me one of his best, if not actually the very
best, of all his poems.'

Unsure of Housman's precise meaning, MacNeice borrowed
his young man, naming him Adam and making him a politician.
The Queen personifies evil. The treatment is more mythic than
in 'The Careerist'; in some ways it recalls 'Pax Futura', in its
message, and the futuristic setting. The sea, forest and desert of
'The Dark Tower' are replaced by a city, with strange subterranean tunnels—a potent image. In this lower world lives

the blind Queen; she will regain her sight only if her power is broken. The setting and the evil Queen are partly reminiscent of George MacDonald's stories (*Lilith* and *Phantastes*); there is an echo of Tennyson in the motifs of curse and mirror. Music makes us feel the strangeness of the Queen's realm:

> Here where there is never a draught, where no fly buzzes
> Where no dust settles, where the light never changes,
> But everything is crystal, timeless, frozen. . . .

Elisabeth Lutyens composed the score; she recalls that MacNeice gave impressionistic instructions—'music like blue velvet, dripping'.

In the upper world the ruler, in the power of the Queen, is Jan Urgarst. Thirty years before he had had a vision, 'to make or break the world'. He had betrayed comrades, taken control of the country by force, caused wars and thousands of deaths. Now he has been defeated in his turn. In his letter to Hugo Schuster, who played the role, MacNeice said that, though old and rather exhausted, 'he ought to show traces of that magnetic quality or dynamism which had made him into a sort of Hitler.' Of Adam, played by Stephen Murray, he wrote that 'he must be played very strong throughout but N.B. in spite of his being possessed by a demoniac and disastrous ideal he should also, at least at times, win the listener's sympathy, even if against the reader's better judgement.' Murray replied that he found the part very exciting.

Adam, chosen by the Queen as her new lover, is accorded the same vision, and becomes a dictator in his turn. He tries to suppress individual freedom, but there are dissenters—professor, peasant, doctor, worker, priest, liberal editor. These are arrested. The priest, for example, is preaching when the door crashes open and, amid the murmurs of the congregation, military footsteps and heelclicks echo on the stone floor. The modern world lends itself to stories of betrayal and surreptitious threat, and to the theme of power misused, destroying what is human. Adam's marriage and a subsequent relationship both fail—the Queen has chilled him for any mortal woman. One of the powerful images in the play is the faceless and ruthless man behind the scenes: MacGregor, played by James McKechnie, 'with a slight Glasgow accent and make him as hard as possible', as MacNeice wrote to the actor. He hides away in a characterless apartment, in a huge nameless block— the inhumanity of the city taken to its extreme.

Neither a hero, like Roland or the captain of 'Pax Futura', nor a suicide like 'The Careerist', Adam resolves to act, after he himself has been betrayed, captured and sent down the long tunnels.

> If the timeless world can sway us for good or evil
> Then we can answer back.

Urgarst's widow, sitting in her chains, has distinguished the lighter patch at the end of the tunnel, and the smell of incense; given a knife by her, Adam breaks through and destroys the Queen and her power. Music helps to build the climax, and accompanies the repetition of Housman's lines. The effect must have been comparable to that of 'The Dark Tower': unfortunately, no copy remains in Sound Archives. It reads well, and at the time of its broadcast (28 March 1949), the radio critic of the *Manchester Guardian* praised the play and its author: 'well worth the attention of anyone interested in new and imaginative writing for the wireless . . . very powerful and sombre . . . he stands pretty well alone in his use of radio as a dramatic medium for serious thought.' MacNeice himself rather underrated the play, and at the time he was aware of possible difficulties. He wrote to Catherine Lacey, who played the Queen, that it was 'a rather strange piece and your part is especially strange! She should throughout be both sinister and glamorous.' To Julia Lang he wrote: 'this is a very peculiar programme in which to my delight you are going to take part. Your part is that of Margaret. . . . Among other things she must be capable of being hypnotised. And we don't of course want any "poetry voices".' Actors found MacNeice very good to work with, not given to much instruction, but what he did give was precise and intuitive.

Immediately after this production, from 1 April, there began the period of leave for the translation of *Faust*. MacNeice's

friend, Ernest Stahl, was to make a line-by-line version, from
which MacNeice could work. They co-operated closely on this
enormous undertaking, discussing detailed and general problems. They met at Louis's London home or BBC office, or in
Oxford; by the summer the families were in France, in a house
at Ménèrbes, lent by a friend—'sun-drenched, mistral-swept',
as Ernest Stahl describes it. In his introduction to the published
text, MacNeice wrote of the 'long and strenuous exercise in the
craft of writing' that the work afforded him. He had to convey
the power and variety of a great masterpiece, and he came to
appreciate Goethe in the process. It was an allotted task, or at
least one offered to him, but it was extremely well suited to his
talents and interests. The story and hero are traditional,
mythic in scope, concerned with evil and redemption. It is a
challenge to the imagination of both writer and listener and
offered fine opportunities to the producer and composer.
Matyas Seiber wrote the music, and Archie Harding produced
the six programmes (eight hours' broadcasting in all). MacNeice
praised the 'sensitivity and imagination' of Harding's production, and called him the 'onlie begetter' of the project. Harding
had suggested the scheme to the BBC, with the comment that
'the Corporation might well be promoting the greatest single
literary and cultural achievement of its history.'

The work was broadcast from 30 October to 21 November
1949; in 1962 MacNeice produced an abridged version of it
himself. The combination of morality and 'saga' was consonant
with MacNeice's work during these years. He found Mephisto
more sympathetic than Faust himself, who seemed too self-
pitying. The devil's speeches are taut and witty. The more
serious sections are effective too—there is great variety in the
verse, which would appeal to so versatile a poet as MacNeice.
The imagery is often strangely in tune with his own: gloomy
passages, the descent to the mysterious 'Mothers', the threat of
desolate loneliness, the search for an ideal beauty and love. The
scene between Helen and Faust is hushed, gentle music in the
background as they enjoy the arcadian retreat; but it is, of
course, an illusion, and Helen bids farewell. The Grey Sisters—
Want, Debt, Care and Need—are eerily rendered, and there is

a hollow spectral sound to Death's name. Faust becomes a tragic figure, sated but unhappy, wishing to be human again. The final section is very beautiful and moving, with Mephistopheles' cynicism over-ridden by celestial power.

The aged Faust, repentant, is helped to salvation by Gretchen, the penitent women, the new-born souls and the angelic figures. The music and poetry create an ethereal uplifting atmosphere: there is one constant star which must shine; the craggy chasm and roaring waters, full of God's love; and roses and grace. Harp, strings and voices bring the work to a fitting climax. The final chorus and solo—the 'Chorus Mysticus'—is especially moving. Professor Stahl has chosen this last section as an example of the great care that MacNeice took in rendering the work into English.

> All that is past of us
> Was but reflected;
> All that was lost in us
> Here is corrected;
> All indescribables
> Here we descry;
> Eternal Womanhead
> Leads us on high.

'MacNeice took a very long time over this . . . elaborating and refining it during one of those extended phases of withdrawn and abstracted concentration when he conceived and shaped his best poetry.'

At the end of 1949 MacNeice was to begin a longer period of leave from the BBC (the *Faust* project had taken six months, an extension of the estimated four months it was thought would be needed). He was to go out to Athens for a year and a half, as Director of the British Institute. The post-war phase of his career in broadcasting was rounded off, as it had begun, with a production of 'The Dark Tower', at the request of Third Programme. It was recorded in December. Cyril Cusack again played Roland, and among the rest of the cast were actors who worked often with MacNeice: Laidman Browne, Mark Dignam, Malcolm Hayes, Allan McClelland, Duncan McIntyre, Esmé

Percy, Marjorie Westbury, Mary Wimbush. Dylan Thomas was the Raven. This production was broadcast twice during MacNeice's absence in Greece: on 30 January 1950, and on 16 May 1951.

Chapter Six

Greek Interval and Return: 1950–1955

To contrive the truth
Or the dawn is the bloom and brief of days ahead. . . .
Autumn Sequel, Canto I

'Having recently lived in Athens for over a year and a half, I find it a hard place to write about.' So wrote MacNeice in *Radio Times*, in November 1951, introducing the first of three radio features he wrote and produced after his return. He had found himself among a small ex-patriate group of artists and writers, and mixed mainly with them; Greek writers, government officials, members of foreign missions. At first the Institute was independent of the British Council, and Louis MacNeice and Hedli arranged parties, concerts, poetry readings, lectures, plays. They brought the British cultural heritage to Greece— including that of Ireland: MacNeice produced and took part in *The Playboy of the Western World* while he was there. A few months after he took up his post the Institute merged with the Council, and something of a feud developed between the MacNeice camp and the new superior. The routine was partly an unwelcome burden but, in the words of a young writer who became friendly with MacNeice, he discharged his duties 'with wit and grace and diligence', while Hedli was 'attractive witty talented and ebullient'.

'I first saw him at a marble-staired reception, looking opaque', Kevin Andrews recalls. He often visited Louis and Hedli in their 'frosty brown flat', Athens circa 1930 style. 'Most of the time he never talked, mostly looked past you at a world you didn't have a place in. So it was matter for astonishment that on two or three occasions he looked me in the eye, or read me a poem just completed, or talked to me in a warm and relaxed manner that I didn't know how to reciprocate. . . . Once too from another room I watched him at a dining-table sitting up till 3.00 in the morning, trying to make suitable for publication a clumsy article I had written on returning from a mountain area in the grip of a guerrilla war.' MacNeice had some unfinished work of his own for Faber, as a letter written in March shows. He apologises for not having sent Part II of *Faust*: 'several circumstances combined have prevented me making the necessary alterations in it but I hope to manage this within the next month.' The news that his *Agamemnon* was to be reprinted pleased him, naturally; he had to consider whether any changes were needed. While in Greece MacNeice wrote a sequence of poems, and developed the idea for three scripts for radio. During the same period were also sown the seeds of three later plays, on themes of imprisonment and betrayal.

The encounter with modern Athens had its shocks, as had his meeting with India. This time he had to set a familiar past against an unfamiliar present. 'Portrait of Athens', the first radio feature, is a 'token patchwork', twenty-four centuries compressed into one day, and that day into one hour. The waking and dreaming thoughts are those of a Visitor, played by a compatriot of MacNeice, Allan McClelland, who came to know Louis well. The 'Portrait' starts with the tinny note of a bell, and the Visitor's comment: 'So this is Athens. A nagging bell and a glaring sky. A box on the ear. A smack in the eye. Crude as a poster. Hard as nails. Yes, this is Athens—not what I expected.' It does not accord with scholarly images of 'a garden in a dream drowsy with bees, mellowed with marbles, tasteful repose'. The Visitor is accompanied by his Chorus (two parts, played by Hedli Anderson and Dylan Thomas) who remind him that there is a 'grain of salt in the nectar' and a merciless light in the birth place of irony. Periclean Athens had seen the morning of Europe, but now its remains are overgrown with thistle and spurge, while Milton's 'studious walks and shades' have been replaced by dull and dusty streets.

Although he went there in 1950—when Greece had been suffering from the civil war that followed the World War—there are only passing references to recent events, to Greece's 'No' to the enemy, and the S.S. setting foot in Kolonaki Square. Modern Athens is suggested by the noise and chatter of streets and market stalls, and by the popular music of the cafeneion where the men seem content to sit all morning, to the dismay of an American official. Lest we should draw the wrong conclusions, from the contrast between past and present, MacNeice brings in Socrates, who does not like the clothes, the buildings or the music, but finds the talk familiar, and, after all, a city is the men in it, not the appearances. He cannot understand our passion for digging up the past; he always welcomed something new. 'Some new thing': the Visitor is reminded of St Paul, and we hear a priest reading the lesson, Paul preaching on Mars Hill, taking his cue from the altar to 'the Unknown God'. The Furies are still in their cave beneath, but 'the whirligig of time' has brought its changes. Back in the present, it is lunch-time, and an afternoon siesta gives the opportunity for a dream sequence.

This takes us gradually back in time: nineteenth-century Bavarian kings, the Turkish occupation; then, as the minarets fade, the Venetian priests appear. Further back is the Byzantine city, its decay lamented by poets—'All is past and gone, the glory of Athens'; then we move back to the golden noonday of the city. Earlier still there was Roman Athens; before that the purest Classical phase; back through the stiff-statued Archaic, into the darkness of legend. Pallas Athena, a hard goddess, gave mixed gifts—the arts of civilisation, and their attendant sorrows. The Chorus describe the silver and grey olive trees, dancing like weird sisters, until the houses reappear, and the metal daylight softens to velvet darkness; we are back in the evening cocktail hour of 1950 Athens, with a satiric vignette of gossiping women. Athens at night is reminiscent of the picture of India, Hymettus turning purple. The place fills with people; there is singing and dancing. The dancers are sketched vividly: 'Looking down at the earth in abstraction, in almost mathematical, almost religious concentration. But with perhaps a cigarette in their mouths.' Finally night lightens into dawn—the sun is about to 'open fire'. Socrates pays his debt to Asclepius, the traditional thank-offering for a recovery; a cockerel crows, and is faded out.

This is a splendid feature, a recapturing of the city that holds good even today. MacNeice's classical learning is lightly worn, but gives perspective to the picture; while the subject inspires some keen observation and striking use of words. What is only touched on is the suffering: the refugees on the outskirts of the city, 'exiles but undefeated'; and the war, a young woman remembers one bright morning when she heard the singing of young men lined up to be shot. Kevin Andrews has written: 'he never got really much involved in any Greek life outside the asphyxiating circle of the English-speaking Athenian Establishment.' More recently he has added that MacNeice 'did see or apprehend enough of the Greece of the time to write a thoroughly and characteristically intelligent review of a book I wrote on the Civil War period'. The impressions of other people in Greece at that time support the view that MacNeice observed, but did not become involved. It seems to have been an introspective phase, a time productive of poetry.

He sent a letter, dated 20 September 1950, to Eliot, at Faber: 'Dear Tom ... I have been working lately on a set of longish poems (averaging *c* 140–150 lines), each in four sections. I call them *Panegyrics* and I think they represent what one calls 'a new development'. I have already written eight (but 4 of these still need considerable tinkering) and am about to start on a ninth.' He hoped, he said, to write twelve poems in all (in fact, he wrote only ten). He felt that they would be more integrated than previous volumes of his poetry, not only because of their structure and length, 'but because they come from a common matrix and so overlap or lead on to each other'. He then summarises his themes: 'Suite for recorders' is to be on the Elizabethans, violence and pastoral; 'Areopagus' on the Eumenides and St Paul; 'Cock o' the north' on Missolonghi and Calydon, Byron and Meleager; 'Didymus' on St Thomas and India; 'In praise of water' on the primal element and its symbolism, hot countries and the Industrial Revolution; 'The island' is to juxtapose Homer and today; 'Aged Forty-three' is to be on the theme of birthdays, time and the timeless; 'Day of returning' on homesickness, Odysseus and Jacob, the evangelicals, this world and the other worldly. The method of contrast, setting of past against present, concern with his actual life and his inner life, all are characteristic. Perhaps 'Panegyrics' came to seem inappropriate as a title; the Biblical phrase 'burnt offerings' was to replace it. (Some of the individual poem titles were also changed.)

The first of the sequence 'Ten Burnt Offerings' provides a link with earlier poems, and with radio works. The Elizabethan age had been the subject of 'Autolycus', and there had been a feature on 'The Death of Marlowe'. The references to Shakespeare's clowns betray a concern with the mature comedies: Feste's phrase 'whirligig of time' occurs in 'Portrait of Athens', and 'Suite for recorders' is headed by part of a sentence by Touchstone: 'When a man's verses cannot be understood, nor a man's good wit seconded with the forward child, understanding, it strikes a man more dead than a great reckoning in a little room.' The poets, 'Elizabethan mayflies in a silver web', are poised over the dark void. Time has to be transcended—this had been a theme of 'The Stygian banks'—and, as in that other poem, spring recurs. Here the mood is less hopeful:

> Great reckonings come, yet cheat nor schemer
> Outlives, outdies, his early beauty,
> Black fingers will bear fruit and spring
> Put paid to every reckoning.

Fate, 'Black Jenny', spins her web, and 'all vision shrinks to dream.' What did the poets leave for us? A bed of flowers? A second best? A starting point? Taking his cue from them, MacNeice ends his poem with a modern pastoral, a lyrical and witty love poem. Perhaps it too has a reminder of Shakespeare's comedies:

> Yet read between those lines and peer
> Down through the mesh of gossamer
> And you will sense the darkness which
> Made either guttering candle rich;

And you, a would-be player too,
Will give those angry ghosts their due
Who threw their voices far as doom
Greatly in a little room.

The second poem may be looked at afresh in the light of the radio feature on Athens. 'Areopagus' begins with St Paul in the city, preaching that new thing that the Athenians loved. 'And they took him and brought him unto Areopagus. . . .' and Paul preached of the Unknown God. There is a clash between the 'Hebrew riddling in the land of olives' and his audience, who mock him. The poem's images are hard: stone, iron, diamond, 'iron faith in the city of irony'. The Furies still sleep in their cave. The second section introduces description of modern Athens, 'seas of electric lights' surrounded by mountains, and the Parthenon's 'ruined playpen'. That metaphor is used in the radio portrait, where we are told that it was the phrase used by an English child (MacNeice's young daughter?). The Furies, hounds or hissing snakes, are still in pursuit. The lines beginning 'Unkind was early' parallel the dream sequence of the radio feature. The close of the section affirms that modern attitudes do not 'cancel out Christ's death or prove the Furies dead'. In Section Three, Orestes and Christ, saviours of Greeks and Jews, are set in the wider scene of 'dark prehistory'. The image of the living rock against the dead sea is matched by lines in the poem 'Mahabalipuram'. Images of risen gods are fused at the end.

The meditation on man and his gods shows that the religion of MacNeice's childhood still had its influence; and that the experience of India was strong. He once made the comment to a friend that he felt that his own talent in poetry was basically a religious one. His admiration for his father must have been bound up with this, and the poem 'Didymus' draws on the example of a devoted pastor, bringing together east and west, as the poet's father had hoped to reconcile north and south in Ireland. Thomas, who doubted, set out to convert India 'armed with two plain crossed sticks'. Paul might present an 'invincible avatar', but Thomas brought the simplicity of Christ against the multiplicity of the Hindu gods. Despite his weakness, Thomas has dignity:

> And beside that sea like a sea on the moon
> He clasped his hands to make sure they were only
> Two and, finding them two but strong,
> Raised them gently and prayed.

Images of dance and dream, frequent in MacNeice's poetry, are combined to express the idea of the ineffable:

> Not strange for all their ingrown iconography, not so strange
>   as our own dreams
> Because better ordered, these are the dreams we have needed
>   Since we have forgot how to dance. . . .

Section Four parallels the radio feature 'India at First Sight': the same evening scene, rivers of people, purple light, but here there is more emphasis on the philosophy, and on Thomas's achievement, the bare church and plaque an 'adequate tribute'.

Another saint is remembered in 'Our sister water': Francis of Assisi, who praised 'my dear Sor Acqua'. Play is made with the word 'water', as noun and verb. Both life and death may be symbolised by the primal element—we find this often in MacNeice's poems. Another frequent theme is the contrast between natural flow and a mechanical world. In this poem the pastoral scene is an Irish one:

>   when a girl in a shawl
> Barefoot and windblown staggers her way through the bog
> With a bucket of windblown gold.

The whole sequence takes us step by step through MacNeice's year in Greece. Now, in summer, he visits an island. Kevin Andrews writes of 'One summer spent in their maid's village at the wild rough end of one of the least known islands of the Aegean (from Byzantine times a place of exile, under the Metaxas dictatorship and again during the Civil War a place of enforced rustication for political prisoners) . . . not enough to spark him off, though some of the prisoners on Ikaria were his contemporaries and most were to go on to places worse. . . .' In the poem, the prisoners are mentioned only briefly after a nightmare passage, in the middle of more personal reflection, with images of water and dryness, shadows lengthening, life passing. 'No freedom, only reprieve' may be more an allusion to his own state than to that of the prisoners. The poem takes us from early morning to night verging on daybreak—as in 'Portrait of Athens'—but the mood is more introspective. This may be partly on account of the poet's approaching birthday, the subject of the next poem.

The idea of prisons remained with MacNeice, however, and was given additional stimulus by two occurrences, which led to later plays. While he was in Greece he read a novel by his friend Goronwy Rees, *Where No Wounds Were*, and wrote to him to say that he would like to adapt it for radio. Then in Athens, in 1951, he was questioned by a policeman who thought he might be the defector, Guy Burgess, whose action was causing such a stir among the London circles in which he had moved; these had overlapped with some of MacNeice's. From this came the germ of a play; first put on by the Group Theatre in Belfast, it was named *Traitors in Our Way*; later he rewrote it for television as 'Another Part of the Sea'. A third play may have had its genesis at this time—the prize-winning radio play of 1954, 'Prisoner's Progress'.

An often-quoted statement is from the birthday poem of 1950, 'Day of renewal':

> This middle stretch
> Of life is bad for poets. . . .

The poem is in reflective mood, looking back to childhood and to other birthdays:

> They told me as a child that ten was a ripe age
> When presents must be useful; which was Progress
> But I felt sad to end each fairy story,
> Kept turning back to the first page.

Other birthdays recall other places: Cushenden, Dieppe and Lahore. In the second section of the poem clever play is made with games and chants of children, and images of bells, candles, the light at the top of the well, a child reaching out for the moon (like the baby wanting the witchball in 'The Careerist'). In Section Three, milestones in 'a vast Forest of marble obelisks' must derive from the cemetery next to the Carrickfergus rectory; there are the child's fears, and the need to grow up.

And now I am forty-three,
At sea in the small hours heading west from the island.

At this time he is returning to Athens; 'But next time what?'
he asks. It is in the fourth part of this poem that the image is
used of burnt offerings, to 'a god who needs no name', in the
smoke of autumn bonfires:

For all my years are based on autumn,
Blurred with blue smoke, charred by flame,
Thrusting burnt offerings on a god
Who cannot answer to his name.

MacNeice said himself that he was steeped in the Bible, and
the phrase is found several times in the Psalms, as in Psalm 66:
'I will go into thy house with burnt offerings; I will pay thee
my vows.'

Birthday reckonings for MacNeice dated to September, and
we have several examples in the poetry: *Autumn Journal*, 'Autobiography', 'Prayer in mid-passage', 'Day of renewal'; sections
of *The Strings are False* also date to the autumn. Certain images
and themes recur, and are found in the next poem of the Greek
sequence, 'Day of returning': Jacob wrestling with God is one
example, and the theme of renewal—also important in 'The
Stygian banks'. The need of fulfilment in human relationships
is affirmed, the importance of one's roots. Odysseus hankers for
Ithaca:

Here could never be home,
No more than the sea around it. And even the sea
Is a different sea round Ithaca.

Jacob welcomes each day with its chance of beginning again,
and remembers his vision.

We all are homeless sometimes, homesick sometimes,
As we all at times are godless or god-fearing.

The last two poems of the sequence focus more closely on home:
'The death of a cat' is set in the MacNeices' Athens home;
'Flowers in the interval' is a 'heartfelt artifice' to Hedli, who
brings him a 'benediction and an end to doubt'.

Another feature for radio, deriving from the time in Greece,

was 'In Search of Anoyia'. In his autobiography, E. R. Dodds
gave an account of a holiday spent in Crete, when with Louis,
Hedli and Dan he climbed Mount Ida. 'It was a long slog,
nothing more, but the MacNeices had had no practice in
mountaineering. Dusk was closing in when we reached the
lofty summer pasture called the Plain of Nida. There we
camped for the night in a roomy cavern with a band of shepherds and their flocks. It was bitterly cold, but the shepherds
were kind: they built a huge fire at the mouth of the cave, lent
us their sheepskin cloaks, and shared with us their accustomed
provision of rock-hard bread dipped in warm sheep's milk. It
was like paying a call on a friendly Polyphemus. In the morning
Dan and I climbed with the guide to the summit while the
others set off slowly downhill. It was late when we reached
Anoyia. . . .' It was Easter, and at midnight the bells rang and
everyone embraced each other in the street. 'Louis, tired as he
was, characteristically insisted on joining in the celebrations.
The experience was later transmuted into one of the most
moving of his dramatic radio pieces.'

'In Search of Anoyia' has as its protagonist an amateur
archaeologist named John, who has a wife and son. What he is
really searching for is meaning in his own life; images of
labyrinth and thread are used, appropriately for Crete, with
Knossos not far from Anoyia. 'One needs intuition. . . . think
yourself back and away.' During an illness he dreams of walking
'down to Phaestos first . . . and then up Ida from the south',
where he finds some shepherds in a cave. Awake again, he
delves into an old book, looking for a reference to Anoyia, for
the place strangely intrigues him. In another dream he talks to
the author of the book, and to an old woman who had been
enslaved by the Turks. There are weaving women (Anoyia is
still renowned for its weaving) and the Easter celebrations.
John still cannot get the place into perspective. Later, there is
the feast of the Assumption (MacNeice paid an August visit to
Anoyia as well); in his dream his wife is transformed into
'Maria'; it is their wedding day. When he wakes he tries to
explain his feelings to his wife: 'I think nothing we've had or
we've been should ever seem far away. We should cling to the

ball of thread that connects the strange and the unusual, the past and the present, ourselves and the others. We should go in search of other men's lives and our own'. His wife does not understand, nor answer him. The programme closes with Cretan wedding music, and greetings in Greek.

Laurence Gilliam went out to join MacNeice for a time, on a semi-official visit in July 1951; they discussed various possible programmes. One was a feature on a current 'dig' at Mycenae, but the excavation proved to be on too small a scale. (This is a pity, since the site has such atmosphere, and would have been particularly evocative for MacNeice with its associations with Agamemnon.) Another sounds attractive, but it came to nothing: a feature incorporating descriptions of certain ancient places as they are today, and translations by MacNeice of poems about those places in antiquity. A feature which was written and produced by MacNeice was on Delphi, where he went for the Festival in August 1951. After an uncomfortable journey, over bad roads and in the extreme heat of summer, he saw Delphi at its worst, overcrowded to the point where many visitors had to be accommodated in tents. At the main event— a performance of *Oedipus*—the actors' beards would not stick on because of the hot weather. Not surprisingly, the feature, 'The Centre of the Earth', registers a certain disappointment. The visitors in this piece are two rather affected and over-sophisticated women, and there is a knowledgeable academic who points out that Delphi became first a political necessity, then, after centuries of silence, a tourist attraction: 'this whole business of the Oracle has been disgracefully romanticised.' The last word is given to a shepherd, who wonders what all the fuss is about.

To end his time in Greece, MacNeice visited 'mountains and islands', including Crete. He was to leave Greece on 31 August, and planned to spend ten days or so in Venice on the way back, arriving home in mid-September. He was in time to add his suggestions to a list of guests that the Third Programme and Features were planning to entertain. Among those already on the list were Alan Rawsthorne, Antony Hopkins, Daniel Jones, Peter Racine Fricker, Donald Swann, Sandy Wilson, Henry

Reed, Dylan Thomas, Lawrence Durrell, Christopher Fry and C. Day Lewis. MacNeice added William Alwyn, Lennox Berkeley, Arnold Cook, Elisabeth Lutyens, Michael Tippett, William Walton, Laurie Lee and Stevie Smith. Alas, the list got too long, and the BBC dropped the idea. The features on Greece were broadcast during November, December and January.

MacNeice now had nothing scheduled until the summer, so he proposed to 'get down to the major Saul project ... a programme which will obviously need maturing'. It was not produced until 1956. He seems to have wanted something lighter to do, and proposed another March Hare feature: 'a fun-and-not-too-vulgar-games piece', in which the Hare would attempt to escape from 'the cold facts of 1952' into myth—Greek, Norse, Irish and oriental. MacNeice gave as an example of the theme the infant Hermes—an incarnation of anarchic and joyful mischief, but destined to grow up into the messenger of the gods, a bureaucrat. At a Features meeting on 31 January the suggestion was put, but not accepted. During the first half of 1952 there were no new original projects for radio from MacNeice, although he was given the solemn task of compiling an anthology, 'Mourning and Consolation', on the King's death in February. In March he wrote to Eliot about the possibility of publishing some of his radio works: the Aristophanes feature, 'The Queen of Air and Darkness' ('a very dour piece and tends to be too much on one note, still I think it has its points'), 'The Heartless Giant' and 'India at First Sight'. Eliot did not think these would make a satisfactory book, but he suggested that a translation of a complete Aristophanes play, perhaps *The Frogs*, would be worth doing; no book ensued.

The minutes of 22 May record that Features Department accepted three suggestions from MacNeice: the Battle of Clontarf, an adaptation of *The Waves* by Virginia Woolf, and a feature provisionally entitled 'The Sports Writer' (the last could be ready any time after 20 July, MacNeice promised). During that summer he was also commissioned by the BBC to make a translation of *The Iliad*; this he proposed to do in his spare time, not during a period of special leave as for the *Faust*.

(He was released from this commitment in 1956.) He did complete work on Spenser's poem *The Faerie Queene*, organising its production in twelve programmes in the last quarter of 1952. In that November he also produced his new play, about the sports writer, as 'One Eye Wild'. (He did not do the Virginia Woolf adaptation until 1955, and the play on Clontarf remained unwritten until 1959.)

How representative of Features Department was this year's schedule? Douglas Cleverdon (who produced a great deal of work himself) has written of Gilliam's inspiring leadership, and of the Department's contribution to creative radio, pointing out, however, the unevenness of the effort. 'There was no fixed output per producer. Some produced a lot of programmes, others only a few. They were unreliable in their office routine and usually congregated with writers and poets and actors in "The Stag" or "The George" for a couple of hours at lunch.' Laurence Gilliam's approach, running his artists on the loosest of reins, made this inevitable; he was anxious to shield his staff from bureaucrats within the bureaucracy. MacNeice's own tilts at the enemy suggest that he could scarcely have survived under a different kind of control. The prestige and the achievements of the Department seem to justify Gilliam. As Douglas Cleverdon has noted, from the inauguration of the Italia Prize in 1949, until 1955, 'of fifteen entries chosen as the outstanding works of these years, fourteen came from Features Department.' Of the dramatised features, five won awards: 'Rumpelstiltskin' by Francis Dillon; 'The Face of Violence' by J. Bronowski; 'The Streets of Pompeii' by Henry Reed; 'Under Milk Wood' by Dylan Thomas; 'Prisoner's Progress' by Louis MacNeice. (Dillon and MacNeice produced their own programmes; the other three were produced by Cleverdon.)

Features which did not win prizes could be very fine too. Douglas Cleverdon regards 'In Parenthesis', based on the book by David Jones, as one of his most important productions; he also produced 'Anathemata'. A 1951 entry by Nesta Pain, 'Spiders', with music by Antony Hopkins, came to be regarded as a classic radio feature. Two works submitted to the Italia Prize Committee in 1953 exemplify other kinds of Features work: Francis Dillon's topical satire 'The Little Gold Shoe', and Dorothy Baker's script about a Belgian woman in the Resistance, 'Who Shall Stand?', produced by Christopher Sykes. In 1950 Gilliam had edited the collection *Features*: these included 'The Last Days of Hitler' by Trevor-Roper, adapted by Terence Tiller; 'The End of Mussolini' by D. G. Bridson; 'Black House into White' (about the Hebrides) by David Thomson; 'The Man from Belsen' by Leonard Cottrell; 'British Justice' by Jenifer Wayne; 'The Brain at Work' by Nesta Pain; 'The Undefeated: Gladys Aylward' by Alan Burgess; 'From Anzio to Burgundy' by Wynford Vaughan Thomas; 'W. B. Yeats: A Dublin Portrait' by W. R. Rodgers. The selection illustrates Gilliam's particular interest in radio journalism, the 'stuff of reality' shaped by a creative mind.

A favourite programme of Gilliam's was the Christmas Day round-the-world link-up, bringing together the various parts of the Commonwealth. This could be very moving, as in the immediate post-war period, or topical and impressive, but it tended to the rhetorical. For those concerned it could be interesting, sending people to foreign places, and taking some three months to plan. Closer to home, and more homely, was the long-running 'Country Magazine', produced by Francis Dillon, introducing traditional craftsmen and the 'fellows in the public bar' (to use MacNeice's phrase), and also putting on record traditional songs—this happened too in Dillon's series about British regiments. There was also a feature on gypsies, made in collaboration with Rupert Croft-Cooke, who knew the travelling people well. Dillon did literary features too, like his fairy tale adaptations; he also introduced the work of Mervyn Peake to radio, producing Peake's own adaptation of *Titus Groan* in 1956.

Other literary features included the 'Radio Portraits' of Maurice Browne and W. R. Rodgers, himself a poet: that on Yeats was broadcast in 1949, and others followed between 1950 and 1954 on James Joyce, George Moore, Synge and Shaw. The eloquence of Irish conversation made these features outstanding. Rayner Heppenstall instituted the 'Imaginary Conversations' for which scripts were submitted by established

writers: there were series in 1946, 1948 and 1952. An offshoot
was the reconstruction of Proustian episodes, from clues in the
novel, by Pamela Hansford Johnson: the first, 'The Duchess at
Sunset', was in 1948, followed by 'Swann in Love' in 1952.
Henry Reed followed up his 1949 plays on Leopardi ('The
Unblessed' and 'The Monument') with his very amusing mock-
biographies and memoirs: 'A Very Great Man Indeed' (1953),
'The Private Life of Hilda Tablet' and 'Emily Butter' (1954),
'A Hedge Backwards' (1956), 'The Primal Scene as It Were'
(1958) and General Gland's war memoir 'Not a Drum was
Heard' (1959). Most of Reed's features were produced by
Douglas Cleverdon.

Geoffrey Bridson continued to produce notable work. Early
in 1951 he carried out a long-held ambition, in adapting for
radio Wyndham Lewis's *The Childermass*. 'Played out under the
towering walls of the Magnetic City across the river, its gates
and battlements rimmed with the circle of smouldering vol-
canoes, the huddling mass of emigrant souls in the foreground
patiently waiting for admission to what they believe is Heaven
—the setting of the drama is only to be seen convincingly in the
imagination. . . .' Following this, Harman Grisewood commissioned Lewis to complete the trilogy: by the end of 1954
Monstre Gai and *Malign Fiesta* were finished, and the entire
trilogy adapted for broadcasting in 1955. Among the works that
he wrote himself for radio, Bridson particularly liked 'The Epic
of Gilgamesh', broadcast in 1956.

Another poet-producer was Terence Tiller: an innovation of
his was the 'literary quest' for origins and meanings of myth and
symbol, at first in the form of dons' Senior Common Room
conversation, following the tantalising thread of obscure allusion. (The dons were dropped after a while.) 'The Baker's
Daughter' (1950), 'The Juniper Tree' (also in 1950, dealing
with tales of the Brothers Grimm), and 'The Symbols at Your
Door' (1953) are fascinating pieces of detection, as the 1975
repeat of the last showed. Apart from producing poetry programmes—including MacNeice's 'Ten Burnt Offerings' in 1951
—Terence Tiller wrote verse plays, and adapted and translated
Middle English and foreign verse and plays. This illustrates the

E

scholarly side of Features Department's output. His own plays included 'Death of a Friend', produced by Robert Gittings, in 1949; 'Lilith' in 1950; 'The Tower of Hunger' in 1952. There were adaptations of some of the Wakefield plays, and the Cornish cycle of Mystery Plays. (BBC logic inferred that Tiller would be a suitable adviser on religious broadcasting; he attended a conference on the subject in May 1952—as did MacNeice and W. R. Rodgers, the son of a bishop and an ex-country parson.) In the 1950s Tiller also did adaptations of Gower's 'Confessio Amantis' and Chaucer's 'The Parlement of Foules'. There were also collaborations with the composer Elizabeth Poston on an original type of ballad-cantata, using traditional verse and tunes. His work for radio continues, maintaining the fine tradition of the best years of Features.

So a 'feature' could be almost anything: Gilliam attracted producers who were innovative and creative, whether journalists or poets, so their programmes defy neat categories. Patric Dickinson illustrates this with an anecdote, from the early days of the Third Programme. At a meeting of Heads of Departments he contributed to an argument as to whether *Paradise Lost* was a Drama, Feature or Talk. 'I said that it was what Milton said it was, an Epic Poem. I am afraid this was not felt to be helpful. I was asked what I would do with it. I said I would have somebody read it. This simple solution appealed to Talks, but was overruled by Drama and Features. At this point Drama had to leave the room and in his absence Milton became a Feature. The lines were split up and cast for actors, like drama, but called readers because it was a Feature.'

So MacNeice returned to Features, in 1951, during a very fruitful period (although his own productions were to be fewer than in the 1940s). His adaptation of *The Faerie Queene*—as a feature—ran for twelve programmes, from 29 September to 15 December 1952. A copy of the script has comments in MacNeice's hand: 'N.B. S. *not* sloppy—avoid wooziness'. There are notes on tempo, stress, precise pointing, manner of delivery. Una, for instance, was to be 'cool v. x precise'; the Sprite sent by Archimago was to be high and mighty, coming from 'supernatural officialdom'. MacNeice wrote several times of Spenser's importance. In a review of a book by Rosemond Tuve, in September 1952, in the *New Statesman and Nation*, he said that Spenser was a great and neglected poet. In the Clark Lectures of 1963 he continued to express his admiration of Spenser—his allegory, variety of theme and style, the dream content. 'In poetry as a reader I have fairly catholic tastes but I would rather read Spenser than most: this is because of his exceptional depth and variety and because his work has the richness and complexity of the best dreams and the truth to life of the best fairy stories.' The significance of this comment can be fully appreciated only by some awareness of the radio work of MacNeice. It must have been very satisfying for him to have been able to present the work of a poet whom he admired to the large audience of radio.

The next work was 'One Eye Wild', broadcast on 9 November. At the beginning of the year MacNeice had been thwarted of his fun-and-games piece of escapism with his Hare, but some of the ideas went into this other feature. In May he had written to Gilliam of an idea which 'sprang already half-armed from my head only a few days ago'. The central figure would be a sports writer and commentator, 'an artist manqué, obsessed by the sad thought that in the modern world there is no place for heroes'. So the character escapes into myth—not the myths that the Hare would have chosen, but, on the one hand, the mystique of sport, and, on the other, 'fantasy proper'. He retreats from his temperamental wife, a nurse who would like to have been a doctor, to a dream mistress, Heliodora. (The name is taken from the poet Meleager: 'pledge her and mix her sweet name with wine.') His wife complains that he has a phoney job, that they have no money or status; she must always deflate him. The day of the play's action brings a crisis in the marriage. As he gives a commentary on the morning's play at Lord's, she prepares to leave with their son. The medium of radio is itself used as part of the mechanism of the play: we can hear her comments as she packs, intercut with his commentary; and later in the day she realises that there must be something wrong because he is not giving the afternoon's commentary. In fact, he has been knocked down, crossing the road to join a figure

whom he mistakes for a friend—it is a kind of *doppelgänger*, his
own cynical and critical other self, the Joker. This figure talks
to the main character, Roger, as he lies in hospital. Finally, he
returns home and is nursed by and reconciled to Margaret, his
wife, a 'more-or-less happy ending', as MacNeice said.

The title of the play comes from cards: a 'wild' card can be
used as the Joker, made into anything. Roger would like his
cards to be wild: 'he would like to be Homer or Hector or
Hobbs without having the hand for it, a man who in default of
myths and heroes has become the ephemeral bard of the minor
heroics of sport, a half-Homer with but one eye blind—but with
also one eye wild.' This gives some idea of MacNeice's quick-
wittedness, liking for plays on words, romanticism, and devotion
to sport; it is also a good illustration of the way he could use
radio both as a medium and as a subject. The feature is narrative, fantasy and parody; it varies in mood from sentimental
nostalgia and wishful lyricism, to wry amusement; so it has
many attributes of its author. The hero-manqué dreams of
scoring at rugby, of being a pre-First World War tennis hero,
adored by a sweet young girl, of jousting for her in days of old
(a running commentary on the medieval tournament provides
a comic pastiche), of horse-riding and enjoying a pastoral idyll.
At every point he is brought to earth—sometimes literally—
and put in his place by the scathing Meg. The play is not fully
a comedy—some of the feeling is too subjective. It may be a
less intense, half-amused, version of the fears and hopes expressed in the last of the 'Ten Burnt Offerings', where images of
loneliness—winds which 'lurk in the night' and the 'frozen
earth'—are dispelled by hope.

> Thus, when once more I round the corner,
> I know your castle is also mine
> And I know your dream defies the sands
> Which count the minutes. . . .
> Returned from a land I did not know
> Making unheard-of meanings heard
> And sprinkling all my days with daylight.

The introvert behaving like an extravert may put us in mind
of MacNeice himself, but the character was typical as well as

individual. Indeed, Howard Marion-Crawford, who played the part of Roger, was upset when he read his script, thinking that Louis had written about him. Margaret, the wife, was played by Brenda Bruce: she only seems tough, MacNeice pointed out—she attacks, but has plenty of provocation. Louis wrote to Richard Hurndall that the Joker was rather a strange part; perhaps they should meet for a drink to discuss it. And he took Cécile Chevreau—Heliodora—to Lord's, explaining that she would understand the game better after a few gins. A new production of the feature was done by MacNeice in 1961, when it still appealed to a sizeable minority. There were criticisms, of its complexity, or its trivial treatment of a serious subject, but some comments by the author, in *Radio Times* of 9 November 1952, had shown his aims. He hoped that the pattern of the story would atone for the ephemeral content. He was hoping for something 'less pretentious' than 'The Careerist' or 'The Queen of Air and Darkness'. Looking back, he felt that these were on 'too high and public a plane . . . too much in the nature of chronicles'. So he now chose sport as a substitute for art and for heroic action. If we reflect on this, we can see that it is consistent with his long-held belief that the poet should be an extension of the ordinary man.

After a routine Christmas feature, 'The Twelve Days of Christmas', and a short stay in Ireland at the end of January 1953, MacNeice spent two months in America, from 18 February to 14 April. This was his first visit there since 1940. He was to give lectures and readings at the Poetry Centre, New York, and Hedli was to give recitals. It is not surprising that the radio feature which arose from this visit should hark back to 1939 and 1940, nor that by the end of the year he should be writing *Autumn Sequel*. He introduced 'Return to Atlantis' himself, acknowledging his subjectivity—'so it's not really safe for me to generalise.' He refers to his various selves, which he personifies as 'Ulster' (played by Allan McClelland) and 'Oxford', recalling the travelling companions of *I Crossed the Minch*.

There are reminders of *The Strings are False* too (not at that time published), in the phrasing—'a magic mountain, a Christmas tree', 'a bit of a spree'—and the detail. The hope of finding

Atlantis, the parties and the intellectuals, the return to London in 1939, and the second visit to America in 1940, after leave of absence had been granted by Bedford College—all are remembered by the Voices. 'Oxford' drawls on about Cornell, and how boring England seemed. After the stay in hospital, and the fall, they embark for England—snow falls the evening before they leave. The ship's siren changes to the air-raid sirens of London, and the Voices wonder if they will ever go back to America. And so to the 1953 visit: the problem of getting a visa, the bureaucracy and paperwork, the United Nations building rearing up like an enormous scoreboard, the talk of investigations. It is a changed world. The programme, broadcast on 5 July, is not only a 'Portrait' of America; it is also a clue to MacNeice's feelings at a time when memories of the past thirteen years were revived, and the idea was growing of a sequel to *Autumn Journal*.

After his return from America, MacNeice had another routine feature assigned to him—to commemorate the accession of Elizabeth II. 'Time Hath Brought Me Hither' is not of great significance, but it employs the familiar method of setting past against present, and shows how the first Elizabethans were still in MacNeice's mind. Of more interest is the fact that he wrote the script for Stobart's film of the climbing of Everest, an equally historic event which coincided with the coronation. Goronwy Rees has a story of being in Wales that summer with Louis, and hearing the locals in a country pub talking of the feat, until a tall quiet man at the corner of the bar intervened: it was Hillary. MacNeice's script for the film, *Conquest of Everest*, was good but, as he knew himself, words could not compete with the awe-inspiring silence of the great mountain range. (He had glimpsed the neighbouring Karokorams himself, when in Kashmir.) He incorporated the Everest conquest into *Autumn Sequel*:

> The icefall tumbling from the Western Cwm
> Above which deserts of unsounded snow
>
> Brood, above which again one ominous plume
> Flies from the crest of what was Peak Fifteen
> Which even now knows fifteen brands of doom,

Twenty-nine thousand and two feet high, a clean
Rebuttal of the verities of Bucks
Where a projector clamps it on a screen

And I write words about it. . . .

MacNeice must have been at work on *Autumn Sequel* by
September 1953—that birthday was his forty-sixth. Eliot wrote
to MacNeice, on 9 October, referring to the publication of the
poem. He ends with the comment: 'I hope that the end of
March will not put you under too much pressure. From what I
gathered from you at lunch, it seemed to me that the poem was
going ahead well, and that only some unforeseen accident
could delay it.' There is a synopsis of the work, probably sent to
Faber at about this time. It would seem that the first ten cantos
were written (though not in their final form), while the rest are
listed under 'probable' headings, 'v. approx.' One irony comes
to light from this: Canto II has for its subject 'Gavin (dead)
lust and death—Gwilym the poet and Poetry—the Fall and the
Devil'. Cantos projected for late October and November include
'Lament for the Folk and for Childhood', 'Lament for the
Middle Ages', 'Lament for the Eighteenth Century'. The
eighteenth canto was to have been about the British Museum,
Egypt, Assyria and Greece; the twentieth about the Pythia;
but that November Dylan Thomas ('Gwilym') died, and
Cantos XVIII and XX are on his death and his funeral, instead
of ancient civilisations and the prophetess of Apollo.

Autumn Sequel was to be broadcast in 1954 as well as published.
Controllers and producers at the BBC considered it a major and
mature achievement. A *tour de force*, it is written in terza rima,
through twenty-six sections (cantos). This is not the only
likeness to Dante: MacNeice's poem is also a journey in the
middle years, involving other journeys, real and dream-like;
during the course of these he recalls people as well as places—
the celebration of friends is a continuation and extension of the
theme of 'The Kingdom'. MacNeice wrote of the later poem:
'What I think myself should be most interesting about the work
is the balance I have tried to achieve between the realistic and
the contemporary on the one hand and the mythical and

historical on the other.' Among the sources of the mythic elements are his own dreams. Some themes and images derive from the radio features, and from his reading, enriching the poem, but sometimes making it a little obscure, especially when he is carried away by the facility of his own invention. It is a stimulating and often moving poem.

The public world is still, as in the *Journal*, interwoven with private feelings and experiences. The new decade was drab and restrictive, but the task was possible:

> To contrive the truth
> Or the dawn is the bloom and brief of days ahead,
>
> In the teeth of ponce and newshawk, nark and sleuth,
> Who deal in false documentaries. August fades,
> Barbicans crumble, Caesar loses his youth,
>
> But we shall find what we make in the falling glades
> And be what we find in the evening; we shall contrive
> A truth to jump the facts of the dour stockades
>
> Garnished with heads that were never, not once, alive.

To counter the false, the lying, the 'senseless beaks' of the Parrot world (a frequent image), he lists gods and heroes: Thor, Krishna, Isis, Pan, Ariel, Puck and Lear. They 'further the drive of life', as do the friends who are 'strange and dear'. Some of these are dead now: Graham Shepard, Archie Harding, Gordon Herrickx; others belong to his past, like the schoolmaster Powys (though he still visits him), or women he has loved (though some are still friends). Many he still saw frequently: Professor Dodds and Ernest Stahl in Oxford; George MacCann in Ireland; Jack Dillon, Bertie Rodgers, Laurence Gilliam and Dylan Thomas in London. Still within earshot of Regent's Park, as when he wrote the *Journal*, he considers man's place in the world, and how little is permanent. So, *Autumn Sequel* begins, with a parade of pun and paradox.

Certain values are represented by 'Gavin' and 'Gwilym': the anarchic and artistic rebel, on the run from the prosaic world (compare the March Hare), relishing life. Later in the poem, 'Devlin' joins their ranks. This attitude recurs in MacNeice's writing—in poems, features, even reviews. In April 1952 he reviewed *Chiaroscuro: Fragments of Autobiography*, by Augustus John who, in MacNeice's phrase, was 'in the best sense, a mixer—hobnobbing with anyone he likes, be it a gipsy or a countess, and evading the people who bore him, but always remaining himself, not mixing so much as to merge'. John's 'gifted successors from his own and other Celtic regions' would continue the fight 'against soulless and fleshless uniformity'. The poet himself will continue to create. Myths and plays, nursery rhymes and folklore, have their important figures: hag, goddess, Knave and Fool, the soldier with the nosebag, Odysseus, the mermaid, the Man in the Moon, and 'old Nobodaddy himself, high god of paradox'.

The poet's everyday life is reflected: the journey to Beaconsfield to see the Everest film, the return to St John's Wood, the routine of the BBC. Images of quest and Eden are drawn from the mountain with its 'abominable Snow Queen', and from Regent's Park. Later these threads will be woven with that of the Three Kings following their star, and used, for example, in the celebration of Dylan Thomas's poetry and death. There are lines about radio work:

> To found
> A castle on the air requires a mint
> Of golden intonations and a mound
>
> Of typescript in the trays. What was in print
> Must take on breath and what was thought be said.
> In the end there was the Word, at first a glint,
>
> Then an illumination overhead
> Where the high towers are lit. Such was our aim
> But aims too often languish and instead
>
> We hack and hack. What ought to soar and flame
> Shies at its take-off, all our kites collapse. . . .

If we pause to examine this we may detect a lack of enthusiasm, an aspect of the sterility which seems to have come on him during the 1950s. In 1952, in the review of Augustus John's book, he had said: 'We are probably in for a puritan and

punctual age where everyone, artists included, must settle down
to work at once, but in art, let us remember, that may mean not
settling down at all. . . . sitting about and self-indulgence may
be necessary for an artist.' In Canto IV the enemy of the word is
identified: 'carapaced Administrators crouch on constant guard
To save it for good business and good taste.'

He leaves for 'a nine days' wondering' during September,
and his birthday slips by amidst refreshing scenery. For the
purpose of the poem, this is in Wales, but the MacNeices'
country 'retreat' during the 1950s was on the Isle of Wight.
J. B. Priestley and his wife, Jacquetta Hawkes, had a house
there, Brook Hill, and a cottage. The cottage they gave to
Hedli—'not to appear too generous', writes Mrs Priestley, 'it
had been condemned, but it did not take very much effort on
the MacNeices' part to get it passed as habitable.' Here they
could enjoy family holidays, relaxed times when they all had
the freedom of the sea and the sun. There was a small 'circle' in
this west part of the island: the Priestleys offered hospitality,
giving parties, especially at the New Year; Gerald Abraham and
his family had a holiday home, and he would help to arrange
concerts at Brook Hill (he was still Professor of Music at
Liverpool). Further north, A. J. P. Taylor and his family had
an old mill, and they would visit and be visited by the
MacNeices, fellow-fugitives from the city. A touch of the
metropolis was brought by MacNeice claiming to be building a
'cocktail terrace', as he laid a few bricks in the mud in front of
the cottage from time to time. He always enjoyed getting away
to the country—the poem 'Country week-end' reveals all that
it meant to him.

The poet returns to London in late September, to the 'murk
and mangle of modernity'. One brilliant day he goes to the
Tate, admiring Renoir, remembering Devlin's comment on a
Rembrandt self-portrait—all the beer and schnapps that had
gone to make that face—as well as the 'Folk' with whom Jack
was at home. After a visit to the ballet he returns home by the
underground, and the escalator and tunnels furnish images of
the age of the automaton, until at last he is 'At home, in the
upper air'. Home is the end of the quest; it is Arcadia—the toad

with the jewel in his head reminds us not only of fairy tales but of Arden; but the idyll may not last. Daily news of Suez, of the Labour Conference at Margate, of trouble in Nigeria and Korea, reminds him of India; and mention of the Inniskillings reminds him of George MacCann and a friend of his, Major Crocker, nicknamed Hobo. (A short story by MacCann, 'The Jolly Dutchman', tells of a drunken night out with 'Finn' the poet and 'The Major'—MacNeice and Hobo.) There are visits to Oxford, recalling undergraduate days, and present meetings with friends. A nightmarish sequence in Canto XIV takes the dreamer up a spiral staircase and through tunnels where slaves in masks and helmets work away at the wall; they break through at last, dazzled by a 'dangerous unknown light'. This is reminiscent of 'The Queen of Air and Darkness'. (The imagery is similar to that of George MacDonald's *Lilith*, but it seems that MacNeice had not at this time discovered that writer, whose symbols sometimes matched his own.) The surreal journey is followed by a more prosaic one to Norfolk, at Hallowe'en, to collect programme material. Another journey is to Wales, to the funeral of Dylan Thomas.

One journey planned from the time he sent his synopsis to Faber, was to the West Country. He went with William Alwyn, who has recorded the occasion in his own journal, 'Ariel to Miranda'. They had been to a poetry recital at Cyril Wood's Everyman Club in Bath. 'The following morning Louis and I were in holiday mood and meandered through the West Country in my car with London our vague and ultimate goal, first calling on an impressive literary Powys. . . . then on to King Arthur's tomb at Glastonbury (with a halt at the George Inn to brood on beer and the *Morte d'Arthur*).' William Alwyn also remembers a visit to Marlborough, and MacNeice's reticence about his childhood. 'Not even when Louis and I were wandering through the deserted classrooms and corridors of Marlborough School did he talk about his experiences there. . . . What he and I eternally discussed was our contemporary world, our plans for the present and the future, and our attitudes and our philosophy of life as it was being lived.' There is a particularly striking recollection of childhood in MacNeice's poem however: the terrible dream in which he climbs a hill with his father, and sees a sight from which he wants to protect him—a strange crucifixion in a fairground.

The poem moves towards Christmas. Despite his disappointment with the drab materialistic world in which he lives, he still looks forward, to meaning and surprise. One day his son appears, before going to America (where he decided to stay with his mother); his ten-year-old daughter comes home for the holiday; a 'festive aura' descends on his colleagues and friends. He manages to get to a rugby match. A visit to the British Museum reminds him of a childhood visit there. With Frazerian synthesis he wonders if the Magi came from Egypt, Babylon and India, only to discover that their Book of the Dead, Epic of Gilgamesh, and Shivan theogony needed to be revised. And how can Bethlehem be linked to Birmingham and industrial England? He hurries home to hang baubles on the tree and to parcel up presents. His love of home focuses on Christmas. The last journey in the poem is to take part in a Christmas Day link-up programme; not a far journey, and he returns home on a nearly empty train which he peoples with memories. Like *Autumn Journal*, the poem ends with blessings, despite the dark wood to be traversed in personal life, and the sombreness of the world.

Home at this time was 2 Clarence Terrace, formerly the house of Elizabeth Bowen. It is the '2 Windsor Terrace' of *Death of the Heart*: 'lanced through by dazzling spokes of the sun, which moved unseen, hotly, over the waxed floors. Vacantly overlooking the bright lake, chestnuts in leaf, the house offered the ideal mould for living into which life so seldom pours itself.' On their return from Greece in 1951, the MacNeices had been looking for a new home; by the beginning of 1952 they were negotiating for the lease of the Clarence Terrace house. Eliot had a hand in this: on 29 January he wrote to tell MacNeice that he had replied to the Crown Estate's enquiry, 'and I hope indeed that they will let you have Elizabeth's house, as it is very charming, looks comfortable, and is very convenient to a taxi-rank.' The MacNeices had moved in by October, after a stay at Canonbury Park.

1954 began with a new production of 'The Heartless Giant', on 3 January; this has remained a favourite play of MacNeice's daughter. Then he started work on the adaptation of Goronwy Rees's *Where No Wounds Were*. This tells of the capture and interrogation of a German pilot, Adam Lipansky. The Interrogating Officer is strangely interested in Adam's past, and the German questions himself about it in interior soliloquy. The probing of memory and motive raises issues of identity, individuality crushed by the Party, the problem of loyalty and betrayal. In the end, we find that the Officer's special interest in Lipansky was so that he could adopt his identity and infiltrate the enemy. So Adam feels betrayed and used by the people among whom he had hoped to find refuge from his past, for we find out also that he deliberately grounded his plane. An attempt to escape from the camp, into Wales, fails and he returns, having grown dependent on the Officer who questions him. The play is interesting to listen to, intriguing and well constructed; although the narrative is quite straightforward, there are underlying suggestions of further significance which add to its effect.

'Where No Wounds Were' was broadcast on 16 March; on 27 April, a second play on prison was produced—'Prisoner's Progress', a parable on the theme. This was the play which won the Radiotelevisione Italiana Prize (of £550) in September, while 'Under Milk Wood' won the Italia Prize itself. Everything is universalised: the opposing forces are labelled 'Browns' and 'Greys'; the scene is a Greys' prison camp, not specifically localised, although 'closely based upon real camps in World War II as described to me by Mr René Cutforth'. There are certain echoes of Kafka, as when the strange foreign voices come over the loudspeaker, or when the Commanding Officer points to the surrounding mountains and tells the prisoners that they are on an island of civilisation. Escape is always in the minds of those confined there—René Cutforth also helped analyse the varying emotional reactions to such camps. One of the prisoners is Walters; as he surveys his life he realises that there has always been the same mountain between him and the sun. He talks to the prison chaplain and to a rather mysterious

airman named Regan about the 'insane muddle' of life, the
madness of the world; about war, power, personal identity.
There are biblical resonances in this play: when the chaplain
offers to read to Walters, he chooses the Book of Job. 'Let the
day perish in which I was born.... let darkness and the
shadow of death stain it. ... Why died I not from the womb?'
The passage from which these phrases are taken expresses a
yearning for peace and repose, and includes the image of
prisoners resting together, safe from the oppressor.

As for use of music in this play, MacNeice tried a new device:
he has an accordionist play and sing nursery songs—'I had a
little nut tree', 'Lavender's blue', and 'What have you got for
dinner, Mrs Bond?' (The refrain of the last is 'Dilly, dilly, come
and be killed', used by Dylan Thomas in 'Over Sir John's Hill',
the poem referred to in *Autumn Sequel*.)

Elements of adventure and romance find expression in the
escape story, when Walters and one of the women prisoners,
Alison, find themselves together and eventually alone on the
mountain. There is the promise of another escape: can they,
together, find happiness, release from personal isolation and
loneliness? We do not know Walters's first name until Alison
persuades him to reveal it. It is Thomas: this may remind us of
Doubting Thomas, but there is also True Thomas, with whom
the Queen of Elfland fell in love. The ballad is quoted by
Alison: the bonny road to Elfland, 'where thou and I this night
maun go'. Like other fairy lands, this one means not only love
and enchantment, but death for mortals. As Alison and Thomas
climb the mountain they are pursued by guards and dogs. (It
was a challenging piece of acting, for Anthony Jacobs and
Cécile Chevreau, to sound as though they were climbing hard.)
Their hope is a slender one, not just because of the pursuit;
Walters quotes from Marvell's 'Definition of Love':

> Therefore the love which us doth bind
> But Fate so enviously debars,
> Is the conjunction of the Mind,
> And opposition of the Stars.

The pessimism is warranted: they have nearly reached the

summit when the dogs are heard getting louder; there is machine-gun fire, then silence. Into this silence steals the song 'Lavender's blue', sung by the accordionist who had himself been killed earlier in the play. It is a most successful radio piece, although MacNeice remarked to Cécile Chevreau that people would probably find it too '*Boy's Own*-ish'. It is more than a mere adventure story, though: the poet's use of words, and the intelligent observer's sense of what is significant, make it a work of depth. The idea had been some years in developing, intensified by the post-war period and the time in Greece. It is in the line of 'double-level writing' that always interested MacNeice —even the nursery rhymes and popular songs are chosen for their double meanings.

During the summer of 1954, from 28 June until 1 August, there were the readings of *Autumn Sequel*, in six parts. MacNeice himself produced work by other writers: 'The Frightened Housekeeper' by Anthony Jacobs, on 6 August, on the Light Programme; and 'The Man Who Stole Children', Dorothy Baker's adaptation of the novel by Jules Supervielle (in Alan Pryce-Jones's translation) in the following February on the Third Programme. MacNeice's own feature on Marlborough, 'Return to a School', was broadcast on 15 October 1954, while he was again in America on a three-month tour of lectures and other engagements.

In March 1955, on the 18th and 19th, MacNeice's version of Virginia Woolf's *The Waves* was transmitted. In his introduction to the 1947 edition of *The Dark Tower* . . . he had said that he felt the work would be feasible on the air: 'The characters, thinking in the first person, say things they never could have formulated, being even as small children endowed with the brilliant introspection and sad philosophy of their creator.' In May 1952 he had put forward the idea, which was accepted at a Features meeting on the 22nd. A programme note in *Radio Times* describes the work as 'not so much a novel as a long prose poem, elegiac and yet defiant'. MacNeice, always a sensitive producer, created a most impressive piece—its rebroadcast in October 1977 has shown that it retains its quality. In July 1955 came a less successful feature, one that would date: 'The

Fullness of the Nile' was based on a three-thousand-mile journey up-river, as far as the Ugandan border, collecting impressions. During 1955, suggestions were invited from producers for possible rebroadcasts as part of the tenth anniversary celebration of the Third Programme. One play that MacNeice said he would like to rewrite and shorten was 'The Queen of Air and Darkness'. He also said that he would like to 'have another go' at 'The Dark Tower': he was not completely satisfied with either of the productions he had done, though he could not envisage anyone other than Cyril Cusack for the part of Roland.

Poet, playwright, producer of Third Programme parable—that was only one side of MacNeice. Some of the 'routine' features brought him in touch with all kinds of people—like Devlin's 'Folk'—whose company he relished. 'The Twelve Days of Christmas' in January 1953, for instance, included a short sequence from the Hastings Winkle Club Children's Party, at the Cutter in the Old Town. Louis, Laurence and the actor John Sharp were photographed with fishermen and other members of the Club. It was with John Sharp that MacNeice made his first visit to Yorkshire, in September 1955. They were collecting material for a feature which was not, alas, to be made. Had it been, it would have been in the best tradition of actuality programmes, with the humour and vigour of the North Country—a latter-day 'Harry Hopeful' (but MacNeice's metaphor for himself and John was of Dante and Virgil, circling around the county). The idea first appears in the Archives in 1954 as a suggestion, apparently from MacNeice, supported by Andrew Stewart, recently promoted from Head of North Region to Controller of Home Service. Writing to his successor, Stewart comments: 'the interest here, as you will agree, is not so much in Yorkshire but in what MacNeice's imagination makes of the theme.' North Region promised all co-operation.

For MacNeice himself the interest was precisely Yorkshire. John Sharp recalls that Louis wanted to take it by surprise, enter by the back door, so he met him at Darlington where Louis arrived from the Edinburgh Festival. It was the afternoon of Saturday, 10 September, just two days before MacNeice's birthday. They went straight to a two-star hotel at Greta Bridge, on the road to Bowes. Both places have literary associations. 'O, Brignal banks are wild and fair, And Greta woods are green.' And Bowes, Scott's 'Rokeby', is the site of Dickens's Dotheboys Hall. On arrival John and Louis made a bee-line for the lounge bar which was at that hour closed for the serving of drinks. No matter, the bar had murals of Dickensian characters. MacNeice suggested, 'If we keep very still with our backs to the door they might think that Boz is talking to Phiz and give us some drinks.' The desire was not immediately satisfied, because it was not the custom to serve even residents with Irish whiskey and Guinness for afternoon tea. After some persuading, however, an ancient porter and a taciturn manager invited them to help themselves, leaving the empties to be counted when the bar opened. 'This first impression of a Yorkshire two-star hotel greatly pleased Louis. I never disillusioned him on this point and happily it re-occurred at several pubs and hotels where we stayed, but it was only because the proprietor or staff wished to go to bed or had other more pressing work.'

Another incident which impressed and moved MacNeice was their meeting at that hotel with the distinguished local squire, who stated that his best friend had been his gamekeeper: 'The moor itself is his true memorial. I spent some of my happiest times in his company.' Louis often mentioned this to John in the years that followed, regretting that he had not recorded the courteous countryman. Later that evening, in the highest pub in Yorkshire, the remote Tan Hill Inn, one of the twist-smoking shepherds tapped MacNeice with his stick, saying: 'Nah then, tha allus wants ter put a Teeswatter tup on a Wensleydale yow ter gie thee a sturdy cross that's thrang i't' fleece. . . .' Some time afterwards Louis had nodded off in the fumes and clatter and woke during an explanation of sheep-counting: yahn, tayhn, tether, mether, mimph, hither, lither, anver, danver. . . . He wondered why they were all speaking Danish. They also found somewhere to stay other than the two-star hotel: this was the Red Lion at Langthwaite, a pub with a congenial landlady —Louis always preferred pubs. They transferred next morning;

a timely move for Louis had burnt some holes in the sheets and the taciturn manager found his tongue.

John showed Louis a great deal of his native county: West Riding towns, East Riding coast, the abbeys, the marvellous caverns at Stump Cross, and the Dripping Well at Knaresborough. This fascinated MacNeice—here was a favourite image realised before his eyes. As he gazed at the bizarre collection of objects, including dead cats and the like, all turned to stone, he faced his companion and suggested they both knew some candidates for the well. In Yorkshire, though, he found plenty of people who were really alive, with character and individuality. He got on famously with Harry Ramsden, owner of the 'biggest chip oil i't' world' (the translation 'fish and chip shop' does no justice to this splendid complex of eating-rooms), whose idea of giving them a drink was to set down a bottle of whisky for Louis, and one of gin for John. Then there was Kit Calvert, a renowned Methodist lay-preacher who revived the cheese-making in Wensleydale, and translated the Bible into the local dialect. Abraham, for example, 'leeted on a tup in a briar'. They were with Kit for a whole morning. There were farmers, shepherds, fishermen, on this bucolic and beery odyssey, with all of whom Louis felt at ease. From Harry Ramsden's they went to Haworth, to the Black Bull where Branwell Brontë used to drink. They were going to spend the night there, and arrived just after the pub shut, so the licensee and his wife drank with them. By midnight John was determined to find the grave of the Brontës' Tabitha Aykroyd, 'Tabby'. 'There we were stumbling about the graveyard striking matches when a voice from nowhere (it was the publican) tried to call *sotto voce*, "You'll catch your death of cold. Come in and have another." '

The last day of their trip would have made a feature on its own—Pateley Bridge Show on Monday, the 19th. 'Show jumping, cats, dogs, cavies, sheep dog trials, kids' obstacle races on horseback, Yorkshire County Cricket Club (i.e. the Yorkshire cricket team) playing Pateley Bridge, and to cap it all Hammond's Sauce Works Prize Brass Band. We were there from ten in the morning to seven at night drinking John Smith's Magnet Draught all day at the rate of about three pints to the hour. We then went back to the Talbot and supped while midnight, to put it in the vernacular. MacNeice was accepted and respected by farmers, landlords, cricketers, cattle drovers, fat and shining women's institute members, instrumentalists, the more staid members of the Upper Nidderdale Agricultural Society, in fact half the county! They loved him.' During those nine days John Sharp got to know Louis better—the 'real' Louis. Trying to sum him up he writes: 'He was a man of simple tastes and basically a countryman and of the people, but he possessed that quality which can only be described with the French word "delicatesse".' Later, Louis wrote to thank John for his 'magnificent mentorship'; he had enjoyed the Yorkshire experience immensely, and if the idea did not stay fresh for him 'perhaps one could slip up there again!' At the time they were re-called to London because MacNeice had to make a journey to the East, to get material for the Christmas Day programme. Several times he tried to revive the plan of a Yorkshire feature, but something always intervened (though he was to return for his last fateful programme). His visit to India, Pakistan and Ceylon lasted from 20 October to 12 November 1955. (Three years earlier, in October 1952, he had been invited by the British Council to make a tour of these same three countries, but he had been unable to go.)

The Christmas Day feature was called 'The Star We Follow' —a traditional theme but this time with a modern aspect. This was during the early days of Jodrell Bank, and a crucial time: what had started as a trailer in the mud was now a station where the largest telescope of its kind in the world was nearing completion. Professor Lovell and his team were to take part in the programme; the publicity might be important for politics and finance. Apart from this, the theme itself is exciting: radio telescopes reaching beyond the Milky Way, sounds from outer space. MacNeice and Ritchie Calder were to write the script, and Gilliam and John Bridges were to co-produce.

Early in November, Bernard Lovell wrote to give Gilliam details of radio signals on Christmas Day: 'the position could scarcely be better', he said, and suggested dates for moon echo recording. Gilliam, Bridges and MacNeice went up to Cheshire on the evening of Tuesday, 29 November, to meet Lovell who had invited them to his home for the evening. (He and his wife still vividly recall the occasion and MacNeice.) The trio were to stay at the appropriately-named Good Companions Hotel.

The script shows the imaginative appeal of the subject: first the audience were taken 'to the upper reaches of the atmosphere, then on to the solar system and right out into the depths of space'. The waves from shooting stars sixty miles up were transmitted; then, from the moon hut, came a different sound; finally sounds came from 'somewhere among the stars of the Milky Way . . . the results of the events which occurred perhaps ten thousand years ago and these waves have been travelling through space ever since'. Later, MacNeice was to write a poem called 'Star-gazer': part of its inspiration may have been this closing feature of 1955.

Chapter Seven

'*The Middle Stretch*': *1955–1960*

and a still small voice in the silence
In spite of ill winds and ill atoms blossomed in pure affirmation
Of what lay behind and before it

'Visitations'

By 1955 the changes we have mentioned briefly were making themselves felt; it is necessary to go back a few years to trace their growth. Television, which was to prove an irresistible rival to radio, had been revived in June 1946, after its war-time shut-down. At the time of its resurrection, however, the BBC was more interested in developments in sound, especially in the newly instituted Third Programme, and in the question of regional broadcasting. During the first few years of its renewed life television had limited resources and facilities, and was subject to post-war restrictions. There was as yet only a small audience: in 1949 viewers numbered only about one per cent of the total audience for broadcasting. In that year the acquisition of the former Rank studios at Lime Grove, and the opening of the new high-power transmitter at Sutton Coldfield, marked the beginning of a more vigorous stage of growth. Between then and December 1952, transmitters were built at Holme Moss, Kirk o' Shotts and Wenvoe, extending the service over most of the country, and adding a potential audience of some twenty million. The number of combined sound and vision licences increased from under 50,000 in 1948 to just over two million in 1953. In that year the televising of the coronation gave a great boost to the medium.

How did BBC radio men react to television? Asa Briggs
records the replies of members of the staff, other than those in
television, to the Senior Controller's (B. E. Nicolls) request for
comments after one year of the new service. 'Perhaps the most
percipient of all the replies . . . came from Laurence Gilliam,
Director of Features, one of the most sensitive and imaginative
people inside the BBC.' Gilliam was impressed most by the
actualities (such as sports) and the conventional plays, but had
seen nothing to compete with 'imaginative' radio drama. One
striking observation was on the lack of news: 'A bulletin, with a
gradually increasing proportion of picture reports from our own
local units, located in key news centres, would surely build up
a regular television audience faster than any other single
development.' This is what we might have expected from a man
of imagination and awareness like Gilliam, but the general
attitude to the televising of news remained conservative and
restrictive for almost a decade after the war.

In 1953, when television was beginning to make its great
impact, meetings were held in Features Department to discuss
how the challenge could be met. Laurence Gilliam wrote to the
Controller of Entertainment (Sound) pointing out the need for
experiment in 'any attempt to make sound broadcasting stand
up to increasing competition from Television'. He suggested
that a team of writers, producers and musicians, British and
foreign, and from all departments, should be set up, and that
new forms of topical broadcasting should be considered. He
wanted such a unit to be tied as closely as possible to output,
and to be as free as possible from controllers. There should be
an 'unrestricted exploration of the combined use of words and
music'. In the autumn issue of the *BBC Quarterly* in 1953
MacNeice made 'A Plea for Sound'. He maintained that, while
television could attempt things that sound could not do, 'sound
can do many fine things which will never be possible on television. We should all therefore hope both that television may
develop to the utmost and that sound broadcasting may survive.'
He argued that poetry would be less effective on television, and
that creative writing for sound 'has more in common with
poetry than with prose'.

As examples of works especially suited to sound, he cites 'any drama which is primarily internal . . . any work such as David Jones' *In Parenthesis* whose significance mainly lies in the colour and rhythm and suggestive aura of the words'. He values the 'goodness of words-as-spoken-and-heard', which radio had restored, and of books, which are still needed despite radio and films. 'Let us pray that all the media survive.' Irony was at work, however, in that there was a new threat to Features Department within the BBC. In 1953 Donald McWhinnie became Assistant Head of Drama; he and Barbara Bray, the Drama Script Editor, encouraged writers like Samuel Beckett and Giles Cooper to write for radio. (Val Gielgud has written that in the early 1950s he felt himself between two worlds, Martyn C. Webster and McWhinnie.) The new spirit that came into the parent department proved competitive to Features. John Morris, Controller of Third Programme, went to Paris to try to persuade Beckett to write for the BBC; Beckett would not accept a commission, but said that if he ever wrote a radio play he would send it along for consideration. Not long afterwards, the script of 'All That Fall' arrived on Morris's desk. The *BBC Hand Book* accorded it the kind of praise once given to Features work. It 'demonstrated powerfully the artistic and emotional potentialities of sound radio'. In 1959 Beckett's 'Embers' won the Radiotelevisione Italiana Prize, the same that MacNeice had won five years before.

As we can see from the article quoted, MacNeice was interested in all media of communication. But he also feared the tendencies of the 1950s—a time which he described as one of 'alarm and redundancy' at Broadcasting House. A poem which he wrote at this time gains in force when read in the context of these changes; it is a message 'To posterity'.

> When books have all seized up like the books in graveyards
> And reading and even speaking have been replaced
> By other, less difficult, media, we wonder if you
> Will find in flowers and fruit the same colour and taste
> They held for us for whom they were framed in words,
> And will your grass be green, your sky be blue,
> Or will your birds be always wingless birds?

At this time, though, 'the lyric impulse did return', and he was writing short poems for the first such collection since 1948. It appeared in 1957, as *Visitations*. This was the Poetry Book Society's summer choice, and MacNeice wrote a piece for the Bulletin. 'I like to think that my latest short poems are on the whole more concentrated and better organised than my earlier ones, relying more on syntax and bony features than on bloom or frill or floating image.'

Some of the poems were about places visited during his BBC journeys. 'The rest house' and 'Beni Hasan' relate to the Nile journey, of which he wrote in *Radio Times*: 'I was exhilarated, saddened, intrigued, confused, and, occasionally, bored.' In 'Beni Hasan' he writes: 'It came to me on the Nile my passport lied Calling me dark who am grey.' During his visit to India and Pakistan he remembered 1947, when 'rivers of men's blood' had flowed; now in 'Return to Lahore' the city is 'At peace and dull'. Among the earliest poems of the new collection are the 'Donegal triptychs' (perhaps dating to 1954) where he voices the fear of middle age and failing inspiration. More explicit than Prufrock's footman:

> the cold voice chops and sniggers,
> Prosing on, maintains the thread
> Is broken and the phoenix fled,
> Youth and poetry departed.

After his return from Athens MacNeice had come to know Dan Davin and his wife better, and Davin's memoir of the poet, in *Closing Times*, gives us a glimpse of him at this time. He was supposed to be editing, with Bertie Rodgers, a book called 'The Character of Ireland'. 'It changed again and again, as the years passed, this plan of ours. Defaulters came and went, and from the margins new ideas infiltrated into the room of the old. . . . the two poets were merciless in their meddling and muddling towards perfection.' Davin failed to pin down his 'editors' who, amid talk and drink, slipped his grasp. There were memorable meetings, at Oddenino's—'still a place then, but now only a diminishing echo'—or Mooney's, or at the Randolph in Oxford, where MacNeice told Davin about his first wife. He also called on the Davins at their home. So the friendship progressed, though the book did not.

Two other writers who knew and on occasion worked with MacNeice were Angus Wilson and Laurie Lee; he produced a script by each of them during 1956. Angus Wilson's 'Left in the Middle' was about left-wing sympathisers of the 1930s. Wilson had complete faith in MacNeice's judgement as a producer, especially for that particular feature—'he understood the subject so completely'. Wilson also had great respect for MacNeice's 'extraordinary sense of what radio could convey that the written word could not (nor the seen play)'. Laurie Lee sent a note with his script, 'Black Saturday, Red Sunday', about Easter in Andalusia, saying: 'Do not hesitate to jettison this script if you feel like it or feel you don't like it.' As for MacNeice himself, Laurie Lee has written: 'Louis I remember as a major presence for which I was grateful in my life and I had some of my best times with him.'

MacNeice's own work for radio in 1956 began with the play about Saul. He had completed the script before leaving for the East in October 1955, a year which he described in an official work sheet as 'somewhat mutilated', half of it being taken up with the Nile journey, and the journey east. 'Also Among the Prophets' is directly based on the Bible story, but themes which interested MacNeice were stressed, such as the corruption of power, 'thrust upon this innocent young man by a prophet who himself was bitterly opposed to kingship. . . . Abandoned by Samuel, Saul becomes gradually madder and unhappier, and his one consolation is in David—till jealousy makes him David's enemy.' Themes of power and corruption are dominant in the serious radio plays by MacNeice, and in his historical feature on Caesar; the Biblical setting gives a greater sombreness—music was to contribute to the solemnity. Although MacNeice first had Britten in mind, the composer was Matyas Seiber, who had written the score for 'Faust'.

The people demand a king, although Samuel warns them of the danger. An Agitator has stirred up the people, telling them that Egypt is great because she has kings, while there are evil days in Israel. Samuel appeals to them: 'Will you sell that star

in your souls for a bauble that shines in the torchlight?' Unable
to convince them, he chooses and anoints Saul; the oil that
seeps into him is used as an image of corrupting power, creeping
into his heart and mind. The chorus of Israel praise Saul, as
they later praise David. Saul becomes more tormented, and the
only thing that can soothe him is David's harp. But he turns
against David, and his own son and daughter leave him when
David leaves. When David parts from Saul's daughter, soon
after their marriage, he remembers her vividly: 'Though I still
smell the perfume of cinnamon and hear her anklets tinkling'—
his words recall those of MacNeice about Mary Ezra. Saul kills
himself after his son Jonathan is killed in battle, and the programme ends with David's lament for them, leading into the
final chorus, 'How are the mighty fallen.' When the play was
broadcast, live, MacNeice decided that the chorus at the end
had to be cut (he had asked Seiber for a shorter version). The
composer had been shocked and upset on hearing the broadcast
to find his music cut, and although MacNeice had written
immediately to explain the necessity of his action, Seiber was
unhappy. It seems to be a rare case of friction, and even this
was conducted in a way that did not impair their friendship.

Making a comparison with 'Faust', Matyas Seiber held that
the music for 'Saul' also needed a 'spaciousness' at the end; but
MacNeice pointed out that 'Saul' was a single piece of sustained
drama and could not afford the lengthy final chorus, for
dramatic reasons. Seiber had written some hard things about
producers, stopwatches in hands, capable of destroying the
effect of the music—he even used the words 'vandalism',
'mutilation' and 'murder'. MacNeice's riposte had a hidden
edge: 'Since you told me that it was the only piece, out of
eighteen, or more, numbers, that you are proud of, I am
naturally prepared to believe that it is a very fine piece of
choral music.' He defended himself against the accusation of
being 'an eccentric barbarian' by seeking opinions from other
people and he quoted Archie Harding on the place of incidental
music. The composers, Harding had said, 'are not there to
write beautiful music, they are there to help us when we need
them'. It emerges from the correspondence in the Archives that

the composer had prepared his score before the actual script
was sent to him; this may explain his emotion about the music
he had written.

The cast included actors who worked frequently with
MacNeice, some of them personal friends after the years of
radio together. Howard Marion-Crawford played Saul, John
Sharp Samuel, and Allan McClelland Jonathan; David was
played by Peter Wyngarde, and the Agitator by John Gabriel.
The script shows some corrections, probably made at rehearsal;
team work could lead to amendments and improvements. The
instructions for the microphones—'open' and 'closed'—illustrate how radio could cope with dialogue, or addresses to the
crowd, or the inner thoughts of an isolated character. This
versatility, and the use of music and effects, make radio very
flexible. At one point Saul, in soliloquy, refers to the cave of his
mind, which no one can enter; this echoes lines in the last
section of the poem 'Visitations':

> Yet after all that or before it
> As he sat in the cave of his mind (and the cave was the world)
> Among old worked flints between insight and hindsight,
> Suddenly Something, or Someone, darkened the entrance
> But shed a new light on the cave and a still small voice in the
> silence
> In spite of ill winds and ill atoms blossomed in pure affirmation
> Of what lay behind and before it.

As MacNeice said in another poem in the collection, 'The
Unknown is There', although all religions deceive and we
cannot prove there is a God.

There is an odd postscript to the 'Saul' broadcast. An
occultist, self-styled 'of the tribe of Judah', wrote from Shepton
Mallet, to praise the programme. He had found it so inspiring
and enlightening that it was as though Saul had been re-
incarnated in the poet as he wrote. He pointed out that they
had now entered the sign of Aquarius: dare they neglect the
fact that seven planets were to meet in this sign in 1963? If
destiny would have it so, he would be happy to meet MacNeice
in London. There is no record of MacNeice's reaction. (Earlier
that year another odd occurrence had inspired a poem, 'Death

of an old lady'—his stepmother, who had died in April. He and his sister had heard 'grey voices Calling three times through the dank fields' the night before her death. He told several people about this—the banshee?—but expected a sceptical reply.)

There were two features for the Home Service, 'Bow Bells' in June, and 'Spires and Gantries', about Rouen, in July. He made a brief visit to France for the Rouen feature. By August 1956 he had sent Faber the set of poems for publication: *Visitations*. There are some fine poems in this volume, including tightly organised ballads with an almost allegorical use of imagery. Sometimes there is disappointment, at other times hope; and sometimes, as in 'Jigsaws', a surreal vision of the world:

> When will the Poltergeist ascend
> Out of the sewer with chopper and squib
> To burn the mink and the baby's bib
> And cut the tattling wire to town
> And smash the plastics, clowning and clouting
> And stop all the boxes shouting and pouting
> And wreck the house from the aerial down
> And give these ingrown souls an outing?

His protests against the modern world found expression in a very attractive radio feature that autumn: 'Carpe Diem', broadcast on 8 October, is based partly on the poetry of Horace. The main character, Quintus, a modern man named after the Latin poet, is being tended in what may be his last illness by Elaine, the last of all his loves. The phrase from Horace 'age iam meorum finis amorum' was to be the epigraph to the next book of poems (*Solstices*, 1961). The feature is described as 'partly the portrait of a modern Horatian and partly an anthology—of translations, paraphrases, and original, but Horatian, English poetry'. It therefore combines lyric poetry and dramatic feature. There is much of the author in the piece, as we might expect: the recall of the past, the protests against the present, the hope of happiness in love. As in 'He Had a Date', snatches of popular songs are used to suggest a period, but this time they are related directly to Quintus's memories. Through his character, MacNeice expresses his kinship with Horace: he 'didn't live in Cloudcuckooland—nor in the

Waste Land. He enjoyed himself on earth—though he saw its drawbacks. *And* he had a sense of human decency. He was civilised. . . .' Horace became part of the Establishment, while Quintus admits that he is an escapist, from a world whose gods are money and power. As well as the poetry of Horace, there is that of Housman—'a romantic melancholic. But also a Latin scholar'—and of Marvell and Sir Henry Wotton. The Latin poems were read by Valentine Dyall, and their translations by Duncan McIntyre, both admirable verse readers.

At the end of 1956 MacNeice wrote and produced a feature about poets, 'From Bard to Busker', broadcast on 30 December. This was built around two street singers, introduced to MacNeice years before by Stephen Murray. Murray and his wife had got to know the Cutlers after they had heard them singing outside their flat. Wyn Cutler was the inspiration for an earlier poem by MacNeice, 'Street scene', in which the 'swan-legged cripple' transports the passers-by 'down a river That has no source nor sea but is each man's private dream'. In the radio feature, the long ancestry and wide range of traditional poetry is shown: the buskers of Camden Town Market tell how they always give priority to a blind busker, and we are led to Homer and Blind Raftery. Like the singer in 'Street scene' all the traditional bards, trouvères, minnesingers could make time stop. From a fourteenth-century tavern we cut to a Kilburn pub (the Admiral Nelson), where Wyn Cutler is singing. MacNeice valued all kinds of people, as this feature reminds us.

How are we to assess MacNeice's place in the BBC at this time? 1957 saw him finally accept 'establishment'—he had refused this when offered it in 1943—but the period was a low one in his work for radio. Since his return in 1951, his plays and radio features had been few; during 1957 he had no programmes put out on the Third, the main outlet for his work since its inception. As for the BBC, in 1957 air time for the Third Programme was reduced. The Controller of the service at this time was John Morris, who had succeeded Harman Grisewood in 1952. (Grisewood became Director of the Spoken Word, until the title was abolished in 1955, when he became Chief Assistant to the Director-General.) In 1952 Haley had resigned as

Director-General and was succeeded by Ian Jacob, like John Morris a Bush House man. The News Division grew in importance in the 1950s; there seems also to have been less rapport between the administrators and Features—some of the work was criticised as old-fashioned. This happened in 1958 to a suggestion by MacNeice for a programme on advertising: the Controller of Programme Planning, Rooney Pelletier, considered it 'out of step with a wide body of public opinion'.

Rayner Heppenstall writes of the setting up, at this time, of efficiency studies; an anecdote tells of MacNeice's reply to a time-and-motion expert who questioned him as to what he had been doing during the blank spaces on his work sheet: 'thinking' was the brusque reply. At this period MacNeice was not at his best: there were bouts of depression, too much drinking, and irritation with bureaucracy. The irritation may be imagined from a memo dated 13 May 1957 from the Features Organiser to MacNeice. It regretted that a message had disturbed him; Home Service were anxious to see his script for 'Nuts in May', an imagined biography, in typical MacNeice style—'to see that its theme does not conflict with other statements made during the Asian year'. This was because his hero was to spend some time in India! A couple of months earlier, the Colonial Office had shown concern over what MacNeice considered an innocuous feature on Ghana. Anthony Thwaite joined the Department in October 1957, 'too late for the Golden Age', as he records in his poem 'For Louis MacNeice'.

> Uncertain of your mood, after an hour
> Of a shared office going slowly sour
> With cigarettes and hangovers, the shelf
> Above your desk capsizing with its load
> Of scripts that date back sixteen years or more,
> I try the Twickenham ploy. . . .
> And yet I play this game only to thaw
> That icy stare, because I'm still in awe
> Of your most private self, that self you spill
> Into the poems you keep locked away. . . .

Anthony Thwaite recalls also the kindness that MacNeice could show, and his courtesy to strangers; but we cannot be surprised at any asperity from a rather disillusioned older man (he was fifty that year) who had been working so long for the institution. There were, too, personal difficulties, and these seem to have been the darkest years.

Escape could be managed, into company, or, from time to time, to Ireland; he could also pit his wits against the Corporation. A letter written to George MacCann in January 1957 mentions a forthcoming visit with Bob Pocock: 'please get in a couple of bottles of whiskey on account of Bob and myself—and we will refund same.' They were going to watch a rugby match, and there was the possibility of Bob doing a feature on the 'Skins', George's regiment, the Inniskillings, so, if 'the BBC High-ups agree', this might 'give the opportunity for several joyous conferences at the Corporation's expense'. He was always happy to visit Belfast, to see George, or work on a programme for John Boyd—usually during the rugby season. At the beginning of 1957 he was also engaged in the staging of his play, variously titled until it became *Traitors in Our Way*, at the Group Theatre in Belfast. Harold Goldblatt produced it, George did the decor, and Denys Hawthorne took the main role. There were joyous meetings for this enterprise. The play was later rewritten for television and will be considered in that context. (In July 1957 MacNeice went again to Belfast, to receive a doctorate from Queen's University.)

The first radio feature of 1957 was 'The Birth of Ghana', on 22 February, but that was a side-product of a script for a film. The Director of the Gold Coast Film Unit, Sean Graham, was to make a film celebrating the independence of Ghana, the first of the British colonies in Africa to attain freedom. The occasion was one of great significance, and the mood one of optimism and enthusiasm for development. Graham remembered having been very impressed by a radio feature that MacNeice had done on India, in 1947, and decided on him as the writer who could do justice to the subject. He contacted Laurence Gilliam, who gave permission for MacNeice to spend some three months working on a script; a month of this period was to be spent in the Gold Coast. Graham met MacNeice in London in August 1956, when they had lunch together and discussed the task. By

mid-October MacNeice was in Accra. His 'thank-you' letter to
Graham, written on 19 November, says that he had greatly
enjoyed the lavish hospitality; in truth, though, it was an unhappy collaboration. MacNeice had changed, and aged, more
than one might expect in the past few years; he came to Accra
ill-equipped for the climate, and more preoccupied with his
own problems than with the political situation. The film unit
was small, and extremely busy all the time; MacNeice had no
car and found it difficult to get about, spending much time with
a few superannuated colonial men, drinking. He was difficult
to talk to, and not fully attuned to the needs of the occasion.
His own comments on his script show that he was more
interested in the symbolism than the actuality; trees and hands
in particular seemed to obsess him (he realised that he may have
'overdone the business' but clung to the motifs), and he wanted
the old scheme of Morning to Evening (as in the feature on
India), although he himself remarked that this was a 'well-worn
device'.

The Ghanaians were much more excited about new techno-
logy than sacred forests; at this moment of their history they
were forward-looking, while MacNeice dwelt on their tradi-
tions. He also used the chance to introduce the theme of slavery,
which had long interested him, but he was not sufficiently
aware of the present-day issues. Perhaps the basic problem,
however, is indicated by another comment: 'this commentary
will obviously remain very fluid till there are some pictures to
attach to it.' The relationship of words to visuals was not
appreciated by MacNeice from a film-maker's point of view. It
was not easy to keep in touch, once MacNeice was back in
England, by means of letter (telephoning was not very satisfactory). After a delay over Christmas, and during the visit to
Ireland, MacNeice wrote to Graham on 4 February: 'Dear
Sean, I have been meaning to write to you for some time but the
BBC has had me distracted. As you know I was expecting to
travel to India for them at the end of January and therefore was
trying to mop up a lot of work before leaving when, at the
eleventh hour, they changed their minds and cancelled the
whole operation.' He would be in London until March and

would not be able to come to Accra for the celebrations; but he could look at any rushes they might send, and do some preliminary work with Elisabeth Lutyens. He had had Graham's comments on his draft; he was glad he had liked the treatment, but agreed that it meandered a little towards the end—he was sure Graham's alternatives would tighten it up. It was not a satisfactory script, and Graham had to 'doctor' it quite a bit; nor was he happy with the film when he had made it.

MacNeice now turned his attention to ideas for books: he suggested to London University Press that he might do an educational book of some kind on Ghana—they liked the notion. And he wrote to Eliot, in February 1957: 'Dear Tom, It has occurred to me that, apart from my memories, I have a mass of note-books that with a number of radio scripts dealing with a wide variety of foreign countries might form the basis for a not too usual kind of travel book. . . . the point of this would be to illustrate the principle—which I am sure is not peculiar to me—that in foreign travel one is much of the time searching for the implementation of certain myths. I would, accordingly, wish to call this book "Countries in the Air".' Eliot and his Faber colleagues liked the idea, and a contract was signed, but the book was not written—it joined the limbo of Louis's unrealised ideas.

There is a synopsis, however, and we have the posthumously published autobiography, *The Strings are False* (put into shape by the late Professor Dodds); the radio scripts suggest the subject matter, and sometimes the treatment, of the later parts. The only completed travel book by MacNeice is *I Crossed the Minch*, written almost twenty years before. 'Countries in the Air' would have started with childhood, the travels radiating from Antrim to the west, and the 'Myth of the West'; Paris at nineteen would bring in the myth of 'Bohemia', while that of the north would begin with a holiday in Spitzbergen, with his father, and continue with Iceland and the sagas. Spain, France and America would have their place. From the war on, there would be the radio scripts and the countries he had visited. As a coda, MacNeice suggests 'the discovery of London—which even now seems to me a foreign city'. This would bring

F

retrospective glances to the late 1930s, and return to the present via the intelligentsia and war-time London. This would have been a very interesting testimony to the decades which his contemporaries have written about: the excitement of the war, and the anticlimax of the drab and materialistic post-war period. Stephen Spender has described the 1950s as a blurred decade, with landmarks of Suez, Hungary, McCarthyism, 'Nuclear Disarmers, Cold Warriors, Angry Young Men. . . . It was a decade of expense accounts, and quick fortunes being made by dubious means.' MacNeice was not alone in feeling out of key with his time.

The next radio play was 'Nuts in May', broadcast on 27 May, 'another dramatised biography of an imaginary man of our time'. The description is particularly reminiscent of 'He Had a Date'. He wanted to create an 'ordinary' man, an extrovert, but the character comes out very much to the MacNeice type. He has a public school education, but joins the army instead of going to university, going to the North-West Frontier in the course of duty, and later to Burma (where George MacCann had served). He has involvements with two women, apparently loving both (and as a child he was told stories of a golden-haired lily-white princess shut in a tower)—one of the women is Irish, like the Princess in 'The Heartless Giant'. A device used in 'Prisoner's Progress' is borrowed: the nursery rhyme 'Nuts in May' runs like a refrain through the play, the question 'Who shall we get to bear him away?' becoming more and more ominous; the hero, Tom Bowlby, is the chosen 'victim'.

Although the play derives many of its details from earlier radio works by MacNeice, there are other points which provided the germ of ideas to be reworked in the last of his plays. Tom remembers incidents from the war against the Japanese—this is to provide a central point in the story of Hank, the artist; Tom wants to try something demanding, a physical challenge (this may have its source in the Everest climb), so he goes to the Antarctic—Hank takes up caving. Tom Bowlby has an unfulfilled need—'I think I want to find something'—which reminds us of the scheme for the travel book. The concluding scenes, set against a cold and howling wind, point forward to

'Persons from Porlock': 'all dark—leading to dark passages'; everything goes black; voices come back from his past, including his former batman who wishes he could save him. Another point of interest is that this play provides a gloss for the poem 'Notes for a biography', in *Solstices*. A further link is with a feature which MacNeice produced the following year, on 16 April. H. A. L. Craig agreed to Gilliam's suggestion for an imaginative programme about Antarctic exploration; Craig said he would use facts, and the actual words of explorers: 'the work would be of a poetic and heraldic nature.' The files also show that MacNeice was 'keen to produce'. This may have been a joint venture, Gilliam and MacNeice perhaps both coming up with the idea; MacNeice had been instrumental in getting Craig to write for radio.

In June 1957 MacNeice put forward a suggestion for a feature about Oxford—to coincide with the Oxford Historic Buildings Appeal. He had had a long conversation with John Snagge; he wrote in a memo to Gilliam, dated 27 June: 'We both feel strongly that a feature programme should be done about it—and in the near future.' Given an appropriately Ruskinian title, 'The Stones of Oxford', it has a Graduate, voicing some of MacNeice's thoughts, like the Visitor to Athens or Atlantis. At times insouciant, a touch snobbish, but aware of it, he is nostalgic for a lost world. He had been 'up' in the 1920s, 'what they now call the decadent era', and he detests the rebuilding, quoting Hawthorne on the picturesqueness of decay. A more robust attitude is represented by the Mason, who points out that buildings were meant to last; he discusses the properties of different kinds of stone, rather like one of Jack Dillon's 'Country Magazine' craftsmen. The Graduate, blasé, asks why they do not let the city be submerged by time, 'a completely useless but beautiful fossil in a world of stream-lined utility'. The 'new face' of the world is not to his taste, but the Mason insists that refacing is not against tradition: 'not unless you do it with synthetic. . . .'

Time was MacNeice's personal enemy too: Dan Davin recalls being with him in the M.L. Club, and Louis pointing to the grey in his hair, smiling ruefully. September brought his

fiftieth birthday. During that month he was preparing the
feature and the Davins took him to Cotswold stone quarries.
The programme was broadcast on 24 September. A companion
programme, 'An Oxford Anthology', takes up the theme of a
lost world: the unreachable golden key to the unreachable
garden, reminding us of *Alice*. A passage from Arnold praises the
beautiful, venerable city with its 'ineffable charm', 'the home
of lost causes and forsaken beliefs'. The Clerk of Oxenford is
there, and an Oxford eccentric, Dr Ralph Ketrell, described in
Aubrey's gossipy prose; so are Pope, Johnson, Gibbon, and
Beerbohm. Beerbohm felt affection and nostalgia: 'Oxford, that
lotus land, saps the will-power, the power of action. But in so
doing, it clarifies the mind, makes larger the vision. . . .' The
narrator comments that, whether one agrees with Beerbohm or
not, Oxford is certainly a hard place to leave.

In October 1957, before going on a month's tour to India,
Malaya and Ceylon, MacNeice was writing to Gilliam about
the next year's schedule: he had 'nothing on his plate' for the
first quarter except three poetry readings, and at the end of
April he would be 'televised away to the misty (London) West',
so he would like to do another April Fool feature. This time the
targets would be journalism and literature. We were by now
into the world of the Angry Young Men and the Outsider.
Earlier that year MacNeice had written a book review, or
protest, about poetry (in the *London Magazine*), and in October,
when he was making his programme suggestions and in the
same magazine, he reviewed books on James Joyce. He used
the occasion to launch an attack against humourless academics.
Shaw, Yeats and Joyce were all three Irish, and all three 'giant
cranks'. His article on Augustus John in 1952 had shown the
same delight in anarchic individuality, in those who were alive
and not fossilised. He castigates 'the ever-growing tribes of
humourless scholars, of Quintilian G. Grinder on his campus,
or little plucky Jim making red bricks without straws and
hoping they will add up to a doctorate'. Irishness is seen as a
defence against grey uniformity, and bureaucratic conformity.
He finds unilluminating a chronicle of all the buildings in which
Joyce, 'a chronic nomad', stayed; of more interest are the

youthful games he played and the periodicals he read. 'Joyce's own work will be waking when his scholiasts have all gone to sleep—if they are not already asleep over their typewriters.'

In such a mood he planned his feature: 'It will irritate a lot of people but it will cheer me up—and perhaps some others', he wrote to Gilliam. In the same way, he had hoped that his March Hare programmes of the 1940s would amuse the 'browned off'. He wrote to George MacCann from the holiday cottage on the Isle of Wight on 31 December, and mentioned that he had just had his suggestion accepted. (He also talks of Ernest Stahl having spent Christmas with them, and of a New Year's Eve party at the Priestleys. There were the inevitable plans for watching rugby—he was to cover the Wallabies' match in Dublin for the *Observer* on 18 January.) His Hare was by now dead, so the Fool persona is a young Ulsterman, part naif, part canny, one Samuel Smiley (his provisional name had been McAnally, and the programme's 'Angry Old Auntie'). Smiley comes to London in search of Culture, so his aunt takes him to the BBC, but he was wanting 'something more sort of poetical'. Instead he finds a new verse play in prose being rehearsed—'The Waste Room'—and meets a famous novelist who deals in 'smog, smut, seediness, sex and spirit'. The musical device in this feature is a variation on that for 'Prisoner's Progress': an accordionist, Tollefson, 'a genius at significant and witty variation', plays theme songs for the characters. The list MacNeice compiled and his comments suggest that he set about his task gleefully. A 'new critic' has 'Wrap me up in a shroud of semantics' as his theme; 'My little grey home in the west' was to be made 'as grey as possible please! It stands for a pretty arid school of younger poets.'; 'J'attendrais' indicates *Waiting for Godot* 'and such things'; and there is a parody of the play in 'The Ferris Wheel', to which the cast (Cécile Chevreau and Anthony Jacobs again) are bound. They are Alpha and Omega. 'As you will observe, as the action fails to progress, there will always be a hundred and eighty degrees between them. Cà, c'est la vie.' In fact, MacNeice admired Beckett, and the skit is good-humoured: the playwright is 'Michael McCarthy Poubelle', just arrived from Paris for the rehearsal. There is

F*

indeed an element of self-parody in the lovers' predicament, which mimics that in 'Prisoner's Progress'.

More heartfelt was the satire on the Red-Brick writers who deal in 'white tiles and dirty talk', although they are willing to accept Samuel as a fellow-provincial. But he still wants poets: the Movement and Lallans poets are a disappointment. So is the northern playwright who hates the middle class and is identified by the tune 'Dashing away with the smoothing iron'. At the end, afraid that the assembled writers may turn on him, as the cards did on Alice, he blows them away. 'Today's been so queer it's all like a caricature. But who's been fooling whom? I'm going to think that one out at home.' Samuel ends with a cheerful song about all the pleasure he has had—a clue to the spirit of the whole thing. The cast enjoyed it, and Louis loved it, curled up laughing at times in the producer's booth. It shows the combination of intellectual wit and youthful humour which was characteristic of him. The programme was called 'All Fools at Home', going out on the Home Service on 1 April.

Less of a joke was the stint in television. Laurence Gilliam had instituted a series of training courses for those Features producers whom he could persuade to go on them, but they generally felt out of place. Gilliam himself had a brief and unhappy interlude there, under his former subordinate, Cecil McGivern. MacNeice was on his course from April to October 1958, and the atmosphere he found is reflected in a letter to George MacCann. He would make enquiries about designing for television, 'provided I can find someone to question about it who doesn't, like many of them, regard me with dark suspicion as a dangerous interloper from sound'. He was glad when he was at last given a production of his own to do. He produced two short Strindberg plays, *Pariah* and *The Stronger*, in August. The most interesting outcome of these few months was a stage play which MacNeice wrote, some four months afterwards, but which he did not see produced and did not revise. He called it 'One for the Dead' but it was retitled *One for the Grave* when it was put on at the Abbey Theatre in 1966, and when it was published by Faber two years later. It is an 'Everyman' play, not episodic as was 'The Careerist', but

following more closely the pattern of the medieval play. Television had suggested the setting: a studio with the Floor
Manager, Morty, and the Production Gallery, with the Powers
Above; communication between floor and gallery is not always
good. There is a good deal of autobiographical content (writing
it may have been partly cathartic at a particularly difficult
time). There is the episode of the chocolates, when his mother
was in hospital, which we find in *The Strings are False*; her death;
the darkness in which the child hears a hymn about the grave,
likened to his bed; an idyllic college affair with Mary—they sit
by the river watching the mayflies dance their one-day life
away, and he gazes at the sunlight on her hair (recurrent motifs
in MacNeice's work). The second half of the play has themes
familiar from radio plays: Admass, Admom, the Electronic
Brain which takes over man's thinking, Sean Bull with his
sentimental Irishry, the Analyst and the Marxist—offering
false solutions—the Scientist putting life under the microscope,
reducing it almost to non-life.

Some of the details were to be used in the plays of the last
few years of MacNeice's life; others are found in the poems:
man's origins in the sea, loss of youth, loss of love. 'And the
ravens croak in Lover's Lane and the telephone is not answered.'
The house is vacated and re-let; Everyman's place is refilled,
his latchkey changed, and the papers in his desk skimmed
through and thrown away. Everyman wants to 'conduct' his
own death, but he is taken over by others. He must, though,
walk his 'long long trail alone', after Conscience and Free Will
have escorted him to the grave. The gravedigger resembles his
father, and offers him life. In the darkness children's voices sing
'Happy Birthday to You', diminishing to a solo singer. The
images are a mixture of darkness and light, of the classical
fates and the Christian promise of new life—an unresolved
paradox.

It is clear that at this period MacNeice was liable to depression, and sought more and more escape in drink and company.
Dan Davin writes of him as 'trying to come to terms with the
laocoön of middle age. . . . In the Irish way, and in the
way of gregarious writers everywhere, he had always made

much use of alcohol and pubs, was at home in them sometimes it seemed more than he was at home.' It is not surprising that his marriage was not to last much longer. As well as the pubs there was the M.L., a survivor among the drinking clubs of Soho and Fitzrovia, many of which were shut down in the late 1950s, leaving disconsolate tea-rooms and modern coffee bars as a poor substitute. The M.L. remains, though much changed in character. On one occasion MacNeice was there with a colleague, Eric Ewens, sitting depressed in the dark and smoky cavern. Eric suggested that they go into the country, to a pub by the river. Louis agreed, and they travelled west from Paddington to Pangbourne, to sit by the Thames, behind the Swan. As they sat, enjoying the peace and freshness of the scene, Louis remarked, laconically: 'Sometimes, Ewens, you have good ideas.' But he did not like the swans who glided up to them: they had cruel eyes, he said. Another time he was in the M.L. with John Sharp, when he put back into Greek, writing on a beer-stained membership form, the epitaph by Kallimachos, known best in Cory's translation: 'They told me, Heraclitus, they told me you were dead. . . .' (Strangely, George MacCann was to recite these lines as he shaped Louis's death-mask, in 1963.)

In the winter of 1958–9 MacNeice returned to radio. The first few programmes that he did reveal the poet and the rugby enthusiast. In an article entitled 'Talking about Rugby', written in February 1959 for the *New Statesman*, he considered the attraction of the game. 'Our code, with its oval ball and unpredictability, must appeal more to the poet than to the scientist. . . . (Association football seems to have more appeal, for instance, to logical positivists.)' This is a glance at the well-known soccer enthusiast, A. J. Ayer, who knew and admired MacNeice. But Ayer does have some interest in rugby too, and remembers going with MacNeice to at least one match at Twickenham. They respected each other but 'our minds worked differently', Ayer says—and he had no wish to join in the prolonged pub crawlings.

In January 1959 MacNeice watched Wales play England at Cardiff. The background to this was his wish to write a feature on rugby, with a Walter Mittyish character dreaming of his lost youth, or a youth that he never had. Hywel Davies, Head of Welsh Programmes, was glad to co-operate, and Cliff Morgan even gave up his ticket for Louis. They were often to discuss the mystique of the game over a 'jar'. As MacNeice wrote in a memo, going to Cardiff was a necessary preliminary. 'I had to wait for the match itself to discover what I was going to invent.' He then wrote the short script, which was to be blended with commentary by Rex Alston and C. V. Wynne-Jones. He ran into Stanley Baker, who said he would like to play the part of Dai (the dreamer); he would be free for only a few days in March. As these happened to include the date when Wales were to play Ireland at Cardiff, MacNeice suggested that they should come down to record the programme, and see the game while they were there, on 14 March. In the event Baker could not make it, but otherwise plans went accordingly. The feature, 'Scrums and Dreams', was broadcast on 3 April, the eve of the France–Wales match in Paris.

By this time Howard Newby had succeeded John Morris as Controller of the Third Programme. He was anxious to get MacNeice to write more of his best work. There were formal meetings, of an editorial nature, where producers could put forward their ideas, but sometimes a more personal meeting was arranged. Such an occasion was the lunch arranged by Newby and Gilliam, at the Zoo (Laurence was a member of the Zoological Society); there they talked with Louis of the work he might do. After this or some other such meeting, MacNeice sent a memo to Newby; it is dated 17 April 1959. 'Following our conversation the other day, I would like to confirm that I am keen on doing a programme on this subject'—he was referring to the Battle of Clontarf. 'I have discussed the possibility of special music for it with Tristram Cary, who lit up to it at once.' After explaining his intended treatment, he added a postscript. 'This is a comparatively long-term project (I could produce it towards the end of the Fourth Quarter) but in the meantime—the other possibility we discussed—I am looking for some suitable folk tale which can carry the sort of symbolism that you noticed in "The Heartless Giant". I have a few other ideas for the Third which I will let you know about as soon as I have got them better formulated.'

This encouragement from Newby seems to have come at the right time. MacNeice had probably recently finished 'One for the Dead', and was to write, during the next twelve months, the poems for *Solstices*. Renewed creativity showed itself in both areas of his writing (and it was perhaps lucky that Newby had commented on 'The Heartless Giant', one of MacNeice's favourite programmes). The first piece that he did for radio after this was a new fairy tale adaptation, of a story from Norway, from a collection of Andrew Lang, found by Louis on his sister's bookshelves; she remembers how fascinated he was by these stories. 'East of the Sun and West of the Moon' was broadcast in July 1959.

This story is a variant of the Cupid and Psyche theme, a tale of love found and lost, and recovered after a difficult quest. The heroine, whose folly lost her her love, must use all her wisdom and courage to overcome the hazards and the wicked spells that separate them. The heroine of this story is Helga who is persuaded to go with a kindly white bear so that her family shall be well provided for. Like Beauty she finds herself in a magic palace with servants; like Psyche she is visited at night by an invisible lover. When she lights a candle one night, she finds a handsome young man, accidentally wakes him, and loses him to the troll who had bewitched him. The Four Winds and three aged Crones help her. (Francis Dillon recommended Patience Collier for the strange voices of the hags—she remembers MacNeice as a wonderfully imaginative producer, a 'conjuror' who understood the microphone perfectly.)

Once Helga has won back her prince, the magic of love takes over, causing flowers to bloom where before there were cinders, and the sun to shine along with the stars. Once again we have a work of considerable charm, the supernatural and strange perfectly adapted to the radio medium. Fairy tales had a lifelong appeal for MacNeice: they attracted the poet and the romantic. Enriching our lives, they can also illuminate them. Bruno Bettelheim, in his study of the genre, *The Uses of Enchantment*, has written that they, 'like all true works of art . . .

possess a multifarious richness and depth that far transcend what even the most thorough discursive examination can extract from them'.

In August and September MacNeice was in South Africa where he gave lectures at the University of Cape Town. Lectures and poetry readings in such faraway places are wittily presented in the poem 'Old Masters abroad'.

> At Bablockhythe the stripling Ganges
> Burns on her ghats the scholar gypsy,
> There's a deathly hush on the rocks of Aden,
> Nine bean rows rise in the Kalahari.
>
> The faces listen or not. The lecturers
> Mop their memories. All over the static
> Globe the needle sticks in the groove.
> It is overtime now for the Old Masters.

But the visit to South Africa brought home to him more serious issues. Bertie Rodgers later recalled that MacNeice had described the experience as like being at a cocktail party on the *Titanic*. Another poem is called 'Half truth from Cape Town': in this he implicitly compares the Irish conflict to that between whites and blacks, viewed from 'this safe hotel Between the goldmines and the padded cell'. He writes of 'each glib airport' and the 'ants' that pour through. He also wrote a radio script (which was not broadcast) which sets its opening scene at an airport. It is much more politically aware than was the film script on Ghana. The suppressed 'Zeros' are black, and treated with brutality; by the end of the play they have risen against their oppressors, in a small-scale incident, while the rigged elections once more put the 'Inners' in power. Worked into the political story is a private one, a doomed love affair between a visitor and a liberal 'Inner', Greta; she too is shot by the Zeros she has tried to help, because the situation has bred only hatred.

Just as he had thought of Ireland when in South Africa, so he thought of the contemporary Irish conflict when he dealt with an episode from its past. 'They Met on Good Friday', that long-delayed play on the Battle of Clontarf, was his major production in the last quarter of 1959. It takes up the story where the saga of Njal ends, the Burners having left Iceland for Ireland after their terrible revenge. Halgertha, one of the cruel women of the sagas, reappears in this new play. Queen Gormlai is also hard and scornful. She describes Ireland as 'this land that is pinned together with thorn trees and still keeps falling apart'. She is the wife of King Brian, whose conquests are sung by his harper; but the old king muses bitterly on the sixty years of strife that have passed. (Patrick Magee made an effective Brian Boru.) The disillusioned voice talks of 'the bog like a purple running sore, the wood like a web of false intrigue, the wind like a whisper of foul intent, the hills like the graves of enormous hopes, the clouds like a tent of despair and death'. Images of ravens and strange weaving women reinforce the sense of doom. The king is indeed killed in the hour of victory; left in his tent, blind, he is deserted by his guards. The Poet, tired of words, envies the Harper: 'Words must be true or false, what you say on those Strings is neither.'

This is a fine radio play, showing a revival of MacNeice's powers. The harp music by Cary is very effective. At the start of the play it suggests the sea beside which an old woman and a child stand, onlookers of the battle, like the watchers in 'Alexander Nevsky'. Advice on church music—the plainsong of eleventh-century Ireland—was given by Gerald Abraham, who responded with enthusiasm to MacNeice's letter. What interested MacNeice particularly about this battle of 1014 were its implications. Although Norse power was broken in Ireland, 'the sands were running out for the Irish as the *Norman* invaders were very shortly to appear over the horizon.' It was not a romantic and heroic episode, but part of the continuity of the ambiguities and tragedy of Ireland. 'There is plenty of evidence that the leaders on both sides were as much the victims of power politics as their counterparts in the twentieth century.' He wanted, however, to retain some of the supernatural elements, and would use heightened language where necessary (these observations are from his memo to Howard Newby). He had not finished with Ireland, and was to write another play with similar but extended themes in an Irish setting.

MacNeice not only picked up once again threads from some of

his best radio writing—the symbolic fairy tale, the sagas—but faced some of the problems of new techniques in radio. Another memo (dated 13 April 1959) had put forward an idea for a kind of programme 'in contrast with the two extremes of pure radio features written for actors and pure "actuality" pieces concocted from tape recordings. . . . This has of course been done already but usually in a merely incidental way. . . . What I am now suggesting is that the interplay of the two elements should be made the *basis* of a programme.' He wanted to achieve 'Unity in Difference', avoiding both contrived effects and monotonous shapelessness. Among the developments which affected Features work was the use of tape, coming in during the 1950s. This made possible actual recordings of people and events, rather than 'actuality' reconstructions written for actors. Some people were rather taken over by the idea of tape-recording, but there was still a place for the writer. MacNeice's memo, and long accompanying list of suggestions for programmes, was an attempt to marry the two techniques. A sample placing was agreed, and 'Mosaic of Youth' was broadcast on 30 December: it interweaves recorded interviews with young people and passages from works written in the past. This was the last production by MacNeice in 1959. The difficult decade had come to an end.

Chapter Eight

The Final Years: 1960–1963

And when the last horn burns the hills
Fetch me far one draught of grace
To quench my thirst before it kills
'Invocation'

The last years of Louis MacNeice's life coincided with the dying years of Features Department, which was wound up in 1964 after the death of Laurence Gilliam. Some rather emotional versions of the last days of Features have, understandably, been given by people who had for years been involved in the work of the Department. The increasing influence of news and current affairs emphasised journalism at the expense of creativity. Drama Department had become more innovatory. So Features Department was threatened on both its fronts, and by the end of the 1950s its best days were felt to be over. Geoffrey Bridson has written that he found himself agreeing less and less with Features policy: documentaries were 'getting steadily drearier and more derivative'. For Gilliam these were sad years of disappointment and illness. Douglas Cleverdon has recorded that 'Laurence Gilliam retained his magnanimity, his breadth of vision, his faith in the radio medium; but that faith was not shared by all his colleagues.'

The Department came to be regarded with disfavour. From reminiscences and anecdotes it would seem that Features retained something of its old style, the easy come-and-go, impatience with bureaucratic routine, extravagance. The self-sufficiency of the producers aroused resentment in other departments; the cost-efficiency worried the accountants.(Stella Hillier, Features Organiser, should be mentioned for the wonderful job she did in keeping the Department afloat.) Moreover, developments in radio meant that the pioneering days were over, and the techniques devised then had been adopted elsewhere, or superseded. It was decided in 1959 that the size of the Department should be reduced; a measure hardly calculated to restore confidence, it seemed more likely to mark the beginning of the end. Features was, perhaps, a luxury that could ultimately be dispensed with.

1960 was the last complete year of MacNeice's full-time career in the BBC. His work sheet for the year indicates the routine: productions, editing sessions, meetings (Third Programme, Departmental, Poetry Committee), interviews with artists and others. He then goes on to summarise his main work, quarter by quarter. During January he was working on his play on South Africa ('The Pin is Out'); he also visited Belfast to discuss with the playwright Sam Thompson, author of *Over the Bridge*, the possibility of doing a 'People Today' programme on him (but this was rejected or delayed 'for reasons of local politics'). South Africa continued to concern him, and he had discussions with South Africans in London. There was also 'preliminary work' with W. S. Merwin and Patrick Kavanagh for forthcoming features. In March he recorded 'Hangman's Helicon', compiled by Merwin; and auditions were held for the reading of Kavanagh's poem 'The Great Hunger'—this was broadcast in April, with an introduction (separately recorded) by the author. 'During this Quarter, though I could not possibly give you dates (and after all some of the work of any imaginative programme is done literally in one's sleep), I was working on the script of "The Pin is Out", which was a 75-minute project.' This script was completed for the third quarter, but there was 'quite a lengthy controversy; it was finally rejected on grounds of policy'. (There was a difference of opinion with Newby; the matter was referred to the Director of Sound Broadcasting, Lindsay Wellington, who turned down the project.) Meanwhile MacNeice revised his television play, worked on an adaptation of *The Odyssey* for radio, and planned another play ('The Administrator'). He also conferred with George Seferiades, the Greek Ambassador in London, about broadcasting modern Greek poetry. From mid-July to September he was attached to television.

In September 1960 MacNeice's marriage came to an end, but a new relationship, with someone he had known for a long while, replaced it. In his poetry the 'lyric impulse' continued. He wrote to Eliot, at Faber, on 20 April 1960, that he had nearly enough poems for a new collection: 'I am having a writing bout at the moment.' The poems appeared as *Solstices* in 1961. In these we find images of renewal and hope, Eden after the Fall, blue sky and a new dawn. Some poems are linked to radio works: for example, 'Dark Age glosses' relate to the sagas and 'They Met on Good Friday'. One subject, suggested as a radio feature but not done as such, provides four poems. These are about Regent's Park, near which MacNeice had lived for most of his London years—his last house was in Regent's Park Terrace, before he moved out of town to the country. The feature on the Park would have had cross-cut internal soliloquies of a few characters; in the poems the poet reveals his own thoughts as he watches these people. One point of description was anticipated in the plan for the feature: the Park as a make-believe countryside in the middle of the city.

The notable element of 'pastoral' in MacNeice's work, in an extended sense of the term, can be seen in nostalgia for childhood, the liking for fairy tales and nursery songs, the enjoyment of and occasional need for escape from the urban life. Ireland was the most important 'pastoral' scene for him, especially Achill, and there had been the Hebrides, Dorset and Wiltshire, Ménèrbes, and the cottage on the Isle of Wight. 'Country week-end' celebrates one such interlude:

> We have been here a thousand years
> Nor yet have reached the age of gas.
>
> And a thousand years of songbirds' bones
> Are pasted in these cottage walls. . . .

The past too is a scene of pastoral, in contrast with the unlovely modern age. The poem ends with this contrast: the poet's

middle age 'Reads better in this light', that is, in the light of an
oil lamp, which has to be tended each night:

> without
> The chance of a failure at the main
> Or a short, without—what matters more—
> The sameness governed by a switch
>
> Which could epitomise our times
> Where everything, not only light
> But food and freedom, thought and life,
> Can be switched on just so—or off.

Some lines recall his childhood home:

> Bustling dead women with steady hands,
> One from Tyrone and one from Cavan
> And one my mother . . .

They, with their 'soft lights' brought nightly out of the pantry,
'spread Assurance'. There is a note of new-found assurance in
some of the poems.

There is technical precision, too, and taut structure, as in
'Nature notes': these four, short, linked poems, on Dandelions,
Cats, Corncrakes and The Sea, refer to childhood and middle
life. The first part of each poem deals with the significance of the
subject to the child; in the second part a parallel is drawn
between the subject and people who reassure the man. The sea,
for instance, is:

> Like something or someone to whom
> We have to surrender, finding
> Through that surrender life.

Childhood is also recalled in a lovely lyric, 'Invocation', with its
simple images of natural beauty, like 'a moon in a tree', seen by
the child in his 'waking day'. The last stanza develops into
symbol, reminiscent of 'The Dark Tower':

> And when the last horn burns the hills
> Fetch me far one draught of grace
> To quench my thirst before it kills.

Religion has its place, a new-found peace being linked to his father's presence in 'The truisms' (although this poem is in the third person).

It is not fanciful to stress this theme of childhood in a reading of the poems of this time. In September 1960 MacNeice produced for television his play on the 'Burgess' motif. 'Another Part of the Sea' (the new title of *Traitors in Our Way*) has as its main character Tom Carstairs, a nuclear physicist on a cruise ship with his wife of a year, Portia, to whom he brings roses. When the hard-drinking Irish doctor, Con Ryan, asks Carstairs what was the worst trouble he ever got into, he relates an early incident. 'It happened when I was five. There was a path at the bottom of the garden. . . .' It is the sad story of the nestlings: 'at the moment it didn't register. It was only the next day there were all the little corpses—hanging among the thorns and they hadn't any feathers.' Con's wife Bridie comments that 'a thing like that makes a dark impression on a child.' The audience would not have realised that the experience was MacNeice's own. Towards the end of the play, when Carstairs feels guilty at betraying his former friend—though the other man is doubly a traitor—he uses the nestlings as an emblem of guilt itself.

The traitor, ex-colleague, former lover of Portia, had defected behind the Iron Curtain; he comes aboard, disguised, at a Mediterranean port, his real motive being to lead Carstairs into a trap. The Suez war forces the ship to head north from the tropics, and it eventually enters the Arctic Circle, thus passing through three zones (though the significance is not fully developed). Images of cold and darkness, and icebergs, suggest other levels of meaning. Portia and the Ryans stand by Tom as the ship moves into enemy territory, and to some kind of imprisonment or annihilation. The play had opened with the tune of 'Loch Lomond'—the song of a man ascending the gallows. But it is the betrayer who is shown with the face of a doomed man as the play ends. One cannot judge it unseen as a piece of television drama, but MacNeice was 'quite pleased' with the revised version of the stage play with which he had become 'very dissatisfied'. It is comparable to radio plays, like 'Prisoner's Progress', which combine naturalism and symbolism and which have powerful images of doom and death. The last radio play was to be in the same mould. Other themes are characteristic of MacNeice's plays: power, corruption and betrayal.

Two of the cast of 'Another Part of the Sea', Liam Gaffney and Margaret Gordon, remember MacNeice with admiration and affection. They both also appeared in his radio plays, and Margaret Gordon took part in programmes of verse. She shared with Louis an enthusiasm for Scots ballads—one is used in the television play. She would play Skerrie in 'The Mad Islands', and MacNeice particularly wanted her to take the main woman's role in 'Another Part of the Sea'. She was also to be in the last of his radio plays. Liam Gaffney, who played the Irish doctor, Con Ryan, stresses what a kind man Louis was, and what clear-mindedness and precision he showed as a producer. He likens him to a blackbird, perched awhile at the edge of a group but slipping away or into his private self if you tried to pin him down.

That autumn, 1960, MacNeice organised the adaptation for radio of *The Odyssey*, translated by divers poets, including Patric Dickinson, Ted Hughes, Terence Tiller, MacNeice himself and Anthony Thwaite who produced the series. There were twelve programmes of 'The Odyssey', through October to December. In December MacNeice produced a feature called 'Night at Lamorran—how to find a poet', by Zofia Ilinska, who wrote to congratulate him on his production, and to praise in particular the acting of Mary Wimbush. He seems to have been busy that quarter, and he had written in October to George MacCann that he would dearly love to come over to Northern Ireland, but there was little likelihood of his doing so for a couple of months as he was behindhand with three jobs at once. Among the items of news was Bob Pocock's having done 'a good programme of tape-recordings about Aneurin Bevan'; and Dominic Behan had had a fight in the George with René Cutforth and the landlord, Martin Sweeney.

The first quarter of 1961 was the last of MacNeice's full-time career in the BBC. It was twenty years since he had done his first free-lance work for Features, just before being taken on to the war-time staff, in May 1941. Now, at his own choice, he went on to a three-year programme contract, whereby he would work for the BBC twenty-six weeks per year; this was to operate from 1 July. This would give more freedom from the institution, but still allow him an outlet for his radio plays, which he would still produce. This would appear a satisfactory compromise, removing some of the irksomeness of being tied to a routine producer-writer's job, but maintaining a rather privileged position within the broadcasting world. In March 1961 he produced his play 'The Administrator', the study of a man who finds himself 'blunted' by being in the wrong job. At first, MacNeice thought of making him a hospital administrator, but changed the role to that of a nuclear physicist (perhaps through reviving *Traitors in Our Way*). He had a compulsion to write this, he said, 'as this sort of painful choice seems endemic in our society'. The choice facing Professor Jerry King is whether to remain in his present position, or to accept promotion to be Director of an Institute and so gain more money and prestige. He is inclined to stay as he is; his wife prompts him to the second course. A postgraduate student, a rather brash representative of the future, thinks that King should take the post because of the power, or at least influence, it would give him. The action begins late one evening, and ends early next morning, much of it taking the form of dreams.

Dreams, in this play, have much of the quality of real dreams: suppressed memories are released; there are surreal images, as of the roses melting in someone's arms; there are illogical links, and symbols. There are echoes of *Alice in Wonderland*: the mock-trial, puns, crossword clues, the symbolism of doors and of figures of authority. The incident of the *Titanic*, recurrent in MacNeice's thoughts, is used imaginatively: the iceberg, manned by scientists, threatens to destroy the ship carrying mankind. Through the dreams we learn of earlier affairs: Jerry's with an American journalist, transformed into a big-game huntress; and his wife Martha's with his friend Robert, before their marriage. Indeed, Martha was pregnant by Robert when he was killed in a car crash—Jerry had been driving and, already in love with her, he marries Martha. They have a child of their own as well. Some of the details and memories of MacNeice's own life are reworked in the play. For instance, the nostalgia of early love, associated with roses and punting on the river, is transferred to the wife. Dreams of husband and wife are intercut, until, in the morning, Jerry King has to make his decision. Originally, MacNeice wanted to leave him undecided, but he was persuaded for the broadcast version to let the wife prevail. However, when he came to prepare the play for publication, he reversed the ending, so that Jerry King seems stronger and more positive.

After his six months off, MacNeice returned to the BBC in the autumn and did a new production of the 1952 play, 'One Eye Wild'. There are in fact points of similarity between this play and 'The Administrator' which may have led to the revival. He produced a new play in December: 'Let's Go Yellow' is the story of a reporter 'in a world of double-think' (as a *Radio Times* note puts it). A young Rugby-Oxonian joins a newspaper, and is shocked by the cynicism with which scandals which may affect the paper are hushed up. Wanting to expose such hypocrisy and self-interest he thinks of writing a satirical script for the BBC, but 'satire doesn't go well on radio'. This hour-long play was put out on the Third Programme.

It received a favourable review in the *Listener* of 28 December 1961; MacNeice was praised for his ear for voices. This drew a reply, in the issue of 4 January 1962, in which MacNeice pays a neat compliment to his actors (many of whom were friends). 'Dear Sir, Like anyone who works in "steam radio" I am naturally very gratified by a favourable notice but I feel I should point out that your drama critic, in giving such a notice to my programme "Let's Go Yellow", handed a bouquet to the producer that was really due to his cast. While I have in fact noticed that "drunks' voices always go up at the end of a song", on this occasion I had no need to explain this fact of life to the actors. I wish it were more generally realised that in any radio production casting is half the battle.' At about this time, too, MacNeice was receiving praise from various reviewers, for his 'old mastery', for the way in which he could combine fantasy and reality, present dreams and subconscious fears and memories, for his 'touch', his sense of what would work, and his dialogue. Terence Tiller later wrote of this last aspect as a 'constant wonder and joy. . . . The short crisp lines, *visually* vivid, heavily-charged with overtones and yet never out of character, would ride the voice like birds—and penetrate the listener's brain like bullets.'

At the end of January 1962 MacNeice was preparing a new, abridged production of his adaptation of *Faust*. There is an account by Ved Mehta of MacNeice at work on this. He gave precise and minimal instructions, with little interruption until the point where Faust's study door opens. It sounded too modern; it should be medieval, stiff on its hinges and heavy. After several experiments they got the right blend of 'effects'. 'It was, however, the arrangement of the effects for Easter Sunday that caused the longest delay. Recordings of bells—from Indian cowbells to the bells of Cologne Cathedral—were assembled and reassembled, until there was an epiphany of sound, a flood of joyous clanging.' A few days after this, Ved Mehta joined MacNeice and his colleagues in Shirreff's Wine Bar. The subject of radio came up, and MacNeice held that the BBC had provided him and others with the opportunity to reach a large audience, the stability of a salary, the company of fellow artists, and a degree of independence. Especially on the Third Programme, one could do interesting work; but the hey-day of the Third was over With cuts in air time, and loss of audiences to television, 'a general depression has set in, and radio, while still the yeast of culture here, is not what it used to be.'

During September 1961 MacNeice had decided to write another 'modern morality', on an Irish theme. 'Seeing that Third are not interested in my Arthurian project, "The Remorse of Sir Gawayne", *and* seeing that for the last decade or more I have been pestered to write "another *Dark Tower*", I have a suggestion to make for the first quarter of next year.' At the end of January 1962 he was writing to the MacCanns: 'things have been hectic'; apart from the new production of 'Faust', he was writing 'a thing of my own, based on the voyage of Maelduin, called "The Mad Islands" '. MacNeice talked about his idea to Denys Hawthorne, now in London at the start of his radio career. He saw a good deal of Louis, who liked him a lot and admired his acting. Denys had had a part in 'They Met on Good Friday', and he was to be Muldoon in the satirical-lyrical adaptation that MacNeice proposed to make of the traditional Irish story. He asked Louis when he could see the script, and MacNeice promised that he would get it done over the weekend. Once he got down to writing, he could work quickly, although he may have carried the idea around in his head for a long time. Writing the poems may have been a more careful process, but the radio plays could be altered in rehearsal, and when he prepared them for publication MacNeice would make revisions. After the production of 'The Mad Islands', MacNeice found himself dissatisfied with his 'hero', and apologised ruefully to Denys for giving him such a weak part. He would have re-written it if, for example, it had been submitted for the Italia Prize. The play was broadcast on 4 April 1962.

MacNeice's chief source was P. W. Joyce's *Old Celtic Romances*, but he made some important changes; he had also read *Celtic Heritage* by Alwyn and Brinley Rees, and he knew the poem by Tennyson. In the original version, after his father is killed by raiders, Maelduin is fostered out by his mother, to her friend, who is a queen. When Maelduin learns of his true parentage he sets off, accompanied by his three foster brothers, for his mother's home in the West—a voyage which takes them to strange islands. Some of these are retained by MacNeice, some transformed, and others invented. The original Maelduin gives up the idea of revenge and is reconciled to the raiders; his episodic travels end with most of his companions still alive. Muldoon is urged on to revenge by his mother, the Queen—a dominant destructive force, like Roland's mother and the Queen of Air and Darkness (she in fact makes a 'reappearance' as the Queen of the Twilight, transformed into a sinister and dangerous creature from the beautiful young lady of the original). And all Muldoon's companions are lost.

Some characteristic touches are the invention of the Jester who warns Muldoon that he is unlikely to find happiness in finding his mother, the outrageous puns on the Island of Foolish Laughter, and the addition of the Seal-Woman Skerrie, an

Irish motif, but not in the original legend. She loves and protects
Muldoon (although he never seems to realise it), saving him,
for instance, from the sisters Olwen and Branwen on the Island
of Rival Beds. At the end she has to bid him a sad farewell: 'I
thought I could break the rules—I could perhaps if you'd
helped me.' A lyrical section elaborates the idea of a crystalline
Country-under-the-Sea: the Drowned Man first heard the sea
'in a singing shell and the music haunted me'; the sea is 'the
first and the last thing, the cradle and grave of life, the mother
and mistress of all of us'.

One point about the play, wrote MacNeice, was its anach-
ronisms. The best illustration of this is the alchemist who
becomes the Inventor (a kind of mad scientist); his dark cell
turns into a shining white room, humming with machinery—
the machines are growing like a cancer. Finally, the Inventor
destroys himself and all the inhabitants in the Port of the
Unwise. The part was played by Richard Pasco, then new to
broadcasting. As a student in the 1950s he had read the works
of MacNeice and Auden, 'and read *about* them avidly'; so
when he was offered a part in a play by MacNeice he was
somewhat overawed. He found him a considerate and kindly
producer, despite a certain distance, and remembers their all-
too-brief working relationship with pleasure. As in 'They Met
on Good Friday', the juxtaposition of past and future is
significant. The Queen 'dying at this moment in the centre of
Ireland . . . is of advanced years but has been well preserved in
hatred . . . She has plenty of venom in her yet—prolong her life
and add a chapter to the annals of Ireland.' Other characters
become faceless (like one of the evil men in 'The Queen of Air
and Darkness'), or they destroy themselves, but Muldoon protests, and at last loses his hatred. 'I thought that vengeance was
mine but the fates took it away from me and what was I
avenging anyway?' At last he is alone, his companions dead,
Skerrie gone; but he sets off once more, affirming hope and
humanity, like Roland.

MacNeice was writing poems for a new collection—the
strength and imagination unchecked, but the note of hope
replaced by more sombre and sinister moods. He had trouble

thinking of a title, and was never happy with *The Burning Perch*;
in one letter to Charles Monteith at Faber he asked if 'Round
the Corner' would do. There are some powerful ballads and
lyrics in this collection, and a dominant note of death. 'The
grey ones' tells of the impassive sisters waiting for men to die;
some will find their Gates of Doom on a mountain, others in an
eastern town. Or the 'Never Yet'

> might be what your childhood swore
> Lay shrined beyond the haunted door
> Or might be where your mentor seems
> To misdirect you to in dreams.

'After the crash' is a strange and elusive poem, set in a weird
landscape where hemlock has grown high on the asphalt, while
the rider sees 'gigantic scales in the sky', both pans 'dead
empty'—and in the 'dead, dead calm' knows that it is 'too late
to die'. Journeys still serve as metaphors, as 'The taxis' and
'Charon' brilliantly exemplify.

Writing for the Poetry Book Society Bulletin, MacNeice made
a comment on the poems. When he assembled them he 'was
taken aback by the high proportion of sombre pieces, ranging
from bleak observation to thumbnail nightmares. . . . I am not
sure why this should be so. Fear and resentment seem here to
be serving me in the same way as Yeats in his old age claimed
to be served by "lust and rage", and yet I had been equally
fearful and resentful of the world we live in when I was writing
Solstices.' His radio works have given us more insight into his
criticism of the world we all live in, and perhaps into the inner
tensions. The poems intensify and crystallise his feelings in
memorable images and incidents, such as the dream-like
croquet game during a Proustian moment of recall, in 'Soap
suds', or the powerfully evocative short poem about the sea,
'Around the corner'. We should perhaps remember, though,
that this melancholy side was 'more than balanced by the
warmth and wit'—to quote words of Denys Hawthorne.

One poet whom MacNeice still admired, and felt in tune
with, was Horace. He translated some of his pieces, and
presented a programme of his verse on the Third in March 1963.

G

One version of 'Carpe Diem' had been used in a radio feature in 1956; it was used again in this 1963 programme, while a second version dates perhaps to that summer, being found in manuscript after his death.

> Do not, Leuconoe, seek to inquire what is forbidden, what
>   End the gods have assigned to you or to me; nor do you
>   meddle with
> Astrological numbers. What shall arise count to your balance if
> God marks down to you more winters—or perhaps this very
>   one is the
> Last which now on the rocks wears out the fierce Mediterranean
> Sea; but be wise and have wine, wine on the board, prune to
>   a minimum
> Long-drawn hopes. While we chat, envious time threatens to
>   give us the
> Slip; so gather the day, never an inch trusting futurity.

In 'Memoranda to Horace' the modern poet communicates over the centuries to his predecessor—posterity will not understand their language. Their would-be audience is

> Caught between cosmic and comic radiation,
> Against which world we have raised a monument
> Weaker and of less note than a mayfly
> Or a quick blurb for yesterday's detergent . . .

But Horace's memory is truly permanent, 'more lasting than bronze'. MacNeice wonders what he and Horace have in common, he with his Irish origins, the Christian framework of his upbringing. But neither of them found the Hesperides, or Tír na nÓg, and both have lived in a noisy, strife-ridden world; so he must emulate the Roman poet and learn to 'gather his day'.

During the early part of 1963, not on duty for the BBC, MacNeice was none the less busy on various projects. He still had not finished a book that he was writing on astrology: 'I wish the stars had never been invented,' he wrote in a letter to the MacCanns. There was also his 'Cambridge chore', the Clark Lectures, begun on 28 February. During the same month he was preparing an introduction for Faber, for 'The Mad Islands'. Writing to Monteith, he says that it 'will range from Celtic saga via the *Faerie Queene* to *The Waterbabies*.' His comments in the same introduction to the play (it was published with 'The Administrator'—MacNeice had suggested they would make 'a nice brace') echo themes of the Clark Lectures (later published as *Varieties of Parable*). He writes of symbolic but not narrowly allegorical double-level writing, and the 'overlapping of references' in the radio play.

He was full of ideas for radio programmes. The book on astrology prompted the thought of a light-hearted comic satire on superstition (possibly to be called 'The Star-Crossed Daughter'). More exciting was a find that he mentions in a memo dated 2 April: 'I have just for the first time in my life read "The Golden Key" by George MacDonald. It has the same extraordinary appeal as the Curdie books. . . . As the story has "got" me, I should very much like to do this but only if I am allowed to have special music. The composer would need to be very sensitive and imaginative. . . .' The idea was approved by Howard Newby, but MacNeice did not live to do the programme—nor an adaptation of *The Confessions of a Justified Sinner*, that strange book by the Ettrick shepherd, James Hogg. It was to be called 'A Justified Sinner'—MacNeice was emphatic about this, just as he was about the title of his next and last radio play, 'Persons from Porlock'.

The link with George MacDonald is worth comment. The evocative symbols of that Victorian fantasy-writer have counter-parts in MacNeice's works—before he had discovered MacDonald. So when in 1961 he read a review of a book on George MacDonald, he must have been struck by this affinity. He asked his sister, Elizabeth Nicholson, who had read the review independently, if she had any of MacDonald's books. Indeed she had, for the house where the Nicholsons lived in Hammersmith, by the river, was next door to that which had been MacDonald's (and, later, William Morris's; the garden was that in *At the Back of the North Wind*) and Elizabeth had made a collection of the stories. In this way MacNeice made his discovery of a writer who was to appeal to him immensely. One has only to read the comments in the Clark Lectures of 1963 to see that MacNeice felt MacDonald to be important: his heroes have 'to prove themselves through action' and also 'to achieve a spiritual evolution'. The caves in 'Persons from Porlock' must owe something to the subterranean tunnels of *The Princess and the Goblin* and the halls of the dead in *Lilith*— but the finding of the longed-for paradise was to have come with his treatment of 'The Golden Key'. In this story two children find a golden key at the end of the rainbow; helped by a lady with magical powers (a frequent figure in Mac-Donald) they find the door which the key fits, and to the sound of Aeolian music unlock it, to find a winding stair (another major image). 'They climbed out of the earth; and, still climbing, rose above it. They were in the rainbow. . . . Stairs beside stairs wound up together, and beautiful beings of all ages climbed along with them. They knew that they were going up to the country whence the shadows fall.'

In a memo dated 7 February, to the Controller of the Third Programme, MacNeice said that he was very glad that his latest suggestion had been accepted, but 'somewhat distressed' to be asked for a different title; 'it would break my heart if either the word "person" or the name "Porlock" disappeared from the title. So much of the time one makes do with make-shift titles and this seems to me to be a really functional one.' It serves as a metaphor for all that distracts an artist from his art, and finally, for Death. In his programme note for *Radio Times* he refers to 'those forces which are always odds on against an artist'. Soon after he had finished writing the script he was at a Faber party for Robert Lowell, remembered by Lowell in *History*:

> A month from his death, we talked by Epstein's bust
> of Eliot; MacNeice said, 'It is better
> to die at fifty than lose pleasure in fear.'

Kathleen Raine was there too, and noted that Louis was 'grey now, but still with something of his former poet's look'. Although they had not met for many years, he greeted her 'with the kiss of friendship'.

In making the character of his latest play a painter, he came closer to his own work; precursors of his character had been a publisher, a soldier, a journalist, a scientist. Now he was writing of one of his own 'profession'. Hank, the artist, follows the line of characters who try to find their way in an alien world: Tom Varney in 'He Had a Date', Tom Bowlby in 'Nuts in May', Thomas Walters in 'Prisoner's Progress'. Like them he seeks challenging physical activity: the others had had war, Antarctic exploration, escape over a mountain—Hank explores caves. The tunnelling to freedom, through a neolithic passage grave, in 'Prisoner's Progress', is an ante-type of this very powerful and evocative theme. There are the relationships with women: one is Hank's false muse, the other his true. He wanders from his path, seduced by commercialism, debilitated by drink, but before the end he returns to his proper calling. His paintings are of caves like cathedrals (recalling MacNeice's childhood dream) and a pitiful dead mole, lying as though praying, a memory associated with Hank's childhood and the loss of his mother. In the cave, where he is to die, voices return from his past—the obvious symbolism of 'back to the womb' is deliberately mentioned, as if to get it out of the way. The dark cave is much more suggestive of the subconscious—source of dreams, poetry, imagination—and of death.

Early in August MacNeice went with the engineers to caves near Ingleton, to check that the effects would be right; it rained and he got soaked. By the middle of the month he was confined to the Hertfordshire cottage, having already recorded the play, and a talk about childhood for his friend John Boyd. He spoke impromptu, sounding ill—it makes poignant listening. From the cottage he wrote to Charles Monteith to ask about the publication of 'Persons from Porlock': 'Because, if you do want to include it in *The Mad Islands*, I'll get it in shape for you. When I pre-recorded the broadcast I had to make a lot of cuts, some of which were improvements.' The writing is unsteady, as it is in another letter written the same day to George and Mercy MacCann: a planned visit was off because of his illness. 'I may still possibly come over on my own for a little in September but that is in the lap of the gods. . . .' His sister Elizabeth visited him and realised he was very ill, so took him to hospital. She heard 'Persons from Porlock' on 30 August, with great foreboding.

Friends were shocked and grieved to hear the news; some were able to visit him. He was considerate, as ever, and attempted to be cheerful, but he had pneumonia and was not responding to antibiotics. Robert Pocock saw 'the utter and, one felt, the ultimate weariness' in Louis's face. He visited with Laurence Gilliam, on the Friday evening—Louis wanted them to describe the view from his window: it was a drab one but the sun was 'going down in stormy colours'. Next day, hearing the news from Laurence, John Sharp drove from Sussex in pouring rain: 'very good of you, John, but bloody silly in this weather'. Dan Davin heard of Louis's illness in the George and stayed the night in London so that he could visit him next day. 'He was very ill, very cold, his face the colour of an Irish winter sea and sky.' Dan told Louis that Oxford University Press wanted to republish his book on Yeats—'His smile glimmered, but only to please me.' At the end only those closest to him were allowed to see him. On Tuesday, 3 September, he died, just short of his fifty-sixth birthday.

His loss was a great blow to his friends—his presence had always enriched and enhanced the company, though he seemed withdrawn and enigmatic to many. William Alwyn was ill himself, and his wife at first kept the news from him; the Davins were greatly shocked; Goronwy Rees arrived back from holiday to hear that Louis was gravely ill—it was only a couple of weeks after the death of another friend, Guy Burgess. The funeral was at St John's Wood, and his ashes were taken to Ireland, to be buried in his mother's grave in the quiet country churchyard at Carrowdore. 'The Dark Tower' was broadcast, as the BBC's memorial to him, on 15 September. The Ulster poet Derek Mahon has written of MacNeice:

> Your ashes will not fly, however the rough winds burst
> Through the wild bramble and the reverend trees.
> All we may ask of you we have. The rest
> Is not for publication, will not be heard.
> Maguire, I believe, suggested a blackbird
> And over your grave a phrase from Euripides.

> 'In Carrowdore Churchyard'

Louis MacNeice is still remembered with great affection, and missed, by his friends. He lies in a quiet grave, but his poetry remains, the greater part of his achievement as a writer. The radio work is relatively neglected, dismissed as ephemeral, but it contains much that is fine, and may help us better to understand the man and the poet.

Terence Tiller, a colleague though not a close friend of MacNeice, made some perceptive comments in his review of *The Burning Perch*. 'It is as if, in his most personal poems, his inward world became appreciable to us only through faintly coloured and slightly twisted glass, or as if it were lit by a sun different from ours. The result is often beautiful, always vivid, always arresting both intellectually and emotionally, but always disturbing, too.' He praises the urbanity, intelligence and superb craftsmanship of the poems, and then adds: 'whether the prevailing tone be apparently classical reasonableness, or a restrained lyricism, or—occasionally—an almost outrageous humour, still there will be undertones of the sub-sardonic, or even of something fiercer.' This, of course, increases the effect of the poems. A comment about the poet himself is also worth quoting, coming as it does from a fellow-poet and colleague in Features: 'what occasionally seemed in him remoteness, watchfulness, wryness, by no means indicated a melancholy or unsociable temperament: on the contrary.' The richness of his inner and outer world, Terence Tiller remarks, was overshadowed by his childhood background. The radio work endorses this, and helps us perhaps to penetrate a little further that strange and complex richness.

Characteristics of his poetry are to be found also in the radio features and plays, though these vary in quality. The deep romanticism of his character, allied to a certain classical coolness and scepticism, produced interesting programmes. The more naturalistic work could be rather weak, even banal, but when insight and feeling are controlled by artistry this kind of play succeeds; 'He Had a Date' and 'Persons from Porlock', the earliest and the last of the 'biographies' of a man of our time, are the best, and most moving. The satirical pieces, though light-hearted, are effective: the 'April fooleries' and 'Enemy of Cant' amuse, but also contain comments on the world—

MacNeice quoted Carroll's work as comparable in this respect. The serious fantasies take the form of the quest: Roland, Adam and Muldoon are variations of the 'hero', impelled by a dominant female will, but asserting themselves in the end against an evil force of tyranny or revenge. The range of MacNeice's original work was wide; to it we must add his adaptations of traditional stories. ('The Mad Islands' is based upon legend, but is so much altered that it may be considered original.) Particular favourites among 'folk' literature were fairy stories and sagas: some of the adaptations make wonderful radio. 'Cupid and Psyche', 'The Heartless Giant' and 'Grettir the Strong' may be singled out. 'Faust' is in a class of its own, and a most impressive piece.

Much of MacNeice's work was routine, but even these features have his personal stamp. If we consider his career chronologically we see that the war period was a concentrated stint, but he did master the techniques of radio—'the space of the air' as Allan McClelland has called it—and 'Alexander Nevsky' and 'Christopher Columbus' gave wide scope for this. From the beginning MacNeice was aware of what 'effects' and music could add to words, and what the voice could accomplish. The most fruitful and concentrated period was that from 1946 to 1950: it included 'The Dark Tower', the sagas, 'The Queen of Air and Darkness' and 'Faust'. The 1950s were less productive; his personal life became more difficult and the climate of the age was less congenial. The last few years brought a renewal, in the poetry and plays, a final burst of creativity before the untimely yet strangely heralded death.

Some critics think that the BBC career destroyed the poet, but it would be difficult to sustain this judgement. Other factors caused a decline, in the life and the work, during the latter 1950s, but the 'lyric impulse' returned, with a new if more sombre strength. Radio is an ephemeral art, but it offered extended opportunities, gave him more 'voices', developed more facets of his talent (including technical expertise, which must have satisfied MacNeice as he admired it in others), and opened for him a more interesting world than would a narrowly academic career, or the life of an isolated writer. There was much disappointment, and years of waste, but they are surely redeemed by the quality of the work that was done, and by the friendships that he enjoyed—the testimony of those who remember the poet with affection is of a rare kind.

Community and communication were two things that MacNeice had looked for since, in the thirties, he became more aware of other people—both were afforded him by the career he so fortuitously took up at a critical point in his life. He hated institutions, and the BBC had its institutional drawbacks, but the spirit of Features Department, deriving ultimately from its remarkable creator, Laurence Gilliam, was more congenial. From its haven, MacNeice could inveigh against the modern world, escape into fantasy, express personal dilemmas, and preach his parables. He could be as scholarly as he wanted to— indeed, at the time of his death, he was about to arrange a sequence of translations of Dante's *Inferno* for a series of pro- grammes like those on *The Odyssey* (the task devolved upon Terence Tiller, the age of Dante being a special interest of his). The poetry is the essence of MacNeice's work, but much of the circumstance is to be found in the radio plays: the two aspects are complementary.

But perhaps we should end in the Irish way (remembering MacNeice's comment at Yeats's Sligo burial) with an anecdote. Eric Ewens had to borrow a few pounds from MacNeice, shortly before the poet's death. He returned it one evening when he was in a hurry, calling in at the M.L., putting the notes into Louis's hand, and leaving. After Louis's death, the barman at the club was commiserating with Eric: 'Sad news about your friend,' he said. Then, leaning forward confiden- tially, 'but I saw how you looked after him at the end.'

Notes on Sources

CHAPTER ONE

This necessarily brief survey of MacNeice's life up to 1941 has been compiled from a variety of sources, primarily the poet's own accounts—in *The Strings are False* and articles listed in the bibliography—and the poems. These have been supplemented from other memoirs, reviews, letters and conversations. Lady Nicholson has been extremely kind in talking to the author about her family and her brother's early life. There is also her account, 'Trees were Green', in *Time Was Away*. The present Rector of Carrickfergus, the Rev. Mr Wright, spent a morning showing the author the rectory, church and town—this was very helpful.

Details of Marlborough and Oxford are to be found in John Hilton's memoir, appended to *TSAF*; Mr Hilton also gave the author advice in letters. Mr Paul Bloomfield kindly talked to the author about his sister, Mary, and his niece, Mary Ezra. The comment by A. J. Ayer is from his autobiography, *Part of My Life* (Collins, 1977), page 94.

Professor E. R. Dodds, in addition to giving permission to quote from his autobiography, *Missing Persons*, also helped the author in conversation and in letters. The quotations from *MP* will be found on pages 114 and 116, dealing with the Birmingham years. Other friends from Oxford and Birmingham days who helped the author are Goronwy Rees, Ernest Stahl, Walter Allen and R. D. Smith; and, from London years, until MacNeice's death, Mrs Nancy Spender. Details of the trip to Iceland come from *Letters from Iceland* and from the account by Michael Yates in *W. H. Auden: A Tribute*. The comments by Auden are from his article 'Louis MacNeice', in *Encounter*, November 1963. Accounts of the Group Theatre are to be found in *The Other Theatre* by Norman Marshall (Lehmann, 1947), *The Thirties: A Dream Revolved* by Julian Symons, and *W. H. Auden: A Tribute*. The comment by Yeats is quoted by Dodds, op. cit., page 132.

The reviews mentioned will be found in *New Verse*, January 1938, and the *London Mercury*, January 1938; Grigson's comment is from a review in *New Verse*, summer 1938. Walter Allen's study of Louis MacNeice, given as the Katja Reissner Lecture in December 1967, and printed in *Essays by Divers Hands (Transactions of the Royal Society of Literature)*, vol. XXXV, is the source of the comment on *Autumn Journal*.

The details of Irish friends were given to the author on a memorable visit to Belfast, at the kind invitation of Mrs Mercy MacCann, who also showed the author letters from Louis MacNeice. John Boyd, John Midgely and Reggie McClure were also very kind and helpful—the quotation from John Midgely is from an article he wrote for the Ulster *TV Post* of 12 September 1963.

The detail about Thanksgiving Day, 1940, is taken from the biography of Carson McCullers by Virginia Spencer Carr, *The Lonely Hunter* (Doubleday, N.Y., 1975; Peter Owen, 1977).

CHAPTER TWO

The background to the growth of Drama and Features has also been drawn from various sources, written and from conversations. The official history is Briggs—volumes I and II deal with this early period. Reith's autobiography has furnished several quotations: these are to be found on pages 90, 99, 95, 100 and 290. To build up a detailed picture, the author went through the *BBC Year Books*, early volumes of *Radio Times*, and Drama files in the BBC Written Archives. Certain personal reminiscences have also been used: books and letters to the author by/from Val Gielgud and Harman Grisewood; D. G. Bridson's *Prospero and Ariel* (the description of E. A. Harding is on pages 30–1); conversations with Geoffrey Bridson, Francis Dillon, Douglas Cleverdon, Robin Whitworth and Grace Wyndham Goldie, who also allowed the author to quote from her *Listener* reviews of 1938. First-hand accounts were invaluable, as the history of these years has not been completely documented.

The comment by A. J. P. Taylor is from his *English History: 1914–1945* (OUP, 1965, 1976), page 307; the quotation continues: 'There is little to be learnt about him from the wireless set, his constant companion. The BBC had been born to caution out of bureaucracy.'

The quotations from John Pudney's *Home and Away* will be found on pages 93–4 and 99. The comment quoted from Harman Grisewood is in *One Thing at a Time*, page 120.

Orwell's diary entries are to be found in *The Collected Essays, Journalism and Letters*, ed. Sonia Orwell and Ian Angus (Secker & Warburg, 1968).

MacNeice's comment in November 1939 is to be found in Dodds, op. cit., page 135; that of August 1940 is recorded in a letter to Dan Davin from E. R. Dodds, dated 11 August 1975. Professor and Mrs

Stahl gave the author details of MacNeice's return from America to
Oxford, immediately before his entering the BBC. Lady Nicholson
confirmed that her brother had met F. W. Ogilvie. Further details
of MacNeice's joining the BBC are from files in the Written Archives.

CHAPTER THREE

The sources again combine written records and conversations.
From this stage on, greater use was made of the BBC Written
Archives, as indicated in the text: there are programme files, Drama
and Features files, and MacNeice's 'Scriptwriter' file. Douglas
Cleverdon kindly allowed the author to quote freely from his unpublished monograph 'The Art of Radio'; he and his wife also
talked to the author about Features Department. Francis Dillon
worked closely with WacNeice and has been of enormous help with
this and other chapters—he and his wife showed the author great
kindness and hospitality. Other friends and colleagues of MacNeice
(and of Gilliam) who gave valuable help were Gerald Abraham,
William Alwyn, Dallas Bower, Patric Dickinson, Robert Gittings,
Antony Hopkins, Elisabeth Lutyens, David Thomson; helpful
comments have been contributed also by Cyril Cusack, William
Empson, Stephen Murray, Sir Victor Pritchett, Kathleen Raine and
Sir William Walton. Philip Donnellan, producer of a television
programme on Features Department, showed the author a re-run
of his programme and sent a copy of the script.

John Lehmann gave permission to quote from his autobiography
and gave advice in a telephone conversation. His account of Stephen
Spender's wedding to Natasha Litvin will be found on pages 105–6
of *I Am My Brother*; his comment about the sense of cohesion in
war-time is on page 165. Stephen Spender's remark about the arts
in war-time is in *The Thirties and After*, page 91. Kathleen Raine's
description of MacNeice is from *The Land Unknown*, pages 163–4.
The comments by V. S. Pritchett are from *Midnight Oil*, page 223,
and from a telephone conversation with the author. MacNeice's
views of the group experience in radio are expressed in his introduction to *The Dark Tower and Other Radio Scripts*, pages 14–15.

Dallas Bower gave the author a great deal of help in talking about
the productions of 'Alexander Nevsky' and 'Christopher Columbus';
he very kindly allowed the author to read 'Pax Futura' and gave
permission to quote from this unpublished script. He also contributed an article to *Time Was Away*, 'MacNeice: Sound and Vision'.

The letter from T. S. Eliot to E. Martin Browne (dated 20
October 1942) is quoted by Helen Gardner in *The Composition of
Four Quartets* (Faber and Faber, 1978), page 21. Gerald Abraham

helped the author with details about his early contacts with MacNeice; and Antony Hopkins spent considerable time and trouble giving help with details of his collaborations with MacNeice—the start of his own career with the BBC. This covers material in the next chapter also.

CHAPTER FOUR

Some very valuable details about MacNeice's stay in Ireland in 1945 are contained in the Written Archives: Mrs Jacqueline Kavanagh and her staff gave a great deal of assistance with this and other matters. Sam Hanna Bell kindly gave information about MacNeice's work with writers for the BBC in Belfast, and showed the author his script with MacNeice's comments. Ursula Eason also contributed her recollections. William Alwyn gave the author an account of the visit to Ireland with MacNeice and Rodgers, in letters (July 1978). The lines quoted are from his 'Dedication, to the memory of Louis MacNeice', prefacing his long poem *The World in My Mind* (printed in a limited edition by the Southwold Press, 1975). Other lines describe MacNeice and 'that slant derisive smile/I knew so well, which means that you approve.'

For the post-war atmosphere, quotations have been taken from Patric Dickinson's *The Good Minute*, page 213; Rupert Croft-Cooke's *The Dogs of Peace*, pages 15 and 25; and John Lehmann's *The Ample Proposition*, pages 95–6.

For the Third Programme background and details, from its earliest days, the author is grateful to Harman Grisewood, Christopher Holme and Leslie Stokes, for information and comments in letters and conversation. Written sources are: Grisewood's *One Thing at a Time*, Briggs's *History of Broadcasting*, vol. IV, and two pamphlets published by the BBC: *The 3rd Programme* (1947) and *BBC Third Programme: The Tenth Anniversary* (1956). Other comments are to be found in D. G. Bridson's *Prospero and Ariel* and in an article written by Francis Dillon for the *Listener*, 5 March 1970.

Commenting on MacNeice's article in the *Year Book* for 1947, Howard Newby writes: 'The practice MacNeice describes here is so much at variance with what came to be normal practice a little later that it is worth a comment. The idea that a theme was approved, a script subsequently read by the Departmental Head and then handed over to a producer was not normal Features practice. It was the producer himself who took the initiative (Cleverdon and Dylan Thomas provide the classic example), Gilliam gave his blessing to the enterprise and it was then offered to a network Controller who, as editor, either accepted it or rejected it. The producer–writer relationship was regarded by Features as of central importance. Drama department, on the other hand, developed a Script Unit where ideas and scripts were swapped around and, on the authority of Val Gielgud, commissions given on the basis of suggested ideas. The resulting script would then be 'processed' by Script Unit and passed on—in the way MacNeice describes—to a producer. Features Department were critical of this procedure. MacNeice is doubtless describing an earlier system, before Drama and Features went their own ways.'

Details of the *Horizon* questionnaire are included in Cyril Connolly's *Ideas and Places*.

CHAPTER FIVE

MacNeice's comments and anecdotes about India are from his article, 'India at First Sight', in *Features*, ed. Gilliam. Sir William Tennant's unpublished memoir, 'Service under the British Raj: 1916–1947, Some Memories of India', was written in 1966–8, and is in India Office Library and Records (ref. no. MSS Eur. D. 846). The author acknowledges the permission given by the IOLR, and is grateful to Miss Sheila Tennant for allowing the use of her father's memoir.

Wynford Vaughan Thomas's description of MacNeice is from *Madly in All Directions* (Longman, 1967), page 188. For most of the details, however, the author is indebted to Francis Dillon who gave a vivid first-hand account of the tour he made with MacNeice.

The account of Yeats's Sligo funeral is given by Maurice Collis in *The Journey Up*, pages 83–5.

Auden's comment is from his *Encounter* article, November 1963. Other impressions of the poet were given to the author by colleagues and friends, in conversation and letters. These include Francis Dillon, David Thomson, Nesta Pain, Dorothy Baker, Bill McAlpine, Allan McClelland, Malcolm Hayes, John Sharp and Mark Dignam.

The description from *Those Vintage Years of Radio* is on page 119. Dan Davin's comment is on page 47 of *Closing Times*. Laurence Kitchin gave his personal recollection of meeting MacNeice in a letter to the author; this supplements information from the Archives.

For the *Faust* translation, Ernest Stahl helped the author in letters and conversation; the quotations are from his article in *Time Was Away*: 'The *Faust* translation: a personal account', pages 67–71.

CHAPTER SIX

For the time in Greece the author has drawn on the features and poems by MacNeice, and the account by Kevin Andrews, 'Time and the Will Lie Sidestepped: Athens, the Interval', in *Time Was Away*. Kevin Andrews very kindly sent the author a copy of his article, with certain corrections, and added to this information in his letter (July 1978). The quotations are to be found on pages 103, 105, 104. The remark about MacNeice's lack of involvement is on page 106, and the qualification was made in a letter to the author. The account of the visit to Ikaria is also on page 106. Others in Greece at that time included Francis King and H. A. Lidderdale; the author is grateful for their help. Goronwy Rees gave the information about MacNeice wishing to adapt *Where No Wounds Were*. The detail about Guy Burgess is given by MacNeice himself in a *Radio Times* note, 6 September 1960. The account of the holiday in Crete is to be found in Dodds, op. cit., pages 185–6. The details of Gilliam's visit and proposed features, and the suggested party at the BBC, are from BBC files; plans for MacNeice's return journey from Greece are in the Faber files.

Douglas Cleverdon's 'The Art of Radio' (unpublished) has been quoted from in the account of Features Department in the 1950s. Other details come from *Features*, ed. Gilliam, and from conversations with former members of Features. Rayner Heppenstall's *Portrait . . .* gives a personal account of these years; details of the programmes are from files in Play Library. The quotation from Bridson, op. cit., is on page 187. Terence Tiller has very kindly helped the author, in conversation, and by giving, on request, details of his own work for radio. (The comment on his work is, of course, the author's own.) The anecdote about *Paradise Lost* is from Patric Dickinson's *The Good Minute*, page 208.

The script of 'The Faerie Queene' with MacNeice's comments is in the BBC Play Library. The Clark Lectures are published as *Varieties of Parable*; the comment on Spenser is on page 8. MacNeice's comments on *Autumn Sequel* are from letters to Faber and an article by Joe Burroughs (who produced the radio readings) in *Radio Times*, June 1954.

MacNeice's review of Augustus John's *Chiaroscuro* is in *New Statesman and Nation*, 5 April 1952, 'The Real Mixer'.

Details of the Isle of Wight have very kindly been furnished by Dr and Mrs Abraham and Mr and Mrs J. B. Priestley.

Mercy MacCann brought to the author's attention the short story by her husband: it is in *Sparrows Round My Brow* by 'George Galway' (The Mourne Press, Newcastle, Co. Down, 1942). William Alwyn was very kind in sending not only details of his journey with MacNeice, in a letter, but a copy of the relevant section of 'Ariel to Miranda', his journal for the years 1955–6. This was published in *Adam International Review*, vol. XXXII (nos 316–17–18). The

impressive literary Powys' is Littleton Charles Powys ('Owen' of
Autumn Sequel), headmaster of Sherborne, who died in 1955.

The comment by Douglas Cleverdon about tape-recording comes
from 'The Art of Radio'.

The splendid account of the Yorkshire jaunt was written for the
author by John Sharp—he has vivid memories of the trip and it is a
pity that space precludes the use of more of it.

Sir Bernard Lovell was very helpful in providing details of the
collaboration for 'The Star We Follow', including copies of correspondence with Gilliam, and of his own script—the quotations are
from this and from Sir Bernard's letter to the author (March 1979).

CHAPTER SEVEN

The background to the developments after the war is to be found in
the most recent volume of *The History of Broadcasting* by Asa Briggs.
Lord Briggs kindly commented on the author's use of his material
and quotations, from page 218 of the volume. Other details come
from Features files, from Douglas Cleverdon's 'The Art of Radio',
and from personal papers lent by Mrs Hedli MacNeice.

Mr Beckett kindly confirmed the details of his early writing for
radio. Angus Wilson and Laurie Lee gave permission to quote their
comments in Features files; their other comments are from letters to
the author (November 1978; January 1979).

Dan Davin helped the author with this chapter, in conversation
and letters; he also gave permission for quotation to be made from
Closing Times. Lady Nicholson told the author of the occasion of
their stepmother's death.

Stephen Murray contributed the information about Bill and Wyn
Cutler (March 1978). The comments by Rayner Heppenstall are
from his *Portrait* ... Anthony Thwaite's poem 'For Louis MacNeice'
is in his 1977 volume, *A Portion for Foxes* (OUP)—he kindly gave
permission for the use of some lines.

Cécile Chevreau, Patience Collier, Eric Ewens, Denys Hawthorne,
Cliff Morgan, David Spenser and James Thomason helped with
recollections of MacNeice and his work.

Sean Graham kindly assisted with recollections of the Ghana
project; papers concerning this were lent by Mrs Hedli MacNeice.
The correspondence about 'Countries in the Air' was made available
by Faber.

The quotation from Spender is on page 155 of *The Thirties and
After*. The quotation from Bettelheim is on page 19 of *Uses of
Enchantment: Meaning and Importance of Fairy Tales* (Thames and
Hudson, 1976).

Howard Newby was very helpful in talking to the author about his time as Controller of Third Programme, and made several useful comments after reading the author's MS. Papers, and a copy of the script, were lent by Mrs Hedli MacNeice for the information about 'The Pin is Out'. The comment by MacNeice on South Africa was recalled by W. R. Rodgers in a radio memorial in 'The Arts in Ulster', October 1963, produced in Belfast by John Boyd.

CHAPTER EIGHT

Various former and present administrators, producers and writers were consulted about the last years of Features. The files are not available, and written accounts tend to be very personal in outlook. Some of MacNeice's papers were kindly lent by Mrs Hedli MacNeice.

Friends of MacNeice who talked to the author include John Boyd, Dan Davin, Francis Dillon, Eric Ewens, Denys Hawthorne, Allan McClelland, Robert Pocock, Goronwy Rees, John Sharp, Nancy Spender, Ernest Stahl. Lady Nicholson, Mrs Hedli MacNeice and Corinna MacNeice also helped with their comments.

Richard Pasco paid his tribute to MacNeice in a letter to the author (October 1978). Ved Mehta gave permission to use his account of MacNeice at work and his comments from *John is Easy to Please*, pages 51–3, 60–2. Kathleen Raine's description is on page 164 of *The Land Unknown*. Terence Tiller has kindly allowed the author to quote from his reviews, and helped greatly in conversation.

Recollections of MacNeice in his last illness were from some of the friends already mentioned. Published accounts from which quotations are taken are: 'The Burning Perch: A Memoir of Louis MacNeice' by Robert Pocock, *Encounter*, November 1969; and *Closing Times* by Dan Davin (page 61). John Boyd and Mercy MacCann were kind enough to take the author to Carrowdore churchyard, to visit the grave of Louis MacNeice, in May 1978. Derek Mahon has kindly given permission to quote from 'In Carrowdore Churchyard', from his book *Night-Crossing* (OUP, 1968).

Terence Tiller's review of *The Burning Perch* is from *TLS*, 27 September 1963. He also gave information about the plans for broadcasting the *Inferno*.

It is hoped that references to archive material and to scripts are sufficiently explained in the text. Comments on programmes *as heard* are the author's own, after hearing tapes and discs in BBC Sound Archives.

Bibliography

A: Published Works by Louis MacNeice (*only those which have been used in this book are listed*)

Out of the Picture: A play in two acts, Faber & Faber, 1937; Harcourt Brace, N.Y., 1938

Letters from Iceland, with W. H. Auden, Faber & Faber and Random House, N.Y., 1937

I Crossed the Minch, Longmans, London and N.Y., 1938

Zoo, Michael Joseph, 1938

Christopher Columbus: A Radio Play, Faber & Faber, 1944

The Dark Tower and Other Radio Scripts, Faber & Faber, 1947

Goethe's Faust, with E. L. Stahl, Faber & Faber 1951, OUP, N.Y., 1952

The Mad Islands and The Administrator: Two Radio Plays, Faber & Faber, 1964

The Strings are False, an Unfinished Autobiography (edited by E. R. Dodds), Faber & Faber, 1965

Varieties of Parable: The Clark Lectures 1963, CUP, 1965

Collected Poems, (ed. E. R. Dodds), Faber & Faber and OUP, N.Y., 1966

One for the Grave, a modern morality play, Faber & Faber, 1968

Persons from Porlock and Other Plays for Radio, BBC, 1969

Selected Articles and Reviews by MacNeice

'A Tripper's Commentary', *Listener*, 6 October 1937

'Traveller's Return', *Horizon*, vol. 3, no. 14, February 1941

'Touching America', *Horizon*, vol. 3, no. 15, March 1941

'The Way We Live Now', *Penguin New Writing*, no. 5, April 1941

'Experiences with Images', *Orpheus*, vol. 2, London, 1949

'Lost Generations?', *London Magazine*, vol. 4, no. 4, April 1957

'When I was Twenty-One', *The Saturday Book*, 21, 1961

'Childhood Memories', *Listener*, 12 December 1963

(References to letters, and film, television and book reviews are given in the text or notes on the text.)

B: WORKS GIVING THE HISTORY AND BACKGROUND OF THE BBC

The official history is:
BRIGGS, ASA, *The History of Broadcasting in the United Kingdom*, vols I–IV, OUP, 1961, 1965, 1970, 1979

BOYLE, ANDREW, *Only the Wind will Listen*, Hutchinson, 1972
BRIDSON, D. G., *Prospero and Ariel*, Gollancz, 1971
ECKERSLEY, ROGER, *The BBC and All That*, S. Low, 1946
EVANS, ELWYN, *Radio: A Guide to Broadcasting Techniques*, Barrie and Jenkins, 1977
GIELGUD, VAL, *Years in a Mirror*, The Bodley Head, 1965
GILLIAM, L., ed., *Features*, Evans Bros and BBC, 1950
GORHAM, MAURICE, *Broadcasting and Television since 1900*, Dakers, 1952
GRISEWOOD, HARMAN, *One Thing at a Time*, Hutchinson, 1968
REITH, J. C. W., *Into the Wind*, Hodder and Stoughton, 1949
SNAGGE, JOHN and BARSLEY, MICHAEL, *Those Vintage Years of Radio*, Pitman Publishing, 1972

C: OTHER PERSONAL MEMOIRS AND AUTOBIOGRAPHIES

COLLIS, MAURICE, *The Journey Up*, Faber & Faber, 1970
CONNOLLY, CYRIL, *Ideas and Places*, Weidenfeld & Nicolson, 1953
CROFT-COOKE, RUPERT, *The Dogs of Peace*, W. H. Allen, 1973
DAVIN, DAN, *Closing Times*, OUP, 1975
DICKINSON, PATRIC, *The Good Minute*, Gollancz, 1965
DODDS, E. R., *Missing Persons*, Clarendon Press, Oxford, 1977
HEPPENSTALL, R., *Portrait of the Artist as a Professional Man*, Peter Owen, 1969
LEHMANN, JOHN, *I am My Brother*, Longman, 1960; *The Ample Proposition*, Eyre & Spottiswoode, 1966
MEHTA, VED, *John is Easy to Please*, Secker & Warburg, 1971
PRITCHETT, V. S., *Midnight Oil*, Chatto & Windus, 1971
PUDNEY, JOHN, *Home and Away*, Michael Joseph, 1960
RAINE, KATHLEEN, *The Land Unknown*, Hamish Hamilton, 1975
SPENDER, STEPHEN, ed., *W. H. Auden: A Tribute*, Weidenfeld & Nicolson, 1974; *The Thirties and After*, Macmillan & Fontana, 1978
SYMONS, JULIAN, *The Thirties: A Dream Revolved*, Cresset Press, 1960

One book of memoirs and articles devoted to MacNeice is:
BROWN, TERENCE and REID, ALEC, *Time Was Away: The World of Louis MacNeice*, The Dolmen Press, Dublin, 1974

Other articles about MacNeice are given in notes on the text.

D: SCRIPTS WRITTEN BY LOUIS MACNEICE FOR THE BBC (*apart from some early scripts, he produced most of his own work—an exception was the series of programmes of 'Faust' in 1949; these were produced by E. A. Harding*). DATES ARE OF FIRST BROADCAST.

'Word from America', 15 February 1941

'Cook's Tour of the London Subways', 25 March 1941

'The March of the 10,000', 16 April 1941

'The Stones Cry Out': 1. Dr Johnson Takes It, 5 May 1941

4. Westminster Abbey, 27 May 1941

5. Madame Tussaud's, 2 June 1941

8. St Paul's, 23 June 1941

10. House of Commons, 7 July 1941

'Freedom's Ferry—Life on an ex-American Destroyer', 16 July 1941

'The Stones Cry Out': 18. The Temple, 1 September 1941

'Dr Chekhov', 6 September 1941

'The Stones Cry Out': 22. Royal College of Surgeons, 29 September 1941

26. Belfast, 27 October 1941

'The Glory that is Greece', 28 October 1941

'The Stones Cry Out': 30. Plymouth Barbican, 24 November 1941

'Alexander Nevsky' (produced by Dallas Bower), 8 December 1941

'Rogues' Gallery', 12 December 1941

'Salute to the New Year', 30 December 1941

'Vienna', 12 March 1942

'Salutation to Greece', 22 March 1942

'Calling All Fools', 1 April 1942

'Salute to the USSR', 12 April 1942

'The Debate Continues', 10 May 1942

'Black Gallery': 1. Dr Goebbels, 14 May 1942

'Salute to the United Nations', 14 June 1942

'The Undefeated' (Yugoslavia), 30 June 1942

'Black Gallery': 10 Adolf Hitler, 16 July 1942

'Britain to America': no. 1, 26 July 1942

'The United Nations: A Tribute', 6 September 1942

'Halfway House', 25 September 1942

'Salute to the US Army', 4 October 1942

'Christopher Columbus' (produced by Dallas Bower), 12 October 1942

'Salute to Greece', 25 October 1942

'Two Men and America' (script lost), 29 January 1943

'Salute to the Unseen Allies', 31 January 1943

'The Four Freedoms': 1. Pericles, 21 February 1943
                    2. Early Christians, 28 February 1943
                    3. The Renaissance, 7 March 1943
                    4. John Milton, 14 March 1943
                    5. French Revolution, 21 March 1943
'Long Live Greece', 25 March 1943
'The Four Freedoms': 6. What Now?, 28 March 1943
'Zero Hour', 3 May 1943
'The Death of Byron', 10 May 1943
'Sicily and Freedom', 18 June 1943
'The Death of Marlowe', 21 June 1943
'Independence Day', 4 July 1943
'Four Years at War', 3 September 1943
'The Story of My Death', 8 October 1943
'The Spirit of Russia', 8 November 1943
'The Fifth Freedom', 17 November 1943
'Ring in the New', 31 December 1943

'The Sacred Band', 7 January 1944
'The Nosebag', 13 March 1944
'This Breed of Men', 23 April 1944
'D Day' (recorded on 30 May 1944)
'He Had a Date', 28 June 1944
'Sunbeams in His Hat', 16 July 1944
'Why Be a Poet?', 13 August 1944
'The Golden Ass', 3 November 1944
'Cupid and Psyche', 7 November 1944
'The Year in Review', 31 December 1944

'A Roman Holiday', 10 January 1945
'The March Hare Resigns', 29 March 1945
'London Victorious', 18 May 1945
'A Voice from Norway', 22 May 1945
'Threshold of the New', 31 December 1945

'The Dark Tower', 21 January 1946
'Salute to All Fools', 1 April 1946
'Enter Caesar', 20 September 1946
'The Careerist', 22 October 1946
'Agamemnon' (broadcast by Drama Dept), 29 October 1946
'Enemy of Cant', 3 December 1946
'The Heartless Giant', 13 December 1946

'The Death of Gunnar', 11 March 1947
'The Burning of Njal', 12 March 1947

'Portrait of Rome', 22 June 1947
'Grettir the Strong', 27 July 1947

'India at First Sight', 13 March 1948
'Portrait of Delhi', 2 May 1948
'The Road to Independence', 23 May 1948
'The Two Wicked Sisters', 19 July 1948
'No Other Road', 19 September 1948
'Trimalchio's Feast', 22 December 1948

'He Had a Date' (revised version), 14 February 1949
'The Queen of Air and Darkness', 28 March 1949
'Faust' (translated from Goethe, with E. L. Stahl, produced by
    E. A. Harding), from 30 October to 21 November 1949

'Ten Burnt Offerings', September–November, 1951
'Portrait of Athens', 18 November 1951
'In Search of Anoyia', 11 December 1951

'The Centre of the World' (Delphi), 28 January 1952
'Mourning and Consolation' (compilation), 8 February 1952
'One Eye Wild', 9 November 1952

'Twelve Days of Christmas', 6 January 1953
'Time Hath Brought Me Hither', 31 May 1953
'Return to Atlantis', 5 July 1953

'Where No Wounds Were', 16 March 1954
'Prisoner's Progress', 27 April 1954
'Autumn Sequel' (in six parts), from 28 June 1954
'Return to a School', 15 October 1954

'The Waves' (from Virginia Woolf), two parts, 18, 19 March 1955
'The Fullness of the Nile', 3 July 1955
'The Star We Follow' (with Ritchie Calder), 25 December 1955

'Also among the Prophets', 5 February 1956
'Bow Bells', 17 June 1956
'Spires and Gantries', 29 July 1956
'Carpe Diem', 8 October 1956
'From Bard to Busker', 30 December 1956

'The Birth of Ghana', 22 February 1957
'Nuts in May', 27 May 1957
'An Oxford Anthology', 22 September 1957
'The Stones of Oxford', 24 September 1957

'All Fools at Home', 1 April 1958
'Health in Their Hands', 7 April 1958

(attachment to television during 1958)

'Scrums and Dreams', 3 April 1959
'East of the Sun and West of the Moon', 25 July 1959
'They Met on Good Friday', 8 December 1959
'Mosaic of Youth', 30 December 1959

('Another Part of the Sea' produced for TV, 6 September 1960)
'The Odyssey', series arranged by MacNeice, some of the trans-
    lation by him, from 6 October to 22 December 1960

'The Administrator', 10 March 1961
'Let's Go Yellow', 19 December 1961

'The Mad Islands', 4 April 1962

(translations of Latin poems for programmes), 3 March and 11
    August 1963
'Persons from Porlock', 30 August 1963

MacNeice sometimes produced scripts by other writers, and presented poetry programmes—some of these are mentioned in the text.

Most of the scripts are in the BBC Play Library. Some were published (*see* Bibliography A).

Index

Wyngarde, Peter, 155
Wynne-Jones, C. V., 169

Xenophon, 48

Yates, Michael, 26
Yeats, W. B., 24, 28, 32, 104, 107, 164, 185, 193
Young, Gladys, 62, 68